THE INVISIBLES

*The Untold Story of African American Slaves
in the White House*

JESSE J. HOLLAND

Guilford, Connecticut

An imprint of Rowman & Littlefield

Distributed by NATIONAL BOOK NETWORK

British Library Cataloguing in Publication Information Available

Library of Congress Cataloging-in-Publication Data is available on file.

ISBN 978-1-4930-0846-9
ISBN 978-1-4930-2419-3 (e-book)

♾™ The paper used in this publication meets the minimum requirements of American National Standard for Information Sciences—Permanence of Paper for Printed Library Materials, ANSI/ NISO Z39.48-1992.

For Carol, Rita, and Jamie, who make it all worth it to me.

CONTENTS

ACKNOWLEDGMENTS

THIS FIVE-YEAR PROJECT IS LOVINGLY DEDICATED TO MY WIFE AND children, who had to put up with me skipping bicycle rides, story times, violin practice, date night, and other assorted activities so I could huddle downstairs in the basement office with my computer and music composing these words. Without Carol June, Rita Elaine, and Jesse James III, none of this would have been worth doing. You three are why I do what I do, and I hope you know how much I love you.

Special thanks go to my parents, Jesse and Yvonne Holland. My father—the first Jesse J. Holland—read an earlier version of this work a couple of years ago and said simply, "It's good." I can feel the smile spreading over my face now as I remember that seemingly offhand comment from him as we sat chatting late one night when I was visiting my childhood home in Mississippi. I don't think I've received a higher compliment in my life. And Mom, you know all of this is you, right? Your curiosity, your determination, your single-mindedness, and your creativity are all reflected in everything I do. The world lost a great writer when you selflessly decided to spend your career teaching English instead of finishing up your own work. And I still think the world deserves to read "The Backwoods of Benton County." We're going to have to do something about that.

I also have to thank my family in Mississippi: My sisters and brother, Twyla, Candace, and Fred, kept me sane and grounded when I felt like banging my head against a wall, and kept pushing when I felt like giving up; my nieces and nephew—Alexandria, Samantha, Fred Jr., Aida, and Annie—I look forward to the next time I'm at home and we get to spend some serious quality time together; and all of my cousins, uncles, aunts, and other relatives who make up the extended Holland and Boga families. You're all the best and I'll see you Thanksgiving and/or at the next reunion.

Dr. Rita Womack is deserving of a special thanks on this page for being there whenever she was needed in any capacity that was required at that moment. I wouldn't get out the door every morning without her help, and so, thank you from the bottom of my heart. My in-laws, Mark and Leslie, also deserve mention here because they always take on some of my burdens when they're here so I can write.

There are so many other people who helped me get to this point: the entire Goucher College community but especially Patsy Sims, the former director of the Creative Nonfiction Master of Fine Arts program, where parts of this work were first refined as an idea and then as my MFA thesis. And then there were my Goucher mentors, each of whom contributed greatly to this project: Jacob Levenson, who came up with the name for this project, a version of which currently adorns the cover; Laura Wexler, who gave me the confidence that you could be a journalist and a long-form storyteller all at the same time (and whose advice on looking at your own family for great story potential I plan to use in my next project); my dearest Diana Hume George, who was always there with a word of wisdom when I most desperately needed to hear it and someone who gives me hope that someday when I grow up I can be a real writer; and Leslie Rubinkowski, the new director of the Goucher Creative Nonfiction Master of Fine Arts program, who got me across the finish line with the inimitable style and grace she brings to everything. And a big thank you goes to my fellow Goucher MFAers (next study hall's on me!), but especially Stef Loh, Becky Lerner, Annmarie Chiarini, Lisa Whipple, Earl Swift, Mike Capuzzo, Fanny Brewster, Becky Lerner, Nena Baker, Magin Lasov Gregg, Lyra Hilliard, Mora Lee, Robyn Barberry, Meredith May, Ann Stader, Mike Freeman, Holly Sneeringer, Lauren Sallinger, and Julie Strauss Bettinger, who all read pieces of this during our two years together at Goucher.

Thank you to everyone at the Carol Mann Literary Agency, but especially to my agent, Joanne Wyckoff. In addition to being my agent, Joanne helped craft the proposal used to sell *The Invisibles* as one of my instructors at Goucher. Her deft touch can be seen throughout this book, and writers, if you get a chance to work with her on a proposal? Take it. She knows what she's doing.

There are so many people who took time out of their day to answer questions and direct me on how to find needed information who need to be mentioned here: the library staff at the Thurgood Marshall Library at Bowie State University for allowing me to use their facilities during my research and writing phases; the now-retired Yvonne Lev at Goucher College for her fabulous researching skills; the library staff at the Bowie branches of the Prince George's County Library; the library staff in the Sojourner Truth room at the Oxon Hill branch of the Prince George's County Library; the library staff at the University of Maryland's Theodore McKeldin Library; the staff at the Library of Congress and the National Archives in Washington, DC, who are probably tired of seeing me by now; and the employees at Mount Vernon, Monticello, Montpelier, The Hermitage, Ash Lawn–Highland, Sherwood Forest, and the Springfield plantations. I was always fearful that people whose jobs depend on making early presidents' lives look good would not be willing to talk about their slaves but everyone—and I mean everyone—was not only willing but eager to help. A special thanks goes to Marsha Mullin at The Hermitage, Beth Taylor at Montpelier, and Nancy Stetz at Ash Lawn–Highland, whose help I'll always appreciate. Thank you to all of those researchers and writers whose work paved the way for this book: Annette Gordon-Reed, Wil Heygood, Clarence Lusane, Garry Wills, Tingba Apidta, Lucia Stanton, Mary V. Thompson, Kenneth T. Walsh, Bob Arnebeck, Sandra Fitzpatrick, Maria R. Goodwin, Dorothy Price-Haskins, William Seale, and William Bushong; Alexandra Lane and everyone else at the White House Historical Association; Richard Baker and Donald Ritchie in the US Senate; and everyone else who has written or helped research slavery in Washington, DC. A special thanks goes to Arthur Johnson, a historical interpreter at Colonial Williamsburg, who helped start me down this road years ago (I couldn't remember his name after I met him the first time, but we reconnected on a second trip to Colonial Williamsburg and I told him I would thank him properly in my second book!).

An extra big thank you goes to everyone at The Associated Press, but especially my three bureau chiefs in Washington, DC: Sandy Johnson,

ACKNOWLEDGMENTS

Ron Fournier, and Sally Buzbee. I also want to acknowledge my editors who helped me through working on all of this while also doing my reporting job during daylight hours: Matt Yancey, John Henry, Jim Drinkard, Mike Sniffen, and Sonya Ross. Also deserving thanks here is Mark Sherman, my writing partner at the Supreme Court, who shouldered so much of the burden there while I was working on my Goucher thesis. Sonya Ross is the only person who gets thanks here twice, because in addition to being my editor she is also a good friend and mentor. On my list of mentors also deserving acknowledgment here are Robert Naylor, Will Norton, Gloria J. Brown Marshall (I'm going to use the spinach-filled Ho-Ho idea in print one day!), and Rod Hicks. And I can't forget all of my writer and creative friends, whose careers make me soooo jealous: Amy Vincent, David Hitt, April Ryan, Del Wilber, Nancy Sharp, Thom Keller, Rene Pedraza del Prado, Lee Eric Smith, and Tim Ivy.

I also would like to thank all of my friends at the National Association of Black Journalists and my brothers of the Eta Zeta chapter of Omega Psi Phi Fraternity, Inc., and my fraternity brother from another mother, Mark Stephens. We'll be hitting the big 5-0 soon, and it'll be time to set it out!

One person I need to mention here at the end is Barry Hannah, the great author whom I had the pleasure of working under while at Ole Miss. Barry's gone now, but all of the advice and knowledge he passed on to me years and years ago still rings true. And Barry, I haven't forgotten your advice and I promise you, I'm working on it.

Finally, there are so many people I need to thank that I'm sure I'm leaving someone out but please, place the blame on my head and not my heart.

FOREWORD

I DECIDED I WOULD WRITE A SECOND BOOK IN 2008 WHILE RIDING ON then-Senator Barack Obama's presidential campaign bus as he made a weekend stopover at his home in Chicago, Illinois. My first book, *Black Men Built the Capitol: Discovering African-American History In and Around Washington, D.C.*, had been moderately successful. But after taking more than a year off, I went back to work at The Associated Press as a political reporter. However, I quickly realized that I still had the desire to write books. The problem was deciding what to write.

I wrote my first book on unsung African American history in the nation's capital in part because I walked into a library one day looking for a book that would describe the black history of the National Mall and couldn't find one. I knew from years of conversations with native Washingtonians, historians, and experts on black history that there were quite a few stories about African Americans that could be told about the Capitol, the White House, and other places in and around the center of Washington. However, no one had bothered to collect and verify these accounts. Since I wanted to read these tales, I decided that I would take it upon myself to write them for anyone else who would be interested.

But what would be next? Was there another area of African American history that deserved exploration in Washington, DC, that hadn't been touched by other authors? Something that I could sink my teeth into without having to rush to publication (I thought about trying to write a book about Obama's candidacy, but knew hundreds of other authors were considering and possibly even working on the same idea, something that would intensify if Obama won). It would have to be something that would justify the many hours away from my family researching and writing, and national enough in scope to draw the attention of publishers looking for a new project. Most of all, it would have to be something that interested me personally, something historically significant that I myself would purchase if I was walking through a bookstore with disposable cash and a yearning to know more about history. Then it hit me.

All through Obama's campaign, people talked about the historical significance of an African American politician having the chance to live inside the White House. But I knew that Obama couldn't have been the first black person to live inside the White House. There had to be some history there. Even better, there had to be a book!

I was so excited I immediately called the editor of my first book on African American history, Maureen Graney, and started babbling ideas over the phone to her about writing an African American history of the White House. Maureen wisely tempered my enthusiasm by telling me to sit down and think about what I really wanted to say. Eventually, I came up with three different ideas about three different eras of African American history in the White House that I wanted to explore: the slaves who lived at 1600 Pennsylvania Avenue with the president, the servants who worked inside the executive mansion for the president, and the African American men and women who wanted to be president. This is the beginning of the beginning: a look at the slaves who worked to build the White House, the slaves who lived inside the presidential mansions in New York City and Philadelphia at the dawn of the United States, and the first slaves to live inside the White House.

I want to be clear that this is only a first look, because we are still discovering who these slaves were, what they were like, and what happened to them after they left the clutches of the president who held them in bondage. Every year, someone finds out something new about these African American men and women. But that should be expected, because until recently, no one has really cared about who these men and women were. Unlike the presidents they served, whose every statement and movement was recorded and studied, very little was left behind to tell us about the lives of the slaves whose work allowed these men to reach for greatness through the wealth that human slavery brought them. Only by reading between the lines, and scouring letters, diaries, and documents left behind by their white masters, can we begin to piece together the lives of the enslaved African Americans who took care of the president and his family while the president took care of the United States. They deserve the attempt.

CHAPTER 1

INTRODUCTION

A SLAVE FROM VIRGINIA ESCAPED HIS BONDAGE, AND CROSSED OVER the Potomac to Washington, DC, hoping to find a friendly soul who would help him in his bid for freedom from bondage. Stealthily wandering through the nation's capital, avoiding ruthless slave catchers, pitiless merchants, and plantation owners, he came upon a large white mansion in the middle of the city. Hoping the owner's heart would be as large as his home, the slave knocked on the front door, seeking shelter and perhaps a few scraps of food to eat before heading upriver toward Baltimore and freedom. A man answered the door, but not the owner—a lackey who spent too much time asking obvious questions, clearly stalling for time. A few seconds later, the slave heard an upstairs window being opened, and a male voice demanding to know what the disheveled man wanted.

"I am a fugitive from one who calls himself my master," the slave said. "I am weary and hungry, and having swam the river, I wish to rest here a while and dry my garments, and get a little to eat. For it is a long way to Canada, and I must rest where I can, and depend on charity for food, for I have no money, and I expect that my master will soon be in pursuit of me."

And then the man in the window leaned out and looked down, with a sneer on his face. "This is the last place in the world for a fugitive slave to find refuge. This is the President's House, and I am the President of the United States, —and a democratic President too, and my chief business is to catch just such fellows as you."

The slave couldn't believe his ears. "That cannot be, for I see on yonder Capitol the flag of liberty, glittering with stars, and the eagle, with wide spread wings, holds in his talons the arrows fatal to tyrants. Surely every man within the shadow of the Capitol must be worthy of carrying such a banner."

The president chortled. "How simple you are. That flag only signifies that this land is the home of the oppressed of all nations except its own. We use it when we march against fugitive slaves."

Leaning from the window, the president rubbed his hands together. "You need not come here for refuge. I am the man who executes the Fugitive Law, of which I know you have heard. And I do it with alacrity. It is natural to me. I like it. I have something of the bloodhound in my own composition—and something of the turkey buzzard. Do not come to me for displays of humanity. I am not a man, but a President—a democratic President. So, away with you, for I will myself take you back to your master."

The slave turned to run, but looked back up at the man in the White House one last time. "If I had known that this was the house of the President, I would not have asked for charity here. But I thought this was the house of a man."

"So, turning on his heel he fled hastily away, and the President shut the window, and the lackey the door, each in great disgust," reported the *Anti-Slavery Bugle* out of Lisbon, Ohio, in its September 27, 1856, edition.

A stirring tale, one likely meant to tug at heartstrings and to express disgust at the hypocrisy of a government system that threw off the shackles of bondage from far away masters to create a free country, but yet condoned and encouraged a system of human chattel throughout its borders. It is also likely completely false, an apocryphal story meant only as propaganda to rile up abolitionists and their allies against the pro-slavery forces in the South who were already discussing possible treason by breaking away from the United States to form a confederacy of states where slavery would remain the cornerstone of the agrarian economy.

However, even in fiction there are some painful truths. With only two notable exceptions, no president in the early history of the United States would have offered succor to a fugitive slave looking for freedom. This is because they were a slave owner themselves, with their Negro maids, butlers, cooks, coachmen, and servants confined to an existence of servitude behind the very walls of the White House itself, or toiling in the fields and barns of the president's home plantations miles away from the capital.

Outside of John Adams and his son, John Quincy Adams—the first father and son presidents, Quakers, and the only early presidents to fervently oppose slavery and back up their words by refusing to keep their fellow men in bondage—none of the early presidents would have been sympathetic to the plight of an escaped slave, simply because they wouldn't have wanted any of their own human property to get the idea that escaping from a life of servitude was possible.

But this book is not about those presidents, as interesting as they are. The lives of the Founding Fathers and the early presidents—their failures, their triumphs, their families, their politics, and their legacies—have been investigated and told and re-told ad nauseam by their descendants and interested academics, politicians, students, enthusiasts, and admirers. This book is about the enslaved people behind those presidents, the ones who made their beds, cooked their food, prepared their clothes, answered the door, and in general made life at the White House work while the presidents and their families took care of the business of America.

This book is about those enslaved African Americans who were first-hand witnesses to history but victims of it as well. These are the accounts of the enslaved cooks, butlers, maids, doormen, body servants, and carriage drivers whose lives were unwillingly dedicated to making the life of the president somewhat easier in the midst of the rough-and-tumble politics of the nation's capital. And like the chief executive, these slaves are among the few who had the exclusive right to call the presidential mansion at 1600 Pennsylvania Avenue their home.

When President Barack Obama and his family first entered the White House following his sweeping 2008 presidential election win, they weren't the first African American family to live inside the executive mansion. That honor—if it can be considered that—was achieved a couple of centuries ago by men and women, most of whose names we don't know, who were not celebrities and much of whose lives have been lost to history. It is likely that Obama himself doesn't know their names, despite walking the same halls that they did and sleeping a mere floor away from where they rested their heads.

It is the lives of these men and women—the forgotten dozens of African American men and women who were held in slavery inside the White House by the executive mansion's occupants, the presidents of the United States—that we explore in this work in an attempt to recover their identities and provide some much-needed recognition to their contributions, not only to the life and comforts of the presidents they served, but to America as a whole.

The election of Obama brought new attention to the African American history of the White House and especially the use of slavery in its construction. The first black president of the United States living in a mansion constructed with the labor of unpaid African American slaves inspired eager reporters and historians to delve into the African American history of the building: the slaves who helped designer James Hoban construct the original building (which was burned by the British in the War of 1812); the domestic servants such as seamstress Elizabeth Keckley, a close friend of Abraham Lincoln, and White House butlers Alonzo Fields and Eugene Allen (whose life story was fictionalized by Hollywood for the movie, *The Butler*) who walked with presidents and founded the upper-middle-class black structure of the District of Columbia; and political figures such as E. Frederick Morrow, the first African American to be officially appointed a White House aide, and Andrew T. Hatcher, the first African American to be named associate White House press secretary.

But lost in this historical exploration are the names of William Lee, Oney Judge, John Freeman, and Paul Jennings, men and women who actually lived inside the White House and other executive mansions as slaves of the presidents, slaves who toiled silently behind the scenes to care for the daily needs of the president, freeing the nation's chief executive and his family from the drudgery of domestic work to concentrate on the cares of the nation in its earliest days.

They lived and they loved outside of their enslavement to the president, but few of their tales have been told.

It always surprises me that the people I've told over the years about this project are startled to realize that slavery was actively practiced inside the White House.

Known interchangeably as the White House, the executive mansion, the President's House, or the presidential mansion, the whitewashed building and all that it entails symbolizes the power and prestige of the United States of America, the truth and honor of the American form of government, as well as the freedom and dignity of all the people who make up this great country. This is probably why few people associate the so-called "President's House," this shining symbol of our American democracy, with one of the greatest scourges of humankind's existence, slavery.

Starting with the nation's first president, Gen. George Washington, and proceeding through the architect of the North's victory in the Civil War, Gen. Ulysses S. Grant, twelve of the first eighteen US presidents owned Africans as slaves at one time or another in their lives. Washington, Thomas Jefferson, James Madison, James Monroe, Andrew Jackson, Martin Van Buren, William Henry Harrison, John Tyler, James K. Polk, Zachary Taylor, Andrew Johnson, and Grant all had different attitudes about slavery during their time as president, but all kept African American slaves.

Grant is revered as the general who led the United States to victory over the rebellious and treasonous Confederate States of America, which wanted to secede in part over its desire to continue legal human slavery within its borders. However, Grant at one point was a slaveholder himself. Given a slave by his father-in-law in Missouri, Grant freed him before the beginning of the Civil War, writing in a court document in 1859 that he does "hereby manumit, emancipate and set free from slavery my Negro man William, sometimes called William Jones . . . forever." Grant in his later life would remember, "We felt that it was a stain to the Union that men should be bought and sold like cattle."

Other American presidents felt the same way, but it did not stop them from using African slaves to enrich their lives both inside and outside the White House. Washington, Jefferson, and Madison all spoke against slavery before becoming president, yet kept slaves at their plantations to help line their pockets and keep them in the American aristocracy. Madison repeatedly said that slavery was wrong, and even spoke against it during the creation of the Constitution. "We have seen the mere distinction of color made in the most enlightened period of time, a ground of the most oppressive dominion ever exercised by man over man," Madison said during a speech at the Constitutional Convention on June 6, 1787. Yet during that same period Madison owned more than one hundred slaves at his Montpelier estate, and refused to release them upon his death as his other wealthy and powerful compatriots did. The only concession he made was to ask his wife, Dolley, not to sell any slaves without their consent contingent upon their good behavior after his death, advice Mrs. Madison didn't even follow.

These same men, once elected president, did not want to incur the expense of paying for a staff to take care of the basic housekeeping functions of the presidential domicile. Congress, during the administration of these first twelve presidents, did not provide funding for a domestic staff for the White House, leaving it to the presidents to figure out how to pay for cooks, butlers, washerwomen, and the other household staff needed for a mansion the size of the White House. So to defray the cost of household help, eight of those twelve slave-holding presidents brought their slaves along to work with them inside the presidential mansions in which they resided: Washington, Jefferson, Madison, Monroe, Jackson, Tyler, Polk, and Taylor. These African slaves began the tradition of African American service to the president of the United States.

The non-slave-holding presidents like John Adams and his son, John Quincy Adams, complained bitterly about the cost they incurred paying for the domestic staff for the White House and other presidential homes. Abigail Adams estimated that she needed at least thirty workers to make the "great castle" in Washington run properly, but since her family was not rich, she made do with six.

The southern slave owners who ascended to the presidency had no such problems. They simply imported slaves from plantations such as Mount Vernon, Montpelier, Monticello, Sherwood Forest, and The Hermitage, and installed them as the domestic staff inside the presidential residence. When a new president moved in, he would bring his slaves with him and his family to Washington, set them up inside the White House, and give them the training they needed to deal with the day-to-day life necessities of the president's family and the entertainment and social functions of the most powerful man in America. Few people today know of these slaves' existence, much less their names, but their tales tell

John Quincy Adams, one of the two first presidents not to hold slaves inside the White House. LIBRARY OF CONGRESS

John Adams, first president to live inside the White House and the first president to live in an executive mansion without the assistance of slaves. LIBRARY OF CONGRESS

us of who we were as a country, who we are now as Americans, and who we might become in the future.

Before we determine our future, we must explore the past and find out who these slaves were. That information is not easily accessible, even for people who have access to the White House. That would seem to be an obvious place to begin since, after all, it's the home of the president and where the majority of these slaves lived. It's one of the best-known structures in the United States, toured by thousands upon thousands of people each year. But even for those who know the White House slaves existed, finding any trace of their existence in today's White House is almost impossible.

We expect today some indication in a southern mansion that slaves were once used to maintain the property. Many southern plantations and mansions now preserve or recreate the outhouses and slave quarters for heritage tourists who want to know how slaves lived and worked in the antebellum era. Mount Vernon, the nearby home plantation of President George Washington, touts its slave quarters as part of the tour for those who wish to see how the slaves owned by the first president lived, and at Monticello, home of Thomas Jefferson, drafter of the Declaration of Independence and the third president, docents offer a tour specifically aimed at those wondering about the lives of the president's slaves "focusing on the experiences of the enslaved people who lived and labored on the Monticello plantation."

But there is nothing inside the executive mansion to mark the existence of the slaves who lived and worked there, despite the fact that hundreds of people walk through the former slave quarters at the White House on a daily basis and never know it.

Each December, the highlight of the Washington social scene is the invitation-only annual White House Christmas party. The executive mansion is exquisitely decorated from top to bottom, and hundreds of dignitaries, celebrities, government officials, and media types gather to see and be seen at the epicenter of political power in the United States. But each year, one person is missing from the party: the president of the United States. Instead of mingling with the guests, the president and the first lady head a formal receiving line for the guests who have abandoned the party to go downstairs for the privilege of shaking hands with them. For Obama, this ritual receiving line has been staged in the formal oval Diplomatic Reception Room, which for the prerequisite photos of the presidential handshake is set up like a photo studio with big lights and white silk screens. Normally, the room serves a very different function: The Diplomatic Reception Room is an entrance to the White House from the National Mall for the family, and a location for important news conferences for the president. For such an important room, its true history is often missed: The millions of people who see that room on television and the thousands who walk through it on tours and at the White House Christmas party don't know they're looking at part of what originally was the slave quarters inside the White House.

The African American slaves most often had rooms in the White House's basement, referred to as the ground floor today because it opens out onto the South Gardens and the National Mall. These were airy rooms directly beneath the principal floor of the house and on the north and south sides of the long groin-vaulted hall that ran from one end of

Daisy Johnson, a free woman working for the president, standing in the basement of the White House in the mansion's kitchen. LIBRARY OF CONGRESS

the house to the other, according to William Seale's *The President's House*. These rooms are now used as a library, China Room, offices, and the formal oval Diplomatic Reception Room. However, this vaulted corridor once accessed a great kitchen forty feet long with large fireplaces at each end, a family kitchen, an oval servants hall, the steward's quarters, storage and workrooms, and the servant and slave bedrooms.

This is where the presidents stashed their slaves, where enslaved Africans ate, slept, socialized and made the best of their imprisonment, all while making the lives of the president and his family as easy as possible so that the affairs of the household could be ignored for the more important affairs of state.

It was likely here where slave women like Fanny Hern and Edy Fossett gave birth to—and lost—some of the first babies born inside the

White House; where enslaved men and women cried for the loss of relatives sold to the South by uncaring masters for seeking their freedom in the North; where bone-tired women and men wearily shed their brightly colored maid and butler costumes, rubbed aching feet and shoulders, and fantasized of a day where the whims of another family did not rule their lives. Little did these souls dream that one day, hundreds of years later, an African American family who looked like them would reside on the top floor of the White House, not in its basement; a family who would be served by White House domestics, instead of being the ones serving; a First Family who could proudly claim slaves like them in their heritage and perhaps close the circle of history for the most recognizable home in America.

But that history—the story of slavery, the presidency, and the White House—doesn't start in Washington. It starts in New York City, the first capital of the United States, and with the first president, Gen. George Washington. While the White House is in Washington, the first presidential residence was actually in Manhattan, where General Washington took the oath of office and served the first term of his presidency. It is also where the first slaves began their service to the American president.

CHAPTER 2

WILLIAM LEE AND
NEW YORK CITY

New York City of 1789 was a bustling, babbling city, jammed to overflowing with Americans from all walks of life: silk-stocking, wig-wearing gentlefolk, destitute and broken-down beggars, and leather-apron–wearing workingmen and washerwomen of all colors, creeds, and religions building what would soon be the nation's busiest seaport and largest city.

For William Lee, looking at the buildings of the growing city and the constant movement and languages of Manhattan must have quickened his heart, for it was a long way from his home at Mount Vernon, Virginia. But unlike many new visitors to New York, Lee knew that he had the most prestigious address in town as his new home: the executive mansion of the new president, George Washington.

Unlike many new citizens of the United States, Lee personally knew the former general and hero of the recently ended War of Independence against Great Britain. He had ridden into battle with Washington against the once-fearsome redcoat army of England, side by side with the Virginia-born general in both bad times at Valley Forge, and good at Yorktown where the great British general Lord Cornwallis surrendered his sword by proxy in shame for having lost to an army of colonists. Lee had been summoned to live in the presidential mansion by Washington. Of course, other Americans had a choice that Lee did not: whether to accept or refuse. Lee did not have that option, because he was not Washington's friend, nor his comrade-in-arms, nor his employee. William Lee was Washington's slave, and when his master called, he had no choice but to come.

Lee, like the man he served, probably would have rather been at home at Mount Vernon. Washington had made clear that he had no desire to be in New York City and no desire to lead his new countrymen. Washington's plans after leading the American colonies to victory over the British were to retire home to Virginia and lead a quiet private life as a wealthy plantation owner. Lee was Washington's favorite slave, and at Mount Vernon, he served as one of the slave overseers, a life much easier than most slaves. Lee likely would have been happy to spend the rest of his days on the Potomac. But Washington's countrymen insisted that they needed the general to lead them again, voting him unanimously as the first president of the United States of America. So Washington packed his bags, gathered his most trusted advisors around him, and left behind his dreams of being a country gentleman to head north to the newly formed country's first capital.

The logical choice for the first capital of the United States was New York City, which at that time was the largest city in the burgeoning new country. With the new government approved by a majority of the former British colonies, the House and Senate immediately moved to the next order of business: the election and installation of Washington as the country's first chief executive.

Washington had watched the newly freed British colonies devolve into a nonworking group of squabbling states in their first attempt at self-governance under the Articles of Confederation, with the agrarian South looking to exert its influence over the still-industrializing North. The Constitutional Convention resolved many of these issues, but required a strong president to hold the new country together. The one man everyone trusted, the only man that everyone agreed would be best for the job, was the now-retired Washington.

Washington had no desire to be called up to service again. "The first wish of my soul is to spend the evening of my days as a private citizen on my farm," Washington said in a letter to Samuel Hanson that preceded his inauguration. He reluctantly gave in to public pressure, and unhappily prepared to leave Mount Vernon with Lee and other slaves to assume

George Washington as a farmer overseeing slaves and workers at Mount Vernon.
LIBRARY OF CONGRESS

his responsibilities to the new nation. "About ten o'clock, I bade adieu to Mount Vernon, to private life, and to domestic felicity and, with a mind oppressed with more anxious and painful sensations than I have words to express, set out for New York ... with the best dispositions to render service to my country in obedience to its call, but with less hope of answering its expectations," Washington wrote in his journal.

His hopes of a quiet life had been dashed, as Americans of all political persuasions and classes turned out to cheer him on his way up the eastern seaboard to the new capital. Although he begged local mayors and governors to accord him no special honors, they completely ignored his wishes, especially as he neared New York City. He had pleaded with the New York governor, George Clinton, to spare him further hoopla: "I can assure you, with the utmost sincerity, that no reception can be so congenial to my feelings as a quiet entry devoid of ceremony." That didn't happen. Sarah Robinson, the niece of the owner of what would become the first presidential mansion in New York City, described a scene of "great rejoicing" in New York City on Washington's arrival in a letter written the day the new president set foot on Manhattan.

"An elegant barge decorated with an awning of satin, 12 oarsmen dressed in white frocks and blue ribbons went down to E. Town (Elizabethtown) last fourth day (Wednesday) to bring him up," she wrote. "A stage was erected at the Coffee house wharf, with a carpet for him to step on, where a company of Light horse, one of artillery, and most of the inhabitants were waiting to receive him; they paraded through Queen street in great form, while the music of the drums and the ringing of the bells were enough to stun one with the noise."

While New York City was celebrating Washington's arrival, Lee was recuperating in Philadelphia. Washington had wanted his longtime valet, body servant, and bodyguard with him as he took on his new responsibilities, but multiple injuries to Lee's knees had made it nearly impossible for the slave to travel past Philadelphia. Lee apparently wanted to be with the new president just as much as Washington wanted the slave to be at his side, so much that he was willing to push on through the pain of two broken knees to get to his master's side.

Tobias Lear, Washington's longtime personal secretary and friend, wrote a family friend, Clement Biddle, in Philadelphia to have him persuade Lee to return to Mount Vernon, "for he cannot possibly be of any service here." Lee was undeterred, and continued to New York City: In June, Lear wrote Biddle, "Billy arrived here safe & well."

Elkanah Watson, a famous world traveler, merchant, and land speculator remembered Lee as "smiling content animate and beamed on every countenance in his presence" when around Washington. And why not? For years, Washington and Lee had been inseparable. The general had owned Lee for decades by the time he ascended to the presidency. He had purchased Lee in 1767, when he was a teenager, from the estate of the late Col. John Lee of Westmoreland County, Virginia, for sixty-one pounds and fifteen shillings, a high price at that time for a Negro slave. Because he was a slave, no one recorded exactly how old Lee was or when he was born, or who his parents were. Washington bought him from Mrs. Mary Lee, the widow of Col. John Lee, one of four slaves purchased by

Washington. There are some black historians who insinuate that he kept the name Lee because he was the son of the colonel and an African slave woman, but nothing has ever been found to confirm that.

Washington was looking for a "body servant," someone to act as his valet, waiter, butler, or huntsman. And he was comfortable with having a slave act in that capacity, having been a slave master since his early adolescence. Washington inherited his first ten slaves in 1743 from his deceased father, although he didn't have personal control until he turned eighteen and bought his first land. That same year, he inherited eleven more slaves, and four years later, in 1754, his brother Lawrence left him six more in his will.

That same year, Washington leased Mount Vernon and its eighteen resident slaves, transferred his slaves there, and bought sixteen more. His marriage to Martha Dandridge Custis took him to an entirely new level, because the richest widow then in Virginia brought along with her eighty-four more slaves under her control (the slaves were dower slaves, under Martha Custis's control but to be divided among the surviving Custis heirs upon her death). Now truly the stereotypical Virginia plantation owner, Washington bought thirteen more slaves and, from 1761 to 1773, another forty-two. Lawrence's wife willed him six more slaves in 1762, but the true increase came through natural procreation from the slaves. As a result, Mount Vernon's slave population grew rapidly, numbering perhaps 150 or more by the time of the Revolution.

Of all those slaves, Lee was Washington's favorite. Lee was at Washington's side when he traveled to the meeting of the First Continental Congress in Philadelphia in 1774, and rode with him during the Revolutionary War. Lee "rode alongside Washington in the thick of battle, ready to hand over to the general a spare horse or his telescope or whatever else might be needed," recalled George Washington Parke Custis, the grandson of Martha Washington and future father-in-law to Confederate general Robert E. Lee. The slave was armed and active in every engagement that endangered Washington's life with British cannon fire or muskets. And he was with Washington at Valley Forge and the famed crossing of the Delaware River to attack the Hessians.

"Was it not cold enough at Valley Forge?" Custis would remember Lee reminiscing later with soldiers who followed Washington into battle. "Yes, was it; and I am sure you remember it was hot enough at Monmouth."

For years, whenever Americans saw Washington, they saw Lee. With his proximity to the nation's most famous American, Lee became the most recognizable African American slave of his time. Early paintings showed the two men together in battle, and Washington even had Lee painted into his family portrait with his wife and grandchildren.

In his book *George Washington and Slavery: A Documentary Portrayal,* Fritz Hirschfeld describes Lee as wearing "a bright red vest with polished brass buttons, long formal tailcoat, and white jersey, standing beside and slightly behind the chair in which Martha Washington is seated" in the painting *The Washington Family.* "His black hair is tied back in a bun, his forehead is high and broad, and a strong Roman nose accentuates well-formed eyes, heavy brows, a jutting chin and a fulsome mouth. Washington's tastes were known to incline toward the elegant and fastidious, and judging from the painting, Billy Lee met the highest standard."

Lee's connection with the general was such that he showed up repeatedly in Washington's portraits, with John Trumbull's *George Washington* portraying him as a young squat boy wearing an exotic turban. Painted from the artist's memory about five years after the Revolutionary War—and in the English tradition of portraying a gentleman with a servant in the background or, in the United States, a slave—this depiction of Lee as a dark-skinned, chubby-cheeked boy is considered inaccurate. Regardless of his portrayals, Lee was undoubtedly recognized on sight by the most powerful men in the US military and government, all of whom would likely have seen him with the general and now-president wherever they went.

And although he was a slave, Lee had to recognize that his life as Washington's body servant was better than the other slaves who toiled in fields of the South. As Washington's butler, body servant, and bodyguard, his job was to do whatever the general told him to do. Luckily, Washington didn't need much.

His mornings would go something like this, according to Hirschfeld's research: Lee "laid out the costume in which Washington would attend to his farms: on a recorded occasion a plain blue coat, white cashmere waistcoat, black breeches and black boots. Washington shaved himself.

George Washington and William Lee. LIBRARY OF CONGRESS

Then Will brushed his master's long hair, pulled it back tightly in what was considered a 'military manner' (as it left no curls at the side) and tied the queue firmly with a ribbon."

Lee would spend the rest of his day attending to Washington's needs, a duty that would bring him as close to the general as any slave could hope to be. Following behind Washington, Lee was present for the two meetings of the Continental Congress in Philadelphia, listening to the debates over freedom from England and the decision to place Washington in command of the colonist forces in 1775.

Lee may have considered himself a member of the Continental Army because of his travels with Washington. But he wasn't, because his master had forbidden slaves from fighting with the Americans. The British had no such reservations. Unlike the American army at the time, the British were more than willing to accept slaves into their forces and use them against the colonists. Even before hostilities had begun, the British were sowing discontent among American slaves yearning to be free with promises of liberty if they worked for the redcoats.

Lord Dunmore, governor of Virginia, proclaimed: "I hereby further declare all indented servants, Negroes, or others (appertaining to Rebels) free, that are able and willing to bear arms, they joining His Majesty's Troops, as soon as may be, for the more speedily reducing the Colony to a proper sense of their duty, to this Majesty's crown and dignity." Dunmore was able to recruit about eight hundred runaway slaves for his Virginia legion, the Ethiopian Regiment, alone. Tens of thousands more fought the colonists with the rest of the British army.

The colonists knew this was coming. James Madison wrote to William Bradford of his conviction that "If America & Britain come to an hostile rupture I am afraid an Insurrection among the slaves may & will be promoted." But the Americans were still hesitant to enlist these men to fight for their cause: Arming men who might turn those weapons against the people holding them and their brethren in slavery might have serious consequences after the conflict ended. But every war needs soldiers, and the Continental Army was no different. By the end of December 1775, Washington had altered his views to accommodate the situation, issuing orders that because "Numbers of free Negroes are desirous of inlisting, he gives leave to the recruiting Officers, to entertain them, and promises to lay the matter before the Congress, who he doubts not will approve of it."

Despite his need, Washington would only go so far so fast: On January 12, 1777, he sent out a general order to instruct recruiters to "enlist none but Freemen." That didn't stop Washington from marching Lee into battle with him. Body servant, such as was Lee's function, was a special category of slaves often used as armed bodyguards in times and places of danger.

For example, Custis recalled that during the Revolutionary War, "Close to his master (wrapped in a blanket, but 'all accoutered' for instant service) snored the stout yet active form of Billy, the celebrated body servant during the whole of the Revolutionary war."

And Washington's needs always came first. For example, at Monmouth, New Jersey, the American forces fought the British to a standstill for one of the first times in the war. But it almost wasn't meant to be. Retreat had been sounded by one of Washington's officers, an order that infuriated the general.

"Sending certain officers to check the advance, he formed the second line himself. A white charger, which he was riding for the first time, wearied, sank under him, and died," author Norman Hapgood wrote in the book *George Washington*. "Washington mounted a chestnut blood-mare, which his servant Billy was leading, and on this he rode along the line, urging the men to receive the enemy, and promising them support from the southern troops."

What did that leave for Lee to ride, in the midst of this major battle? The slave likely had to keep up the best he could on foot until he could procure another animal for himself.

Lee's life wasn't in danger from only the British. He also had to keep up with Washington, who was called by Thomas Jefferson "the best horseman of his age." And Lee apparently was no slouch, because he matched Washington in horsemanship in the field. Custis described the slave valet's horse skills as such:

"Will, the huntsman, better known in Revolutionary lore as Billy, rode a horse called Chinkling, a surprising leaper, and made very much like its rider, low but sturdy, and of great bone and muscle. Will had but one order, which was to keep with the hounds; and mounted on Chinkling, a

French horn at his back, throwing himself almost at length on the animal, with its spur in flank, this fearless horseman would rush, at full speed, through brake or tangled wood, in a style at which modern horsemen would stand aghast."

One example of the recklessness they showed came as they tried to break up a fight in Cambridge, Massachusetts, between Virginia riflemen and New England fishermen, perhaps prompted by the presence of African American soldiers in the northern unit. The fight came to Washington's attention as it threatened to break out into a riot.

"The General threw the bridle of his horse into his servant's hands, and, rushing into the thickest of the fight, seized two tall, brawny riflemen by the throat, keeping them at arm's length, talking to and shaking them," said Samuel Adams Drake in his book *Historic Mansions and Highways Around Boston: Being a New and Rev. Ed. of "Old Landmarks and Historic Fields of Middlesex."* "His commanding presence and gestures, together with the great physical strength he displayed,—for he held the men he had seized as incapable of resistance as babes,—caused the angry soldiers to fall back to the right and left. Calling the officers around him, with their aid the riot was quickly suppressed. The General, after giving orders appropriate to prevent the recurrence of such an affair, cantered away from the field, leaving officers and men alike astonished and charmed with what they had witnessed."

Given the description and the time frame, it is likely the slave was none other than Lee.

Despite the close calls, Lee survived all of his wartime travels with Washington unscathed. But his peacetime life was not as tranquil, with two serious injuries disabling him for life.

Lee was out with Washington on one of his surveying trips when his first serious accident happened. Washington wrote about it in his diary on April 22, 1785: "After having run one course & part of another, My Servant William (one of the Chain Carriers) fell, and broke the pan of his knee, wch. put a stop to my Surveying; & with much difficulty I was able to get him to Abingdon, being obliged to get a sled to carry him on, as he could neither Walk, stand or ride." Three years later, Lee fell again and broke his other knee, according to Washington's diary: "Having sent my Waiter Will to Alexandria to the Post Office he fell at Mr. Porters door and broke the pan of his other Knee & and was not able to return."

But when Washington was elected president in 1789, he insisted on taking Lee with him. Lee attempted to make the journey to New York City for the inauguration, but had to be left in Philadelphia for medical treatment.

Lee had "his knee examined by several local physicians including Dr. William Smith . . . and Dr. James Hutchinson," Washington's agent in Philadelphia wrote to the new president. Billy improved under the ministrations of the two doctors, and Biddle wrote to Lear, on May 25: "I shall have a Steel brace made this day by directions of Dr. Hutchinson to strengthen Billy's Knee which will not only render his traveling more safe but enable him in some measure to walk & I shall send him on some day this week by way of Bordertown & Amboy of which I shall advise."

There may have been a second reason for Lee to linger in Philadelphia.

Lee's time with Washington wasn't all horse riding and wig brushing. He also found time for gentler pursuits. While in Philadelphia at Washington's military headquarters, Lee met a free black woman who worked as a washerwoman for the colonial army, Margaret Thomas. She joined the staff at Washington's headquarters in February 1776, according to the accounts of his household manager Ebenezer Austin. At that time, Washington was living in the Cambridge mansion, now known as Longfellow House, trying to push the British military out of Boston. Thomas's duties included washing and mending clothes, and she apparently followed Washington's headquarters throughout the war, sending at least one bill for her services from Valley Forge.

Sometime during the Revolutionary War, Lee wooed and won Thomas for his own, even though she was a free woman and Lee a slave. But there is no record of Thomas ever joining Lee at Mount Vernon, despite attempts by Washington to get her to come down to stay with Lee. In 1784, Washington tried to help out his longtime slave by sending for his wife, even though he apparently did not have a great relationship with Margaret Thomas. In a letter he wrote on July 28, 1784, Washington said:

The mulatto fellow William, who has been with me all the War is attached (married he says) to one of his own colour a free woman, who, during the War was also of my family. She has been in an infirm state of health for sometime, and I had conceived that the connection between them had ceased, but I am mistaken; they are both applying to me to get her here, and tho' I never wished to see her more yet I cannot refuse his request (if it can be complied with on reasonable terms) as he has lived with me so long and followed my fortunes through the War with fidility. After premising this much, I have to beg the favor to procure her passage to Alexandria, either by Sea, in the Stage, or in the passage of boat from the head of the Elk, as you shall think cheapest and best, and her situation will admit; the cost of either I will pay. Her name is Margaret Thomas allias Lee (the name by which he calls himself). She lives in Philada. with Isaac and Hannah Sile—black people, who are oftern employ'd by families in the city as cooks.

While it's not mentioned, it is possible that Thomas stayed in Philadelphia and was there when Lee stopped in the city while on his way to join Washington after his inauguration. And who could blame him? He considered himself married to a woman who likely knew that she could be sold into slavery if she stepped below the Mason-Dixon Line, and therefore would never join with him at the place Lee called home. It is not known what happened to Margaret and Lee's relationship, whether she joined him in New York City or stayed in Philadelphia for the remainder of her days. What is known, however, is that Lee eventually left Philadelphia and joined Washington in New York.

This wasn't Lee's first time in New York City. Washington had been elected as the Continental Army's commander-in-chief in 1775, and he and Lee had been present for the successful Siege of Boston and the retreat of the British army to Canada. Washington correctly predicted that the British general Sir William Howe would regroup and make the newly bustling Manhattan his next target. Rushing his troops south from Boston, Washington occupied New York City in March 1776, which was then limited to the southern end of Manhattan.

Washington made his headquarters the house called Richmond Hill, the former home of Maj. Abraham Mortier, paymaster of the British army in the colony. The colonial estate likely reminded Lee and the general of their Mount Vernon home, "a wooden building of massive architecture, with a lofty portico supported by Ionic columns, the front walls decorated with pilasters of the same order and its whole appearance distinguished by a Palladian character of rich though sober ornament." This house was the scene of many conferences that determined the early strategy of the American Revolution, and here William Lee likely met many of the future leaders of the new country they were fighting for, some of whom would remember the slave in his later years.

Richmond Hill was also likely Lee's first residence in New York City, with Washington making Richmond Hill his headquarters from April until August 1776, staying there until being forced to evacuate the city by the impending advance of an overwhelming British force. Given their relationship, it was not unusual for the new president to demand Lee's presence when he returned to New York in his new position, even though New York City and New York State were in the midst of divesting themselves of the evil of slavery.

Slavery was a part of every American colony until outlawed in the first Vermont constitution of 1777. Pennsylvania gradually abolished slavery, beginning three years later. Court decisions freed all Massachusetts slaves by 1783. But in New York, slavery remained economically important. Emancipation came grudgingly, and not completely until 1827. By the time Washington arrived to take the presidency, slavery was on the wane in the city. The British, who had used New York City as their headquarters during the Revolutionary War, sheltered many African slaves who had escaped from American slave masters in the city and evacuated as many as three thousand of them to Canada when it became apparent that the Continental Army would win the war and demand their slaves back.

Deborah Squash was one of these escapees, described by one of Washington's employees as "a woman about sixteen years old," and the British later described her as a "stout wench, thick lips, pock marked." Like many escaped slaves, Squash headed to British-occupied territory, of which New York City was the headquarters. After arriving in New York, she married a man named Harvey Squash, who belonged to a man named Lynch, who had bought him from a British officer.

When the British abandoned New York City after losing the war with the colonies, the commander in charge, Sir Guy Carleton, refused to return the newly freed slaves to their owners despite demands from plantation owners like Washington. One of Washington's aides later noted that Carleton "insisted that he conceived it could not have been the intention of the British government by the Treaty of Peace to reduce themselves to the necessity of violating their faith to the negroes who came into the British lines."

Washington apparently was furious. "I was surprized to hear you mention, that an Embarkation had already taken place, in which a large Number of Negroes had been carried away," he said in a letter to Carleton. "Whether this Conduct is consonant to, or how far it may be deemed an Infraction of the Treaty, is not for me to decide. I cannot however conceal from your Excellency that my private opinion is, that the measure is totally different from the Letter and Spirit of the Treaty." But there was nothing he could do, because Squash was on one of the first British ships headed toward Nova Scotia, where she lived out the rest of her life.

Given his access to Washington, Lee had to be privy to his master's efforts to return Mount Vernon's escaped slaves, but there is no record of what he thought about the general's attempts to get his war slaves back. It is also likely that Lee noticed the antislavery feelings that were surging through New York, considering that some of the groups were bringing their complaints directly to Washington.

In 1796, Edward Rushton, a prominent English antislavery advocate, called Washington out on his slavery views in a public letter.

"My business is with George Washington of Mount Vernon in Virginia, a man who not withstanding his hatred of oppression and his ardent love of liberty holds at this moment hundreds of his fellow being in a state of abject bondage," Rushton said. "Yes: you who conquered under the banners of freedom—you who are now the first magistrate of a free people are (strange to relate) a slave holder . . . Shame! Shame! That man should be deemed the property of man or that the name of Washington should be found among the list of such proprietors . . . Ages to come will read with Astonishment that the man who was foremost to wrench the rights of America from the tyrannical grasp of Britain was among the last to relinquish his own oppressive hold of poor unoffending negroes."

In addition, antislavery forces were badgering the new Congress to ban slavery nationwide behind arguments from Benjamin Franklin, president of the Pennsylvania Society for Promoting the Abolition of Slavery and the Relief of Free Negroes Unlawfully Held in Bondage. Unfortunately, Congress wasn't ready, and the antislavery petition was sent to a committee, where it died.

Washington never said anything publicly as president about freeing slaves, worried that attempts to emancipate the South's slaves would drive a wedge into the fledgling country, whose survival was his chief goal. While Washington said nothing publicly, privately he was glad to see the Quakers' bill fail. "The memorial of the Quakers (& a very mal-apropos one it was) has at length been put to sleep, from which it is not (likely) it will awake before the year 1808," Washington wrote in a letter.

This is the situation Lee found himself approaching as he headed toward New York and his new home. Did escape cross his mind? Or did his two injured knees prevent him from hoping for escape and a better life than as a slave to Washington?

What Lee knew as he headed toward New York City was that he would be staying in the new nation's first presidential mansion. But what he didn't know was that his new home was no Mount Vernon. The Franklin House apparently wasn't even the best house in New York City. It was, however, the best home available for rent to the American government at the time it was needed.

After Congress unanimously affirmed Washington as president, lawmakers quickly began searching for a suitable workspace and living quarters for the new president before his arrival in Manhattan. One of Washington's former Revolutionary War officers, Samuel Osgood, offered his residence at the corner of Cherry and Pearl (now known as Franklin) Streets off Franklin Square in what is now called the Bowery. Merchant Walter Franklin built the mansion, one of the finest in the city at that time, in 1770. Upon his death the property near the port along the East River became Osgood's through his marriage with the widow of Mr. Franklin.

Judging by illustrations of the 1850s, it was a foursquare three-story house with five bays of rectangular windows on each side, a broad frieze with bowknots and blank panels, and a roof balustrade with panels at the corners. The dwelling was similar to comparable elite New York households of the late eighteenth century, with a combination of "plain" and "fancy" furnishings.

Washington, a meticulous record keeper, noted at the end of his two terms that his executive furniture included both inlaid and plain furniture left over from his stay in New York. Those with inlay, including a breakfast and tea table, were presumably in the fashionable neo-classical style and placed in the best rooms of the house. The objects specified as "plain" included three of the six groupings of mahogany chairs Washington identified, and were probably either simply finished examples of Hepplewhite designs or of the more established Chippendale style.

One observer noted that the Franklin House "partook of all the attributes of our republican institutions, possessed at the same time that degree of dignity and regard for appearances, so necessary to give our infant republic respect in the eyes of the world. The house was handsomely furnished; the equipages neat, with horses of the first order; the servants wore the family liveries; and with the exception of a steward and housekeeper, the whole establishment differed little from that of a private gentleman."

That was good enough for Congress, who rented the house from Osgood for $845 a year. A joint resolution of the Senate and House of Representatives directed Osgood to "put the house and the furniture thereof in proper condition for the residence and use of the President of the United States." Congress then appropriated and spent eight thousand dollars preparing the executive residence for the Washington family. Substantial alterations were made, including expanding the drawing room in order to accommodate presidential entertaining. Osgood's niece, Sally Robinson, described in a letter the effect this sum had on the dwelling, and its final appearance with "every room furnished in the most elegant manner."

"I went the morning before the General's arrival to look at it," she said. "The best of furniture in every room, and the greatest quantity of plate and china I ever saw; the whole of the first and second stories is papered and the floors covered with the richest kinds of Turkey and Wilton carpets. There is scarcely anything talked about now but General Washington and the Palace."

The Washingtons were so besieged with callers, officials, ex-soldiers, and with both high and low in social and private life that it became necessary to set aside certain days for the president to receive. Tuesdays were exclusively for men, especially foreign ministers and other distinguished callers who sought an introduction. State dinners were on Thursdays, and Friday nights were when Mrs. Washington entertained, events that the president attended in an unofficial capacity. At these evening receptions light refreshments were served, but the guests were not permitted to linger overlong. Mrs. Washington is said to have reminded them: "The General retires at nine, and I usually precede him."

But the memory of those parties struck their grandson, who attended the soirees with his famous family.

"Persons visiting the house in Cherry Street at this time of day will wonder how a building so small could contain the many and mighty spirits that thronged its halls in olden days," he said. "The levees of the first President were attended by these illustrious patriots and statesmen, and by many other of the patriots, statesmen, and soldiers, who could say of the Revolution, 'magna pars fui,' while numbers of foreigners and strangers of distinction crowded to the seat of the general government, all anxious to witness the grand experiment that was to determine how much rational liberty mankind is capable of enjoying, without said liberty degenerating into licentiousness."

With all of those visitors, Lee wasn't the only slave whom Washington brought up to New York City from Mount Vernon. The house of a president, especially one who needed to entertain dignitaries, politicians, military officials, ambassadors, plantation owners, and other important figures, needed a staff. So after Washington arrived in Manhattan, the new president sent back to Virginia for his wife and a retinue of slaves to occupy the first executive mansion. In mid-May 1789, after the inauguration, Martha, two of their grandchildren and seven house slaves—Lee, Austin, Giles, Paris, Christopher Sheels, Molly, and Oney Judge—left for New York City to join Washington.

Unlike Lee and Oney Judge—who became famous later on in life for becoming one of the few slaves to escape from a president—little is known about most of the other slaves who traveled from Mount Vernon to New York City. For example, all that is known about Molly is that she was a nursemaid to Martha Washington's two grandchildren. And there isn't much information about Paris other than that he was a dower slave and stable hand, and eventually displeased Washington because he was returned to Mount Vernon in 1791.

"Paris has become so lazy, self willed, and impudent that John (the Coachman) has no sort of Government of him; on the contrary, John says it was a maxim with Paris, to do nothing he was ordered, and every thing he was forbid," Washington said. "This conduct, added to the incapacity of Giles for a Postillion, who I believe will never be able to mount a horse again for that purpose has induced me to find Paris some other employment than in the Stables." Paris died three years after being shipped back to Mount Vernon.

Giles was also a dower slave and footman for Washington's carriage at Mount Vernon. Giles accompanied Washington and Lee on their trip to the Constitutional Convention in Philadelphia from May to September 1787. When Washington visited the South from March to July 1791, Giles drove the baggage wagon. During this tour Giles sustained an unknown injury that left him unable to ride a horse, as noted by Washington. He was sent back to Mount Vernon, where he doesn't appear on the 1799 slave rolls, most likely because of his death in the intervening years.

Austin was Oney Judge's half brother and a favorite of Martha Washington, with his mother Betty coming to Mount Vernon with Mrs. Washington after her marriage. During the Revolutionary War, Austin is believed to be one of the slave chaperones who traveled with Martha Washington when she visited her husband on the battlefield. In addition, Austin was one of the waiters at Mount Vernon and a footman for Washington's carriage, making him useful inside the presidential household.

Austin stayed in the New York executive mansions with the Washingtons, and transferred with the presidency and the nation's capital to Philadelphia. When he left for New York City, Austin left behind a wife on Mount Vernon named Charlotte. In a sign of how much the president's family trusted Austin, they gave Austin twenty dollars to go visit his family in Virginia but on December 20, 1794, while trying to cross a river on horseback near Hartford, Maryland, he fell from his horse. He was pulled from the water in serious condition and died soon after.

The slaves the president brought to New York City also represented him in public when they escorted him around the country or simply up and down the streets of Manhattan. So with his high profile and social schedule, Washington wanted his slaves to look their best. As a president's property, Lee and the others couldn't be seen in the hand-me-down and homemade clothing that other slaves at Mount Vernon were issued once a year. Instead, the slaves who traveled with the new president to the first capital in New York City were issued uniforms called livery, which were based on a three-piece suit of an eighteenth-century gentleman, and included a coat, waistcoat, or vest and breeches.

Livery was usually made of fine wool in the colors of the slave owner's coat-of-arms and would be edged with woven "livery lace." George Washington's first surviving order for livery dates to the end of 1755, when he asked his British agent to send "2 Compleat Livery Suits for Servants," with enough extra cloth to make a second set for each man: "I wou'd have you choose the livery by our Arms; only, as the Field of the Arms is white. [sic] I think the Cloaths had better not be quite so. . . . The Trimmings and Facings of Scarlet, and a Scarlet Waistcoat . . . If Livery Lace is not quite disus'd, I shoud [sic] be glad to have these Cloaths Laced. I like that fashion best. and [sic] two Silver lac'd Hats for the above L[iver]y."

Washington was always concerned about how the slaves looked to the public, as could be seen when he returned to Mount Vernon and was scheduled to attend a dinner in Alexandria, Virginia.

"Upon examining the Caps of Giles and Paris I find they (especially Paris's) are much worn, and will be unfit to appear in with decency, after the journey from hence is performed, I therefore request that you will have two handsome ones made, with fuller and richer tassels at top than the old ones have. That the maker of them may have some government in the size the enclosed dimentions of their heads, will I presume be sufficient," Washington said in a letter to Lear.

Demands upon the hospitality of the first presidential mansion constantly increased, and at best space was lacking for the comfortable accommodation of the family and their nine-slave entourage. Eventually, Washington would abandon the Cherry Street house and move into the much larger McComb mansion on Broadway, only a few blocks from Federal Hall, making that residence the second presidential mansion.

Leila Herbert, in her 1900 book, *The First American: His Homes and His Households*, said the McComb mansion was considered "the finest private dwelling in the city, in the most fashionable quarter . . . four stories high—and larger in every way. It was of double brick, the front handsome. The usual brass knocker was on the heavy entrance-door, which opened immediately upon the street but for a short flight of steps. Long glass doors led from a drawing-room to the inviting balcony, and from the rear window the eye delighted in an extended view of the Hudson and the Jersey shore."

The change in addresses wasn't the only alteration in the Washington household. The injuries to Lee's knees became worse, causing Washington to look for a replacement for his favorite slave. The president knew how difficult that would be. "I do not yet know whether I shall get a substitute for William; nothing short of excellent qualities and a man of good appearance, would induce me to do it," Washington said in a letter dated November 8, 1793. "And under my present view of the matter too, who would employ himself otherwise than William did; that is as a Butler as well as a Valette for my wants of the latter are so trifling that any man (as Willm. Was) would soon be ruined by ideleness who had only them to attend to."

But eventually, Washington promoted one of the other New York slaves, Lee's nephew Christopher Sheels, as Lee's replacement, and he retired his longtime companion back to Mount Vernon, where Lee was retrained as a shoemaker. Sheels apparently wasn't a good replacement; Washington remarked in November 1793 that Sheels was "too little acquainted with the arrangement of a Table, & too stupid for a Butler." But Sheels would last until after Washington and the federal government moved to Philadelphia and a third presidential mansion.

Sheels would eventually become one of Washington's favored slaves, perhaps because of his parentage. He was the son of Alice, a spinner, and an unknown father, and the grandson of Doll, the first cook for Mount

Vernon. Maybe that was why Sheels got treatment few other Mount Vernon slaves would ever have expected.

First, Washington showed an unusual amount of concern about Sheels's health, and even paid for his slave to go on an out-of-state doctor visit. Months after Washington retired from the presidency and left Philadelphia, Sheels was attacked by a rabid dog at Mount Vernon in 1797. After sending him to a doctor in Alexandria, who Washington noted "has cut out so far as He could, the place Bit, applyed Ointment to keep it open, And put the Boy under a Course of Mercury," the former president decided that something more must be done.

Washington remembered a "hex-doctor" in Lebanon, Pennsylvania, Dr. William Henry Stoy, "celebrated for curing persons bitten by mad animals." Not only did Washington send Sheels back to Pennsylvania to be cured, but he also gave him twenty-five dollars to cover all of his possible expenses and a letter from the nation's greatest hero and first president to present to the doctor to urge him to take on Sheels's case. "For besides the call of Humanity, I am particularly anxious for His cure, He being my own Body servant," Washington said in the letter. Stoy's remedy consisted of "one ounce of the herb, red chickweed, four ounces of theriac and one quart of beer, all well digested, the dose being a wine glassful," and the doctor wrote Washington on October 19, 1797, that Sheels was no longer in danger because he had taken his "medicine." Sheels, once he returned to Mount Vernon, declared himself cured, and unafraid of any other rabid dogs.

"Christopher continues to do well, & I believe is now free from apprehension of any bad consequences from the bite," Washington said in a letter.

For Sheels, this had to be a golden opportunity for escape. It is unknown for sure whether the slave was sent to Pennsylvania by himself or with a member of the Washington family to watch him (George Washington Lafayette, the son of Marquis de Lafayette accompanied him part of the way, having become friends with the slave during visits by his famous father to Mount Vernon) but most likely Sheels was on his own, since Washington gave the twenty-five dollars directly to him (Washington later noted that Sheels returned twelve dollars to him upon his return to Mount Vernon). With that money in his pocket, what brought a possibly unsupervised Sheels back to Mount Vernon?

Like Lee, Sheels was married, and that likely tied him to Virginia in a way that even his desire for freedom could not break. In September 1799, Sheels had requested Washington's permission to marry a slave from another plantation, a request that apparently was granted. "Sometime ago the Servant who waits upon me, Christopher (calling himself Christopher Sheels) asked my permission to marry a Mulatto girl belonging to you," Washington wrote in a September 19, 1799, letter to neighbor Roger West. "As he had behaved as well as servants usually do, I told him I had no objection to the union, provided your consent (which was necessary) could be obtained."

But once Washington agreed, Sheels decided that he had had enough of slave life. Like many of Washington's house slaves, Sheels was literate, and apparently the woman he chose as his wife could also read and write. Sheels's plan to escape with his wife was foiled not by slave catchers or slave turncoats, but by a simple mistake—a lost sheet of paper. A note discussing the plan was inadvertently dropped and Washington discovered it and alerted the owner of Sheels's wife.

"I was in hopes that this connexion (as I heard the Girl well spoken of) would have been some brake upon his future conduct; but the reverse is to be apprehended from the enclosed note, which was found in my yard; dropped it is supposed, by him," Washington said. "Whether the girl can write, or not; and whose writing it is, are equally unknown to me; but it undoubtedly came from her to the Husband, from the purport of it. He is unacquainted with my possession, as I think his wife ought to be, until proper measures can be taken."

History does not record whether Washington ever confronted Sheels about his escape plan or what punishment the slave's wife—who may have been on the verge of being freed according to Washington's letter—may have suffered. It can be assumed that his privileges of traveling away from Mount Vernon on his own—even to see his wife—were revoked, but there is no proof of that.

Washington had a track record of dealing harshly with slaves who attempted to escape: In 1766, after recapturing the escaped Tom, who the general admitted was "exceeding healthy, strong, and good at the Hoe," Washington now described the slave as "both a Rogue & Runaway (tho. he was by no means remarkable for the former, and never practiced the latter till of late)" and immediately sold him off to the island of Saint Christopher in the West Indies. And just to be sure, Washington warned the slave captain to "keep him handcuffed till you get to sea" lest Tom attempt to escape being sold away across the ocean away from everything he had ever known. Washington did the same five years later when he sold Will Shag to Port-au-Prince in Saint Domingue after the slave whipped a slave overseer who tried to discipline him and kept running away.

With that history, one would suspect that Sheels would be in deep trouble with Washington for even thinking about escaping Mount Vernon. Unfortunately, there is no record of whether Washington told Sheels that he knew about the escape plan or that Sheels even went beyond planning and tried to escape with his wife. What is known is that Sheels stayed on as Washington's body servant, and was with Washington on the day he died.

Washington fell sick in December 1799 after deciding to go outside to check his farms in snowy weather. No one noticed any change in his health when the sixty-seven-year-old ex-president returned to Mount Vernon, but when he woke up on Friday, December 13, he complained of a severe sore throat. Early that Saturday morning, he complained of chills to Martha Washington and by daybreak, Lear found him breathing with difficulty and hardly able to utter a word intelligently. He would only get worse as the day went on.

With Washington feeling poorly, Sheels apparently felt he needed to be close by in case the president needed anything, even though there apparently was nothing anyone could do for Washington. Sheels propped Washington up next to a fire while others sent out for physicians in hopes that something could be done. Doctors attempted rudimentary herbal treatments like gargling with sage tea and vinegar or a mixture of molasses, vinegar, and butter. None of it worked, and Washington's doctors next tried bloodletting, an ancient process where the blood is drained from a body in hopes of banishing ailments. An amazing five pints of blood were drained from Washington's body (the average adult body has between eight and ten pints of blood), and by the time the doctors were finished, blood was draining slowly and thickly from the president's body.

While all of this was going on, Sheels stood alertly at Washington's side. In between treatments, Washington noticed Sheels standing there at attention, and in his last gesture to a slave, the former president motioned for Sheels to take a seat beside his bed. Sheels would sit there for the rest of Washington's life, with the president dying between 10:00 and 11:00 p.m. December 14th, 1799. Performing one last service for Washington, Sheels emptied Washington's pockets and passed the keys to Mount Vernon over to Lear. After Washington's funeral, Sheels is recorded as continuing working at Mount Vernon through 1792, but he disappears from the slave rolls in 1802. As a dower slave, Sheels could have been sent to the plantation of one of Martha Washington's children, but there is no indication of what happened to him after the former first lady's death.

Even though Lee was at Mount Vernon during this time, the president never asked to see his previous body servant in the last hours of his life. There is no recorded interaction between the ex-president and his longtime companion after Washington left New York City and the presidency behind and returned to Mount Vernon. Instead of Lee, it was his brother Frank, the Mount Vernon butler who also had been purchased by Washington at the same time as William Lee, who was allowed into the room. But Sheels and Frank Lee weren't the only slaves present for Washington's last moments, because standing in the doorway of his room were the black slaves Caroline, Charlotte, and Molly. The next day, Sheels likely performed his daily duties for Washington one last time, washing and preparing the body for the funeral on December 18. After he was finished, Sheels, Lee, and the other slave butlers inside Mount Vernon were outfitted with new shoes—probably to look extra-special while waiting on guests attending the Wednesday funeral.

Despite Lee's banishment back to Mount Vernon, Washington did not forget his long service. The president, after retiring back to Mount Vernon, became one of the few slave-holding Founding Fathers to attempt to free his slaves. While he couldn't free all of the slaves at Mount Vernon (the majority of them belonged to the estate, and not him personally),

George Washington and his family, with slave William "Billy" Lee standing in the background. LIBRARY OF CONGRESS

Washington wrote into his will that they would be freed upon Martha Washington's death. "Upon the decease of my wife, it is my Will & desire that all the Slaves which I hold in my own right, shall receive their freedom," Washington said. But there was one caveat, one exception, for one person.

"To my Mulatto man William (calling himself William Lee) I give immediate freedom; or if he should prefer it (on account of the accidents which have befallen him, and which have rendered him incapable of walking or of any active employment) to remain in the situation he now is, it shall be optional in him to do so: In either case however, I allow him an annuity of thirty dollars during his natural life, which shall be independent of the victuals and cloaths he has been accustomed to receive, if he chooses the last alternative; but in full, with his freedom, if he prefers the first; & this I give him as a testimony of my sense of his attachment to me, and for his faithful services during the Revolutionary War," Washington wrote.

After Washington died, Lee chose to stay on at Mount Vernon. But Lee never forgot all of the places and people he had met during his life, and made sure they didn't forget him, Custis said. "Billy carefully reconnoitered the visitors as they arrived, and when a military title was announced, the old body-servant would send his compliments to the soldier, requesting an interview at his quarters; it was never denied, and Billy, after receiving a warm grasp of the hand, would say, 'Ah, Colonel, glad to see you; we of the army don't see one another often these peaceful times,'" Custis wrote. "'Glad to see your honor looking so well; remember you at headquarters. The new-time people don't know what we old soldiers did and suffered for the country in the old war. Was it not cold enough at Valley Forge? Yes, was it; and I am sure you remember it was hot enough at Monmouth. Ah, Colonel, I am a poor cripple; can't ride now, so I make shoes and think of the old times; the General often stops his horse here to inquire if I want any thing. I want for nothing, thank God, but the use of my limbs.'"

After all of the things he'd seen and done, Lee's life ended on a sad note. He became an alcoholic, perhaps to battle the pains from his injured knees. His drinking would lead to delirium tremens, a severe form of alcohol withdrawal that involves sudden and severe mental or nervous system changes. Custis was present for Lee's inevitable end.

"His master having left him a house, and a pension of one hundred and fifty dollars a year, Billy became a spoiled child of fortune," Custis said. "He was quite intemperate at times, and finally delirium tremens, with all its horrors, seized him. Westford frequently relieved him on such occasions, by bleeding him. One morning, a little more than thirty years ago, Westford was sent for to bring Billy out of a fit. The blood would not flow. Billy was dead!"

Even in death, Lee was accorded one last honor. He was laid to rest at Mount Vernon, one of the few slaves buried at the home of George Washington.

Like the rest of the slaves at Mount Vernon, Lee's final resting place is unmarked. But in 1983, Howard University college students designed and delivered to Mount Vernon a memorial for the plantation's slaves to mark their gravesite. The memorial, which consists of a granite column, on top of three circles with the words *faith, hope,* and *love* engraved on them, is adjacent to a 1929 Mount Vernon Ladies' Association marker noting the site of the slave burial ground. Lee is the only slave Mount Vernon historians can definitively say is buried in that plot.

CHAPTER 3

THE BEGINNING OF AFRICAN SLAVERY IN THE UNITED STATES

By the time William Lee was born, African American chattel slavery was a full-fledged institution in the British colonies in North America. Slavery had been in existence in Virginia and other colonies since the early 1600s, likely making Washington's body servant part of the fourth or fifth generation of African American slaves, people who no longer had firsthand experience in their native Africa, knowing only bondage in the nascent United States. In fact, the American institution of slavery had its British roots only hours away from Washington's Mount Vernon plantation.

In August 1619 a pirate ship sailed into the harbor at Jamestown, heavy laden with the spoils of an earlier raid on the high seas. While sailing looking for prey, the *White Lion*, a Dutch pirate ship from Vlissingen and its partner, the British man o' war the *Treasurer*, had come upon a Portuguese ship heading for Mexico.

The Portuguese slave ship, the *San Juan Bautista*, had acquired a cargo of Angolan slaves in the Ndongo region of Africa, and was heading across the Atlantic to sell them to the Spanish living in Veracruz on the east coast of modern-day Mexico. The Portuguese had been importing slaves from Africa for over a century, and the Spanish were using them, along with the Indians in Central and South America, to work the mines and to grow crops.

The two British ships, which were flying Dutch flags, attacked the *San Juan Bautista* in the Gulf of Mexico, intercepting it from its destination.

After hours of cannon fire, the *San Juan Bautista*'s captain, Manuel Mendes da Cunha, wisely surrendered. The *White Lion* sent twenty-five men to board the slave ship, expecting to find silver, gold, and other precious jewels. Instead, when they opened the hold, they saw 350 black faces peering up at them, hoping against hope that their freedom was near.

Being pirates, the crews of the *White Lion* and the *Treasurer* likely had no idea of what to do with their prize. So, taking some of the *San Juan Bautista*'s tallow and wax and at least sixty of the slaves, they released Captain da Cunha to deliver his remaining cargo at Veracruz.

The *White Lion* and the *Treasurer* headed back out to sea, but the battle against the *San Juan Bautista* had taken its toll. The *Treasurer* was damaged and slow, and food and supplies were beginning to run low for both ships, likely because of the extra mouths the pirates took on with their raid of the Portuguese slave ship. The *White Lion*, captained by privateer John Colyn Jope, docked at Bermuda and bartered with the islanders the only things it had left of value: fourteen Africans for supplies. And then it headed up the east coast of North America, toward the first English colony to be permanently planted on the soil of the future United States, Jamestown, Virginia.

Almost two decades before this battle, King James I agreed to give a charter to a group of English businessmen called the Virginia Company to establish a permanent British settlement in the Chesapeake region of North America. In December 1606, more than one hundred settlers departed London with instructions to tame the new continent, discover a new lucrative path to the riches of the Orient, and obtain treasure for king and country. In May 1607, the English landed on Jamestown Island on the banks of the James River, sixty miles from the mouth of the Chesapeake Bay. In a little over a month's time, the newcomers managed to "beare and plant palisadoes," enough to build a wooden fort with walls protecting a storehouse, church, and a number of houses. This fort was erected partly out of fear that Great Britain's enemy, the Spanish, would attack, and partly in response to ongoing attacks from one of the Virginia area's native tribes, the Algonquians.

Life was not easy for the British. Disease, famine, and continuing attacks by neighboring Algonquians took a tremendous toll on the colony, with only sixty of the original 214 settlers at Jamestown surviving even with the help of a friendly tribe, the Powhatans. Trade with the Powhatans revived the colony, with the Native Americans providing food and farming expertise in exchange for glass beads and implements of copper and iron. Eventually, the British made peace with other tribes, sealed by the wedding of Pocahontas, the favored daughter of the Algonquian chief Powhatan, to tobacco entrepreneur John Rolfe.

Pocahontas's famous trip to Great Britain, where she met King James and was feted by royal society, was aboard the *Treasurer*, perhaps explaining how and why that ship and the *White Lion* turned their rudders toward Virginia before heading back to Europe.

The *White Lion* sailed up the coast to Virginia, laden with its cargo of Angolan slaves. But these slaves were not the stereotypical African slaves that many would envision today. The land from which they were captured, Ndongo, was one of several sophisticated Iron Age states in Angola, a bustling kingdom of settled farmers, craftsmen, and cattle-herders. Angolans had embraced Christianity and were trading with Europe, and aboard the *White Lion* were several second- and third-generation Christians with names such as Mary, Isabella, Anthony, Antonio, Pedro, John, Katherine, and Angela.

By this time in Jamestown, the colonists were finding success growing tobacco, but needed more bodies to help harvest the "sweet-scented" leaves that were in demand in Europe. The Africans had arrived at harvest time. The colonists did not think twice about buying the slaves in exchange for some food that the pirates needed to make the long journey back to Europe.

"About the latter end of August, a Dutch man of Warr of the burden of a 160 tunes arrived at Point-Comfort, the Comandor name Capt Jope, his Pilott for the West Indies one Mr Marmaduke an Englishman," Rolfe said in a letter. "They mett wth the Trer in the West Indyes, and determyned to hold consort shipp hetherward, but in their passage lost one the other. He brought not any thing but 20. and odd Negroes, wth the Governor and Cape Marchant bought for vietualle (whereof he was in greate need as he p'tended) at the best and easyest rate they could."

The famous Capt. John Smith also noted their arrival in his log. "About the last of August, there came to Virginia a dutch man of warre that sold us twenty negars," Smith wrote.

The *Treasurer* limped into port a few days later, but kept its load of slaves for a trip down to Bermuda. The very next year, having sold many of the Angolan slaves in the Caribbean, the *Treasurer* returned with a few more than a half dozen of those same slaves, who were then sold to Virginia colonists before the leaky, tired old ship overturned and sank in a creek off the James River.

In all, thirty-two African slaves (seventeen females and fifteen males) were purchased by Jamestown settlers.

In the beginning, the first group of Africans was split up and sent to a handful of tobacco plantations along the James River. They were put to work mostly planting and harvesting tobacco, but records show they also raised cattle and acted as traders, selling produce to Indians and to European ships arriving in Jamestown. During the next two decades, some were permitted to raise crops and cattle to purchase their freedom. They married, sometimes to their fellow Africans and sometimes to English settlers, and they raised families. By the 1640s and 1650s, a handful of families from the *Bautista* bought their own farms around Jamestown.

Two of the Angolan Africans, Isabella and Antonio, stayed in Hampton and became servants in the household of William Tucker, who was the commander at Point Comfort. They are believed to have become indentured servants serving a term of seven years. In 1624 they would give birth to William Tucker, the first documented child of African descent born in America.

It's not clear if the Angolan Africans were considered slaves or indentured servants in the beginning. (An indentured servant would be required to work a set amount of time, then granted freedom.) Records of 1623 and 1624 list them as servants, and indeed later records show increasing numbers of free blacks, some of whom were assigned land. Most likely some Africans were slaves and some were servants. During their indentured servitude, they were obligated to work for a master for five to seven years and learned carpentry, blacksmithing, or other skills. After that time, they became free and were usually given "freedom dues," such as a plot of land and supplies.

Some found success. In time, John Graweere became a respected officer of the Jamestown court. Margaret Cornish charmed the son of a Jamestown legislator. John Pedro became a member of the militia. And then there was Anthony Johnson. Called "Antonio the negro" in the 1625 Virginia census, he was brought to Jamestown in 1621 and worked on a plantation for a wealthy white family. He married, had four children, and eventually became free. To proclaim his freedom, he changed his name to Anthony Johnson, because most servants did not have last names or used their master's name. Johnson soon owned land, cattle, and even indentured servants from Africa.

Whatever the status of these first Africans to arrive at Jamestown, it is clear that by 1640, at least one African had been legally declared a slave. This African was ordered by the court "to serve his said master or his assigns for the time of his natural life here or elsewhere." This was the first documented African American slave, John Punch.

Punch was one of three servants working for a Washington, DC–area farmer named Hugh Gwyn. Punch and his two white compatriots, John Gregory and Victor, felt mistreated by Gwyn, so they decided to run away. They were captured and returned to Jamestown, where a court sentenced them all to thirty lashes. The two white men were sentenced to an additional four years of indentured servitude, one more for Gwyn and three more for the colony for their escape. But the punishment was different for Punch. Punch was ordered to "serve his said master or his assigns for the time of his natural Life here or elsewhere." John Punch no longer had hope for freedom. He became the first documented slave.

It would get worse. By 1625, ten slaves were listed in the first census of Jamestown. The first public slave auction of twenty-three individuals was held in Jamestown square itself in 1638. In 1705, the Virginia General Assembly removed any lingering uncertainty on whether blacks were servants or slaves; it made a declaration that would seal the fate of African Americans for generations to come.

All servants imported and brought into the Country . . . who were not Christians in their native Country . . . shall be accounted and be slaves. All Negro, mulatto and Indian slaves within this dominion

*. . . shall be held to be real estate. If any slave resist his master . . .
correcting such slave, and shall happen to be killed in such correction
. . . the master shall be free of all punishment . . . as if such accident
never happened.*

The code, which would also serve as a model for other colonies, went even further. The law imposed harsh physical punishments, since enslaved persons who did not own property could not be required to pay fines. It stated that slaves needed written permission to leave their plantation, that slaves found guilty of murder or rape would be hanged, that for robbing or any other major offense, the slave would receive sixty lashes and be placed in stocks, where his or her ears would be cut off, and that for minor offenses, such as associating with whites, slaves would be whipped, branded, or maimed.

Whatever the original status of the first Africans to enter the American colonies, slavery had taken hold, and it would take a war between American brothers to loosen its grip.

CHAPTER 4

ONEY JUDGE AND PHILADELPHIA

EVERY EVENING, MARTHA WASHINGTON WOULD BID GOOD NIGHT TO President George Washington and retire to her room in the president's mansion to prepare for bed. And every evening, Oney "Ona" Judge followed behind her.

Every night, Martha and Oney prayed and sang hymns together. Upon Mrs. Washington retiring to her room, Oney would remove the elaborate caps that Martha favored in hopes that they would make her seem taller and carefully unbutton the fine colonial-style dresses the first lady felt she had to wear as the wife of the first American president. Oney would bathe her in one of the mansion's bathtubs, brush her hair, care for her clothing, and get her comfortably into bed.

The two women, sometimes joined by the first lady's granddaughter, would then sing hymns and pray, and Martha would read from a Bible until she fell asleep. The next morning, the routine would begin again. Oney would wake Martha, brush her hair again, help her mistress dress and powder for official receptions, and prepare her for her social calls and outings. This was Oney's life, and for a while, she appreciated what privileges she had, because she knew it could have been much worse.

As a child of Mount Vernon, Oney began her life in the slave quarters with the rest of the Washingtons' African slaves. But as a child, she had been selected to live in the big house, perhaps because of her fair skin and pleasant demeanor. As she grew older, she became a master at Martha's favorite craft, sewing, and the two women became inseparable. They worked together as part of Mount Vernon's sewing circle, with Oney learning weaving, spinning, fine needlepoint, and cloth making. When

George Washington became the first president, Martha refused to leave Mount Vernon without Oney. Whenever the first lady ventured out into New York or Philadelphia society or to fine stores, Oney was at her side.

In return for her loyalty and skill, Martha exempted her from strenuous work, occasionally giving Oney her own room in the President's House, allowing her to dress in fine clothes and rewarding her with money for theaters and circuses. In fact, Martha Washington later in life would tell people she considered the slender teenager a surrogate daughter.

With the Washingtons, Oney Judge saw the countryside, met America's leading citizens, and lived better than most people of her time, black or white. It was a life that many Americans of her time would have loved. That made it more shocking when one evening, as President Washington's term of office was coming to a close, Martha Washington made an announcement.

Her eldest granddaughter, Elizabeth Custis, had married English expatriate Thomas Law on March 20, 1796. The Washingtons were unable to attend the Virginia wedding, but invited the couple to visit Philadelphia and honeymoon with them. When the Laws left, Martha Washington told Oney, her time with the Washingtons would be done. There would be no more shopping trips or social calls or carriage rides. No more fancy clothes or trips to the theater or sewing circles. There would not even be a return to Mount Vernon life with the Washingtons for Oney.

The slave would be going with the Laws—as the First Family's wedding gift.

Oney Judge was born in 1773 at Mount Vernon to Betty, one of the slaves brought to the plantation through the marriage of George and Martha Washington, and Andrew Judge, a white indentured servant at the plantation. As the child of a dower slave, Oney was not the property of George or Martha Washington, but the property of the estate of Martha's late husband, Daniel Parkes Custis.

When Martha married George and moved to Mount Vernon, the Custis slaves and the Mount Vernon slaves and servants commingled, and Judge, a white English tailor, impregnated Betty. Judge never claimed Oney or her sister Delphy as his children, and left them behind after fulfilling his four-year contract at Mount Vernon. But Oney never lacked strong male figures in her life, because by the time she was ten years old, she had another man she could observe: George Washington. The Washingtons could never have children of their own, so they informally adopted Martha's granddaughter, Nelly Custis, and moved her to Mount Vernon. And as Nelly grew older, she needed a playmate.

Oney's mother may have pushed Martha Washington into making her child her mistress's playmate. Betty had a longstanding relationship with Martha as one of her seamstresses. Betty was an expert at textiles and spent much of her time spinning thread, weaving cloth, and tailoring clothes for both the Washingtons and her fellow slaves. That gave her superior status among the slaves and preferential treatment from the Washingtons for her and her daughters. There would be no backbreaking plantation work or household drudgery for Betty and her daughters, but Betty knew that their situation, like any slave's, could change in a moment.

Moving Oney into the big house, even if it meant separation from her mother and sister, could only be good for the girl's status with the Washingtons, so Betty had to be pleased when Martha had Oney moved into a room in the mansion, a room that she sometimes shared with Nelly. Martha also promoted Oney to the Mount Vernon sewing circle, a favorite pastime of the mistress of the house. Spending more and more time with Oney, Martha soon became fond of her and her skills. And by the time Oney was ten, she had been promoted once again to Martha's personal maid—and her relationship with the future first lady blossomed.

George Washington himself noted that Oney "was brought up and treated more like a child than a servant" by Martha. For years, the young black slave would be the last person Mrs. Washington would see at night and the first thing she would see in the morning. Whether at Mount Vernon, in Philadelphia, or New York City, Oney and Martha would follow the same routine.

So when George Washington won the presidency, there were only seven slaves who left Mount Vernon with them to move to New York City to live in the presidential residence, and Oney was among them. And when the national capital was transferred to Philadelphia in 1790, she transferred right along with the president and his family and continued to lead her charmed life. (The compromise that settled the question of where the new capital of the United States would be—on a plot of land between Maryland and Virginia on the Potomac River—also required the federal government to leave New York City and relocate to Philadelphia.)

Oney wasn't the only slave taken to Philadelphia. The Washingtons also brought from New York City Molly, Austin, Giles, Paris, and Christopher Sheels, and they added new slaves to their retinue: Hercules, Richmond, and "Postilion" Joe Richardson.

Postilion Joe Richardson was a footman for the president, and worked in the stables in Philadelphia. When it came time to go to Philadelphia, left behind at Mount Vernon were Joe's wife, Sall, a seamstress at Mount Vernon, and his three young sons, Henry, who was seven, Elijah, three, and Dennis, one.

Joe was a dower slave, one of the 153 enslaved Africans inherited by Martha Washington's grandchildren after her death in 1802. Sall and their children were owned by George Washington and freed after the president's death. Although he remained enslaved, Joe and Sall Richardson managed to stay together and had at least seven children, all of whom were free.

Unlike the slaves who worked in the stables, Oney's workload was light, and several times a week Oney accompanied the First Lady on her visits to the wives of other legislators and political leaders. While Martha traded gossip and news in the receiving rooms, household servants entertained Oney in the kitchen with refreshments and stories of life in Philadelphia. For the first time, Oney got to know people outside of the Washingtons and the Mount Vernon slaves.

Philadelphia was the right city for a black slave to learn about her options. It had the largest northern free black community in the United States with more than two thousand free African Americans. While not a wealthy community, the black Philadelphians boasted a sizable working class, with many able to find work as mariners, day laborers, domestic servants, doctors, teachers, clergymen, hairdressers, shoemakers, bakers, tailors, sail makers, teamsters, food caterers, carpenters, musicians, and many other professions, often serving a predominantly black clientele. In

1816, the city directory listed 180 black men who owned their own businesses. Most women worked as domestic laborers, but some were teachers, or owned their own businesses.

Only blocks away from the President's House, some of these black Philadelphians were banding together to help each other and their community. In a small brick house on North Fifth Street, free blacks met and founded the Free African Society, the nation's first black self-help and civic organization. They opened up private schools for black children, operated food programs for the poor and widowed, issued marriage licenses for black couples, and bought pre-paid medical plans for Free African Society members and their families. One of its members, Richard Allen, even started the first independent African American religious denomination in the United States, the Bethel African Methodist Episcopal Church, in 1794.

Some of these men and women likely became part of Oney's circle of friends, and they answered some of the slave's questions about liberty, self-sovereignty, and her right of freedom. They were the ones to know, because Pennsylvania was the first former colony to take steps to abolish slavery in 1780. By the time Washington moved into the President's House in Philadelphia in 1790, the state not only was on its way to freeing its slaves but the slaves of any plantation owner who crossed the state line.

Under Pennsylvania law, slaves could demand their freedom after their master spent six months in the state. Washington, as leader of the government and a citizen of Virginia, claimed that Pennsylvania law didn't apply to him. But just in case, the president employed a legal trick that would allow him to work in Philadelphia and keep ownership of his slaves.

The six-month clock restarted each time the slave owner and slave crossed the Pennsylvania state line. So, between March 1791 and October 1796, the Washingtons made fourteen trips from Philadelphia to Mount Vernon, rotating their slaves in and out of Pennsylvania to keep them under their control. Martha herself took part in this plan. Washington was on his southern tour in May 1791 when the first six-month deadline approached. To interrupt their Pennsylvania residency, Martha

Washington took Oney and another slave to Trenton, New Jersey, for two days, and sent other slaves back to Mount Vernon before the deadline to prevent them from obtaining their freedom.

While the Washingtons made sure Oney stayed in their possession while leading the new nation, Oney must have hoped to be freed after their death. The Washingtons were known as kind slave owners, recognizing slave marriages and family relationships and refusing to sell slaves off the Mount Vernon plantation without the slave's consent. Washington may have even told some of his slaves about his plan to free them all after he and Martha died. But that was not Oney's fate.

The wedding of Elizabeth Custis to Law brought the couple to Philadelphia and inside the President's House. Soon after, Mrs. Washington informed Oney that she was to be given as a gift to the bride.

The certainty of unending slavery under another family changed everything for Oney. The Laws planned to make Virginia their permanent residence, eliminating any chance Oney had of legal freedom. Even worse, Elizabeth was known for her "grim moods" with the slaves.

So on May 21, 1796, Oney made her move. The Washingtons were preparing to leave Philadelphia one final time to return to Mount Vernon. Oney had prepared for weeks, surreptitiously packing her clothes and personal effects and delivering them to her friends in Philadelphia's free black community.

"Whilst they were packing up to go to Virginia, I was packing to go, I didn't know where; for I knew that if I went back to Virginia, I should never get my liberty," Oney recalled later. "I had friends among the colored people of Philadelphia, had my things carried there beforehand, and left Washington's house while they were eating dinner."

Oney slipped out one of the mansion's doors and went into hiding until her transport out of the city, the northbound ship, the *Nancy*, was ready. The *Nancy*, after making a brief stop in New York City, deposited Oney in Portsmouth, New Hampshire, in May 1796, where the former slave walked down the plank and took her first breaths of air as a free woman.

Judge's example rippled through the rest of Washington's slaves, with some who knew her personally likely looking at her successful escape and planning their own attempts. At least two other slaves who worked with Judge at the New York residences and the Philadelphia "President's House" also made breaks for freedom.

Hercules is by far the most famous. Also called "Uncle Harkless," likely because the children at Mount Vernon couldn't pronounce "Hercules," his cooking was known around the nation, and when it came time to leave New York City and set up a new presidential household in Philadelphia, Washington decided to call up the slave chef from Mount Vernon to participate in the cooking and entertaining of the cream of Philadelphia society.

Like many Mount Vernon slaves, there is little information about Hercules's early life. It is thought that Washington bought Hercules in 1767 when the young man was thirteen and working as a ferryman. But his calling made itself clear, with the young chef apprenticing himself under Martha Washington's longtime slave cook, Old Doll, the grandmother of Christopher Sheels. Soon, Hercules was head chef, and was described by G. W. Parke Custis as "a celebrated artiste . . . as highly accomplished a proficient in the culinary art as could be found in the United States."

In addition to being a great cook, Hercules was also a family man. He married a dower slave named Lame Alice, a seamstress at Mount Vernon, and they had three children, Richmond, Evey, and Delia. Alice died in 1787, and Hercules seems to have had another child, a girl, by another woman, but her identity and whether he married her mother is unrecorded. Alice's death left Hercules to raise their three children on his own, and he seems to have taken care of them the best he could. That made Washington's Philadelphia assignment a bit of a problem for Hercules.

When Washington moved to New York City to accept the presidency, he brought along some of his Mount Vernon slaves, but left behind both Old Doll and Hercules. Instead, Washington hired Rachel Lewis, a white woman, to work as the first presidential chef. However, the president wasn't pleased with her work. As they got ready to transfer the government to Philadelphia, Washington decided it was time to make a change from the tasteless cooking and unsanitary habits of his chef.

"With respect to Mrs. Lewis and her daughter, I wish it may not be done, especially as it is in contemplation to transplant Hercules or Nathan from the Kitchen at Mount Vernon to that in Philadelphia; and because the dirty figures of Mrs. Lewis and her daughter will not be a pleasant sight in view (as the Kitchen always will be) of the principal entertaining rooms in our new habitation," Washington said in a letter to Lear.

Washington eventually decided he wanted Hercules in Philadelphia. But when the slave learned that he was to be transferred to Philadelphia, Hercules asked Washington's permission to at least bring his son Richmond with him as a kitchen scullion and chimney sweep. Washington agreed, "not from his appearance or merits, I fear, but because he was the son of Hercules and his desire to have him as an assistant."

As seen by Washington's decision to bend his rules, Hercules was a clear favorite of the Washington family, who described him in glowing terms for years afterward. "He was a dark-brown man, little, if any, above the usual size, yet possessed of such great muscular power as to entitle him to be compared with his namesake of fabulous history," Custis said of him. Upon Alice's death, Martha Washington ordered that Hercules be given three bottles of rum "to bury his wife."

And his skill and discipline in the kitchen was legendary. "The chief cook gloried in the cleanliness and nicety of his kitchen. Under his iron discipline, woe to his underlings if speck or spot could be discovered on the tables or dressers, or if the utensils did not shine like polished silver. With the luckless wights who had offended in these particulars there was no arrest of punishment, for judgment and execution went hand in hand," Custis said.

Because of his skills, Hercules got privileges other slaves could only dream of. There were tickets to see a play at the Southwark Theater and the spectacular riding acrobatics at Ricketts' Circus, according to account books. Hercules also was allowed to open his own business in Philadelphia and keep the money he made. The slave chef sold the kitchen "slops"—leftover food like animal skins, used tea leaves, and rendered tallow that were not used in the president's meals—to outsiders to make a little money of his own, apparently with the Washington family's blessings. And for a slave who was unused to having any money of his own, Hercules's little side business was apparently very lucrative.

Money "from the slops of the kitchen were from one to two hundred dollars a year," Custis reported. What did Hercules do with that money?

He apparently decided that he was tired of the clothing that Washington provided him, and went out and purchased all new clothes of his own. "His linen was of unexceptionable whiteness and quality, then black silk shorts, ditto waistcoat, ditto stockings, shoes highly polished, with large buckles covering a considerable part of the foot, blue cloth coat with velvet collar and bright metal buttons, a long watch-chain dangling from his fob, a cocked-hat, and gold-headed cane completed the grand costume of the celebrated dandy (for there were dandies in those days) of the president's kitchen," Custis said.

Hercules soon became known for his dapper wardrobe, in which he would stroll proudly down the streets of Philadelphia to see and be seen. "Many were not a little surprised on beholding so extraordinary a personage, while others who knew him would make a formal and respectful bow, that they might receive in return the salute of one of the most polished gentlemen and the veriest dandy of nearly sixty years ago," Custis said.

Hercules's status vaulted him to the top of slave society and into the eyes of white American society. There is a portrait believed to be of Hercules painted by Gilbert Stuart, the same artist who did the most famous portrait of George Washington. Hercules gazes out across history, "a large, cinnamon-colored man in immaculate chef whites with a kerchief tied around his neck and a toque," says Jessica Harris, culinary historian and author of *The Welcome Table: African-American Heritage Cooking*.

But despite his fancy clothes and wondrous culinary creations for the president, his family, and their guests, Hercules was still a slave. He chafed at his life's restraints, one of which was the frequent back and forth trips to Mount Vernon required by the president to ensure that his Philadelphia slaves never became free. And then Judge escaped from the President's House, which apparently changed Washington's attitude toward his beloved slaves.

Judge's escape brought questioning of the rest of the President's House slaves about their loyalty to their master. They obviously knew about the six-month limit, but Hercules tried to quell any doubts that Washington had about whether he was thinking about following Judge's example, according to Lear, Washington's secretary in 1791.

*Somebody, I presume, insinuated to him that the motive for sending
him home so long before you was [sic] expected there, was to prevent
his taking advantage of a six months residence in this place.—When
he was possessed of this idea he appeared to be extremely unhappy—
and altho he made not the least objection to going; yet, he said he was
mortified to the last degree to think that a Suspicion could be entertained of his fidelity or attachment to you. And so much did the poor
fellow's feelings appear to be touched that it left no doubt of his Sincerity—and to shew him that there were no apprehensions of that kind
entertained of him, Mrs. Washington told him he should not go at that
time; but might remain 'till the expiration of six months and then go
home to prepare for your arrival there. He has accordingly continued
here 'till this time, and tomorrow takes his departure for Virginia.*

And then there was Richmond. Hercules's son clearly was not a
favorite of Washington's. Around fourteen when he came to Philadelphia, Richmond only lasted one year and was sent back to Mount Vernon
in 1791. And because of Richmond, Washington got his first inkling that
Hercules might not be as content in captivity as the president thought.
Richmond was caught stealing money at Mount Vernon in November
1796, according to a letter sent to Washington while the president was
wrapping up his affairs in Philadelphia. Washington clearly hoped that
Hercules had nothing to do with it, but decided to warn the overseers
just in case the slave cook was concocting something with his son. "I hope
Richmond was made an example of, for the Robbery he committed on
Wilkes Saddle bags I wish he may not have been put upon it by his father
(although I never had any suspicion of the honesty of the latter) for the
purpose perhaps of a journey together," Washington said in a letter to
William Pearce on November 14, 1796. "This will make a watch, without
its being suspected by, or intimated to them, necessary; nor wd I have
these suspicions communicated to any other lest it should produce more
harm than good."

Richmond eventually was demoted to a simple laborer, and now
Washington was worried about Hercules. So during his final months in
Philadelphia, when he sent his slaves back to Mount Vernon to ensure

that they stayed his property, he ordered that Hercules be left behind when it came time to bring his entourage back to Pennsylvania. This had to come as a shock to the chef, who by now had become accustomed to city life. Hercules, who had been known for his fine silk clothes, suddenly found himself that November in the coarse linens and woolens of a field slave. Washington ordered him placed out in the fields with his other slaves digging clay for one hundred thousand bricks, spreading dung, grubbing bushes, and smashing stones into sand to coat the houses on the property, according to farm reports and a November memo from Washington to his farm manager.

"That will Keep them," Washington wrote, "out of idleness and mischief."

By February 1797, Hercules had had enough. Before dawn on February 22, 1797, the slave chef made his break for freedom from Mount Vernon. Interestingly enough, Hercules chose George Washington's sixty-fifth birthday as the day of his escape, perhaps hoping that the festivities going on around the president's celebration would mask his disappearance, or perhaps thinking that anyone who saw him out on the open roads would assume the well-known chef was simply out to procure an item for Washington's party. Regardless of his reasoning, Hercules's plan was successful. He simply vanished, with no one the wiser. There has not been found any evidence of a manhunt nor even acknowledgement of Hercules's departure for at least four days. A February 25, 1797, weekly farm report discovered recently by Mount Vernon historian Mary V. Thompson simply says, "Herculus absconded 4 [days ago]."

Lest we think that his escape was an easy decision, Hercules had to leave behind at Mount Vernon his children, including Richmond, who had worked with him in Philadelphia, and a six-year-old daughter by his relationship after his wife's death. That leads to the assumption that his escape was on foot, because taking his children along would have been an easier task with transportation. It's not hard to assume that Hercules would have wanted them out from under Washington's thumb, because Richmond had already gotten on the president's bad side. Richmond would never escape, but his father had, and by all accounts, headed north.

The Washington family was much inconvenienced by Hercules's escape, having become dependent upon him for the preparation of their food in Philadelphia and at Mount Vernon. It was a double blow to Martha Washington, who had lost her personal maid, Oney Judge, and now the plantation's cook, Hercules. She complained in a letter to her sister, Elizabeth Henley: "I should have written to you last week but companey prevented. I am obliged to be my one Housekeeper which takes up the greatest part of my time—Our cook Hercules went away so that I am as much at a loss for a cook as for a housekeeper—altogether I am sadly plaiged."

Washington never said he was sad over Hercules's escape, but he did note that things were not running smoothly without him. "The running off of my cook, has been a most inconvenient thing to this family; and what renders it more disagreeable, is, that I had resolved never to become the master of another slave by purchase, but this resolution I fear I must break," Washington said in a letter to James Ross in November 1797.

Washington assumed that Hercules headed back to Philadelphia, where the slave chef likely made both black and white friends who were willing to help him in his quest for freedom. In a letter from March 10, 1797, the traveling Washington writes from Head of Elk, Maryland, to Lear in Philadelphia: "I pray you to desire [steward Frederick Kitt] to make all the enquiry he can after Hercules, and send him round in the Vessel if he can be discovered and apprehended . . ."

They never found him, but Washington refused to give up the search. He sent two notes to former steward Kitt the following January, nearly a year after the escape, urging him to hire men to keep up the hunt. "We have never heard of Hercules our Cook since he left . . . but little doubt remains in my mind of his having gone to Philadelphia, and may yet be found there, if proper measures were employed to discover (unsuspectedly, so as not to alarm him) where his haunts are," Washington said. "If you could accomplish this for me, it would render me an acceptable service as I neither have, nor can get a good Cook to hire, and am disinclined to hold another slave by purchase."

In 1933, Stephen Decatur Jr., a descendant of Tobias Lear, would write: "Although diligent inquiries were made for him, he was never apprehended."

At least one of Hercules's children left behind was happy for her father, although they would all stay in slavery at Mount Vernon until after Washington's death. Prince Louis-Philippe of France, who would go on to become the last king of that country, visited Mount Vernon during his exile from his home country and came across Hercules's daughter. The then-prince likely knew Hercules from his time on Washington's staff in New York or Philadelphia, and wanted to speak to the slave chef again. But being told that Hercules was no longer at Mount Vernon, the prince was directed to his daughter and recorded the conversation in his book, *Diary of My Travels in America*.

"The general's cook ran away, being now in Philadelphia, and left a little daughter of six at Mount Vernon," he said. "Beaudoin ventured that the little girl must be deeply upset that she would never see her father again; she answered, 'Oh! Sir, I am very glad, because he is free now.'"

And Hercules was free, with Washington's slave catchers unable to find him. But that doesn't mean that Hercules had completely vanished. Col. Richard Varick, Washington's former recording secretary who later became mayor of New York, spotted the chef in late 1801. In responding to his alert, Martha Washington wrote "to decline taking Hercules back again."

No wonder. By then, Hercules was already free. On January 1, 1801, Martha Washington had decided to free all 123 of her late husband's slaves, despite his wish that they would not be freed until both he and his wife were dead. Mrs. Washington, however, felt she had no choice. The will Washington left behind specified that his slaves were to be freed upon the death of both George and Martha Washington. With the former president already dead, the only thing standing in the way of the freedom of 123 African slaves was Martha Washington's life. And for a woman who spent large amounts of time alone with her slaves and depended on those same people for all of her food (slaves had been known to poison food of masters they didn't like or wanted to get rid of), she felt that caveat placed her in an untenable position.

Abigail Adams, while visiting Martha Washington at Mount Vernon, noted that the mistress of the plantation was well aware of her precarious position with the slaves. "The state in which they were left by the General, to be free at her death, she did not feel as tho her Life was safe in their Hands, many of whom would be told it was there interest to get rid of her—She therefore was advised to set them all free at the close of the year."

But even though George and Martha Washington intended to eventually set their slaves free, while they were alive they were not going to tolerate runaways.

The next time anyone connected to the Washingtons would see Oney would be several states away, and quite by accident. A chance encounter would put the president back on Oney's trail again, and a single shouted word would send her on the run for her freedom.

"Oney!"

The sound of her name being shouted in public while walking along Strawberry Banke in Portsmouth must have sent shivers of fear down Oney Judge's spine and visions of slave catchers through her head. It had been only a few weeks since she had quietly slipped out of the Washingtons' Philadelphia residence and into the night.

Like other escaped slaves, Oney likely stayed hidden because of the fear that their former masters would send slave catchers to bring them back. Oney knew this was a distinct possibility, since she lived in the house where the law mandating this was first put into effect. While Oney and his family lived in Philadelphia, Washington signed into law the Fugitive Slave Act of 1793, which provided for the return of slaves who had escaped and crossed state lines. The law allowed a slave owner to seize an escaped slave, present the slave before a federal or local judge, and, upon proof of ownership, receive a certificate authorizing the slave to be retaken. It also established a penalty of five hundred dollars for obstructing an owner's efforts to retake a slave, or for rescuing, harboring, or concealing a fugitive slave.

As the summer progressed, Oney must have felt more and more confident that she had successfully escaped. She probably first ventured out in Portsmouth's free black community, where her masterful sewing skills would have made her a valuable commodity. Oney likely became braver and braver as no one from Mount Vernon or from the Washingtons' household was sighted in New Hampshire. Oney knew that while still in the former thirteen colonies she had a precarious grip on freedom, but after several months, walking around Portsmouth probably seemed relatively safe.

Until she heard someone calling her name.

A quick examination of the street didn't show men with guns and chains running toward her, just a young impeccably dressed white woman whose face was familiar. Waving to her from down the street was Elizabeth Langdon, daughter of US senator John Langdon of New Hampshire, close friend of Nelly Custis and frequent visitor to the president's mansion in Philadelphia. Her time visiting with Nelly and the Washingtons meant Elizabeth knew Oney was rarely without Martha Washington, but the young Langdon hadn't seen the First Family in a while, so the word of Oney's escape hadn't reached her.

"Why, Oney, where in the world have you come from?"

Oney must have considered running, but decided that not making a scene would be better. "Come from New York, missus."

Upon seeing Oney, Elizabeth was no doubt eagerly scanning the area and shops for Martha Washington or perhaps Nelly Custis, perhaps hoping that her friends had come to visit her. But the truth quickly became apparent to Elizabeth, and when confronted, Oney hung her head and decided not to lie. "Run away, missus."

Nelly Custis was one of Elizabeth's closest friends, so she was familiar with the inner workings of the Washington household, including the comfortable life that Oney led as Martha Washington's chambermaid. "Run away! And from such an excellent place! Why, what could induce you? You had a room to yourself and only nice light work to do and every indulgence." Of course, Oney knew this quite well. But there was something more important to her than how she lived. "Yes, I know, but I want to be free, missus; wanted to learn to read and write." That apparently wasn't enough for Elizabeth, who thought that appealing to Oney's sense of duty and love might make a difference. "How can Mrs. Washington do without you?"

Oney didn't care. She somehow slipped away from Elizabeth and disappeared into the alleys of Portsmouth. Elizabeth recounted her discovery of Oney Judge to one of Martha Washington's friends, and now, her former masters knew where she was and made plans to get her back.

Back at Mount Vernon, Martha Washington felt betrayed. Oney was not just her slave, she was also her friend, Martha told George. There was no way she would run away on her own, so it must have been someone else's idea. Oney, Martha said, must have been seduced and abducted by a Frenchman. No one knows what George Washington thought of his wife's theory. But what is clear is that the former president wanted Oney back for financial as well as personal reasons.

Since Oney was a dower slave, Washington had to either give to or purchase for the Custis estate another slave to take her place, something he didn't want to do. He already was down one slave, having given Oney's younger sister, Delphy, to the Laws as their wedding present. And if he let Oney's escape stand, the other slaves at Mount Vernon might try the same thing.

Washington also had a reputation to uphold. It would be unseemly, he thought, for his name to be linked publicly with an attempt to drag a former slave back into chains. So, much to Martha's chagrin, he refused to use his powers as the country's first leader to track Oney down. He did place one advertisement in a Philadelphia newspaper, offering ten dollars to anyone who brought her back.

The advertisement made clear that the Washingtons had no idea where Oney had gone: "As there was no suspicion of her going off, nor no provocation to do so, it is not easy to conjecture whither she has gone, or fully, what her design is," the ad said.

It must have seemed like a stroke of luck when Elizabeth Langdon informed them that she had bumped into Oney on the streets of Portsmouth. The former president, now that he had a place to use his influence, decided to enlist the collector of customs in Portsmouth, John Whipple, in his attempt to find Oney. Whipple tracked her down, and must have explained to Oney the precarious position she was in. Washington would be within his legal rights to send slave catchers to New England, and few people would likely stand against the first president. Whipple likely suggested that Oney negotiate as good a deal as possible for herself before returning to Virginia. The two of them put their heads together and sent Washington a letter expressing Oney's willingness to return, on one condition.

May 23

No. 43, Fourth Water Street.
6 tot

Advertisement.

ABSCONDED from the houshold of the President of the United States, ONEY JUDGE,
a light mulatto girl, much freckled, with very black
eyes and bushy black hair. She is of middle stature,
slender, and delicately formed, about 20 years of
age.

She has many changes of good clothes, of all forts,
but they are not sufficiently recollected to be described—As there was no suspicion of her going off, nor
no provocation to do so, it is not easy to conjecture
whither she has gone, or fully, what her design is;—
but as she may attempt to escape by water, all matters of vessels are cautioned against admitting her
into them, although it is probable she will attempt
to pass for a free woman, and has, it is said, wherei-
withal to pay her passage.

Ten dollars will be paid to any person who will
bring her home, if taken in the city, or on board any
vessel in the harbour;—and a reasonable additional
sum if apprehended at, and brought from a greater
distance, and in proportion to the distance.
                    FREDERICK KITT, Steward.
May 23   a2t

To-morrow will be landed,

Advertisement placed by Frederick Kitt, steward of the President's House, after the escape of Oney Judge from George Washington in Philadelphia. *The Pennsylvania Gazette* [PUBLIC DOMAIN OR PUBLIC DOMAIN], VIA WIKIMEDIA COMMONS

Oney "declared her willingness to return and to serve with fidelity during the lives of the President and his Lady if she could be freed on their decease, should she outlive them," Whipple wrote in an October 4, 1796, letter. "But that she should rather suffer death than return to slavery and (be) liable to be sold or given to any other persons."

That his slave would have the nerve to attempt to negotiate her freedom with him, especially one that he and his wife had so favored for so long, probably infuriated Washington. He replied to Whipple on November 28: "It would neither be politic or just to reward unfaithfulness with a premature preference; and thereby discontent before hand the minds of all her fellow-servants who by their steady attachments are far more deserving than herself of favor."

But his time with Oney brought about a change in Whipple. After listening to Oney and hearing about her desire for freedom, Whipple refused to arrest her and have her shipped south, saying he feared a riot on the docks from the abolitionist New Englanders. He also officially punctured Martha's theory about a man abducting Oney.

"After a cautious examination it appeared to me that she had not been decoyed away (by a Frenchman) as had been apprehended, but that a thirst for complete freedom which she was informed would take place on her arrival here and Boston had been her only motive for absconding," Whipple said.

Oney still was not safe. Washington's nephew, Burnwell Bassett Jr., came up to New Hampshire on business and stayed with the Langdons, the same family that had informed the Washingtons of Oney's whereabouts. He mentioned to them that while he was there, he hoped to track down Oney and take her and any children she might have had back with him to Mount Vernon to return them to slavery. Bassett had tracked Oney down once before and tried to convince her to return on her own. He told her the Washingtons would set her free when she arrived at Mount Vernon.

Oney didn't believe him. Her reply was: "I am free now and choose to remain so."

Barrett's second trip was not to negotiate, but to kidnap. But this time the Langdons decided to help the runaway slave. They quickly sent word to Oney that Bassett planned to kidnap her, and she fled Portsmouth for a neighboring town. She hid with a free black family until after Bassett had left.

Three months after this incident, George Washington died and Oney was finally free. But she would have no happy ending. Her husband and three children would all precede her in death. Outliving her daughters by fifteen years, the aged Oney became a pauper, depending on yearly donations of firewood and other sundries. But she said she wouldn't have done anything different. Asked later in her life if she ever missed her life at Mount Vernon and with the Washingtons, she said, "No, I am free."

CHAPTER 5

SLAVERY AND THE CONSTRUCTION OF THE WHITE HOUSE

While Washington and his slaves were living in New York, the work on a new capital city was underway. Winter in Washington, DC, in 1792 was bitterly cold, making travel treacherous around the swampy vistas of the new federal city and work impractical for the men paid to raise a new metropolis out of the land Washington chose for the new capital of the still-young United States of America.

Washington, though modest about his namesake city (he preferred to call it the "Federal City" and only once wrote the name "the city of Washington" during his lifetime) was strident about getting construction going on the new capital on the land he had personally chosen between Maryland and his beloved Virginia. The embryonic United States was still fragile, having won its freedom from the colonial rule of Great Britain only a few years earlier. The construction of a permanent home for the federal government, scheduled for completion at the turn of the century in 1800, would strengthen the new nation and free the legislature and president from the whims of sometimes greedy and self-important state lawmakers.

Despite knowing Washington's desire to move the nation's capital south, New York City and Philadelphia were constructing versions of the President's House in hopes of keeping the federal government in the North. New York at one point offered Congress the use of the city of Kingston, New York, "one of its most thriving towns, beautifully situated on the romantic Hudson," one observer reported, while Maryland offered the use of its state capital, Annapolis, "already distinguished for the charm of its climate and the culture and elegance of its inhabitants."

New York City was not a popular choice for a permanent capital, with lawmakers shunning large, already existing cities and disliking the idea of placing the new capital so far from the existing center of the new country. Philadelphia, the site of the meeting of the Continental Congress and the writing of the Declaration of Independence, was considered but control of the city was an open question to lawmakers, who did not want to depend on independent and sometimes obstinate state-level officials for their protection.

This fear had become real in 1783, when the remnants of the Continental Army stationed near Philadelphia sent a missive to the Congress of the Confederation demanding payment for their services during the Revolutionary War. Congress ignored the message, but could not ignore the four hundred soldiers who mobbed Independence Hall demanding their money and refusing to allow the delegates to leave. After some fast talking by Alexander Hamilton, members of Congress were allowed to leave the building later that night. Meeting in secret, a congressional committee led by Hamilton appealed to the Pennsylvania government to call out the state militia to protect the national government from the mutinous military, but its request was turned away. The next day, Congress left Philadelphia for Princeton, New Jersey, and a vagabond existence.

Congress soon tired of itinerancy, having bounced around the former colonies meeting in cities such as Princeton (June 30, 1783 to November 4, 1783), Annapolis (November 26, 1783 to August 19, 1784), Trenton, New Jersey (November 1, 1784 to December 24, 1784), and finally New York City for the ratification of the US Constitution and Washington's inauguration.

Three of the nation's most prominent Founding Fathers negotiated a compromise solution for a permanent capital, one that would balance the agrarian interests of the South and the industrial concerns of the North: a capital site that would be square in the middle. The states of Virginia and Maryland both ceded ten square miles to Congress for use for a capital city (and $120,000 and $72,000 for that purpose, respectively), leaving it up to lawmakers to decide which spot along the two states' borders to place the city.

Slavery also played a part in the decision, with the final compromise struck by Alexander Hamilton, Thomas Jefferson, and James Madison at a dinner party in New York City. The federal capital would be moved from Philadelphia to Washington in return for southern votes and support for the federal assumption of state debt. Southern leaders were angered over the idea of having to pay off northern states' Revolutionary War debt, and moving the federal capital to a slave state suggested that the North would not continually complain about slavery.

Washington gave his approval to this deal, and soon, he and his hand-selected architect, Pierre L'Enfant, selected the perfect spot for the new city: land between the banks of the Potomac and Anacostia Rivers that yielded thick forests of oak, sycamore, and cedar, irregular hills and plains, and swamps and marshes. That vista would give him plenty of room to design a new metropolis to rival any of the great cities of Europe.

L'Enfant was pleased as he climbed "the heights," an irregular ridge of hills that rambled from the Anacostia to Georgetown. From the heights to the Potomac, wrote a delighted L'Enfant, the hills "sink as the waves of a tempestuous sea," flattening to a nearly level plain. Just back from that ridge, the Frenchman found an apple orchard and a farm cottage. The view to the Potomac must have been memorable, for L'Enfant noted that it made the ridge an ideal site for a public building. When his plan materialized, he reserved one of the best spots for the "palace" of the president.

Eager to get started, the commission in charge of building the federal city established the White House's first official relationship with slaves, ordering L'Enfant in 1791 to hire "good labouring negros by the year, the masters cloathing them well and finding each a blanket, the Commissioner finding them provisions and paying twenty-one pounds a year wages, the payments to be made quarterly or half yearly." Their job: "To throw up Clay" at the construction sites of the Capitol and the President's House.

For these first White House workers, hired away from neighboring plantations, "to throw up clay" was backbreaking but important work because brick was the most reliable construction material in the eighteenth century. Brick was sturdy and attractive, and its raw material, clay, was abundant in the District of Columbia, situated between two rivers. With the invention of steam shovels still several years away, these slaves dug for the clay on site with hand shovels, working day and night to get the raw material to the skilled brick makers and at the same time, opening up ground on the site for the space that would become the White House's foundation and cellar. "By the first of October gangs of men were employed in getting out this material for building in the vicinity of the two public buildings and later on kilns were erected there where the brick used in those structure was made," Wilhemus Bogart Bryan wrote in 1914.

The identity of these slaves and where they came from has been lost. There were thousands upon thousands in the Washington area at that time, with the largest single slave population in the United States being in Virginia at 292,627, according to the 1790 census. But the city commission, made up of President Washington's allies, never bothered to record the names of this first crew or which plantations they came from. Digging up clay was unskilled, tedious, and backbreaking work, and the men who did it were just laborers, not skilled artisans whose work could be signed and remembered. Washington himself must have seen them digging, but there is no mention of these slaves in his letters or diaries. Instead, all the president noticed was newly hired Irish architect James Hoban, who "has laid out the foundation which is now digging and will be back in a month to enter heartily upon the work."

Hoban, a noted South Carolina architect and slave owner, was on site because L'Enfant's haughtiness and temperament led to his firing before he could complete his dreams of a luxurious palace for his one-time patron, Washington. Instead, a commission of Washington's friends put in charge of the city decided a competition would be the best way to get an appropriate design for an executive mansion, advertising in newspapers a "premium of five hundred dollars or a medal of that value to the person, who before the 15th of the following July, should produce to them the first approved plan, if adopted by them, for a President's House." The winner was Hoban, and by the time the first slaves started digging the foundation, the Frenchman was out, the Irish-born South Carolinian was in, and work on the President's House was well under way.

As stated in their advertisement, the commissioners in charge of the city were in charge of finding food and shelter for their rented slaves, with the owner only responsible for providing a "blanket" to sleep on during the hot summer nights and to sleep under during the long cold winter. Where did this sleeping take place? With transportation around the city difficult because of the swamp Washington was being built on, the commissioners knew that workers would have to stay on site for them to get their money's worth out of them. They authorized Hoban to build himself a home on the land set aside for the President's House. For the actual work force, a barn, fifty feet by twenty-four feet, with a nine-foot entrance, was built on the site, likely providing the first on-location shelter for the slaves. These, however, were not the only buildings on the future site of the White House.

In January 1792, the commissioners contracted out to an Elisha Williams the building of eight huts on the President's House square. A few weeks later came an order for more. "We also wish an additional number of huts to be set up against the Spring making the whole number 20 these to be added to the same size, and on the lines of the present with 20 feet intervals, which may if necessary be filled up with others," the commissioners said in a letter to Williams. Records don't reflect whether white skilled workers or black slaves slept in the huts around Hoban's home, which was located just about where the statue of Andrew Jackson now sits in Lafayette Park, across Pennsylvania Avenue from the White House.

What we do know is that the bitter winter forced a halt to the clay-making at the White House. These slaves had been hired for a year, and therefore could not sit idle waiting for spring. So the commission hired them out as "axe-men" to chop down trees to clear land around the future site of the White House and the Capitol, and to make the broad avenues that city planners wanted for the new city as they waited for the spring thaw.

The working conditions of the slaves at the beginning of the construction of the White House were suspect. James Dermott, an Irishman recently arrived in the new country, was hired to help with the surveying and was placed in charge of the slave axe men. James Dermott was described by the commissioners as one who "now and then drank to access (sic) and when enebrated (sic) . . . is unruly and quarrelsome." While there was some concern on the part of the city commissioners as to whether Dermott was qualified to manage slaves, it seemed that the Irishman took to his work with enthusiasm. By 1799 Dermott was a slave trader, offering nine women and children, including three girls from six to ten years old, for sale. He even advertised a service to help planters get back their runaway slaves, and advertised for the return of one of his escaped men. He offered a reward for jailing or flogging his man, Fidelio, "well known about the city" and probably lurking at an old farm in the city along the Anacostia, "where he has a wife."

But even with problems, the work the slaves were doing around the White House seemed to be valuable enough for the city commissioners to seek more the next year. "Wanted at the city of Washington a number of Slaves to labor in the Brick Yards, Stone quarries &c, for which generous wages will be given. Also Sawyers to Saw by the hundred or on wages by the month or year," the advertisement read.

Now that the trees were clear and the foundation was under way, the city commissioners turned to finding enough stone for the walls of the White House. Once again, they turned to slave labor to ensure that everything got done on time. The closest quarry that had the freestone they needed was at Aquia Creek, Virginia, about forty miles downstream on the Potomac in Stafford County, Virginia, and they quickly locked it up for use in the White House and other federal buildings. "On the 16th day of November, 1791, L'Enfant on behalf of the Public hath rented from John Gibson for ten years to commence on the 10th day of next month, all quarries of freestone on the land on Aquaia Creek at a yearly rental of Twenty pounds current money to be paid to the said John Gibson on the first day of December in every year," the orders read.

The stone at this quarry was exactly what the commissioners were looking for, pale gray arkose sandstone with some reddish tint. Time would prove that this sandstone was not the best, absorbing water and cracking in freezing temperatures, leading workers on the executive mansion to decide to seal the stone, which in the eighteenth century usually meant applying a coat of lime wash or paint. When this was done in 1798, the executive mansion was for the first time actually colored white, leading to the future nickname the White House.

The city commissioners had sorely overestimated the attraction of the new federal city for workmen. Construction was prevalent in New York City, Boston, Philadelphia, and other major cities following the devastation of the Revolutionary War, and workers simply weren't willing to give up high wages and better living conditions up north to move down to the swamp of the federal city.

So once again, the city planners turned to the local slave workforce to get things done. In the spring of 1792, the commission ordered the hiring of "twenty five able bodied Negroe men slaves to be employed at the quarries." A daily ration of one pint of whisky each was furnished through the hot summer and a steady diet of pork and bread was guaranteed. These men dug the stone out of the ground, cut it into the desired size with picks and sledgehammers, and then dragged it down to Aquia Creek to be sailed down to the Potomac and up to Washington.

"They chiseled (actually picked) a vertical face on the outcropping of the stone which would serve as a working plane from which they could measure and begin to plan their removal of blocks of stone," according to Lee H. Nelson, author of *White House Stone Carving: Builders and Restorers*. "Using hand picks, they then cut two trenches four to six feet deep into the stone, perpendicular to the face of the stone and roughly ten to twenty feet apart. To minimize waste, these trenches were only about twenty inches wide, providing barely enough room for a man to work with a pick and cut a relatively smooth surface on each side of the trench."

Working along with White House master mason Collen Williamson, who had to "train hired slaves on the spot in the quarry," these slaves and their white coworkers provided most of the stone that would be used for the foundation and walls of the White House. This work, however, did not automatically mean that Williamson was enamored of slave work, his opinion of which would show up later. Regardless, the slaves who worked there must have been decent workers, because in December 22, 1794, the men left in charge of the quarries, Brent and Cooke, advertised for "sixty strong, active Negro men for whom good wages will be given—they shall be well used and fed."

The basement and foundation of the White House were finished by the winter of 1793, leading a commenter to note that the "Basement story was laid & built of greyish white free Stone handsomely polished." Hoban now started work on the inside of the White House, and once again slave labor would be a part of the efforts. The earliest payroll for skilled workers at the White House dates from January 1795 and showed that nine white carpenters, three white apprentices, and five slave carpenters were at work. The white carpenters made $1.09 a day, the apprentices from eighty-four to ninety-seven cents a day, and the slaves from fifty-three to eighty-four cents a day for their masters. Just like the unskilled labor that cut down the trees and dug up the clay for bricks, the skilled slave workmen who labored on the White House did not earn any money for the work that they did.

But unlike earlier unskilled slave gangs, the African slaves who worked on the inside of the White House were not just rentals from nearby slave plantations. They were the property of the driving force behind the construction of the "President's Palace," James Hoban. Hoban learned the art of building in Dublin, and then immigrated to Charleston, South Carolina. Once he had secured his job at the White House, Hoban returned to South Carolina and recruited some Irish carpenters to come with him to the new federal city. He also brought along his slaves: Peter, Ben, Harry, and Daniel, whom he immediately put on the payroll as workers on the White House. Judging from the payrolls, only slaves brought to the city by Hoban and his assistants got skilled work with the commissioners. Other slaves from nearby plantations ended up at the White House doing the brute work while Hoban's slaves worked on the inside.

For example, in November 1794, John Slye applied to be an overseer, claiming "his friends . . . have engaged to hire to the city thirty valuable Negro men slaves." The commissioners did not pass up Slye's offer and hired him to oversee laborers at the President's House for fifteen dollars a month. What percentage he took of the annual rental made by the thirty slaves he brought to the city is not known.

Middleton Belt, who supervised the overseers, rented the two slaves he owned, Peter at the Capitol and Jack at the President's House. Even one of the commissioners, Gustavus Scott, rented two slaves, Bob and Kitt, who worked at the President's House. And local plantation owners also got their slaves work, with Edmund Plowden, who lived in nearby Saint Mary's County and owned sixty-four slaves, sending his Moses, Len, Jim, and Arnold to work at the White House.

The commissioners also hired free blacks, and one of them, Jerry Holland, did make an impression. In January 1795 he worked as one of nine laborers on the surveying crew. "Pay Jerry the black man," the chief surveyor wrote to the commissioners, "a rate of eight dollars per month for his last months services; he is justly entitled to the highest wages that is due to our hands—being promised it and the best hand in the department." The commissioners ignored the recommendation.

This did not mean that everyone was happy about the use of slaves as labor at the White House, although the first complaints were not about the horrors of slavery but about work being taken away. When Williamson, a Scottish stone mason, was fired from his job supervising the stone work on the public buildings, he complained about the Irish and their slaves, including the Irishman who engineered his dismissal, Hoban. Hoban replaced Williamson with an Irishman who demanded that the commissioners supply fourteen slaves to assist his crew of eighteen masons. Williamson fumed to President John Adams that twelve blacks could not do the work of two good hands and that because of Hoban's "Irish vagabons . . . there is nothing here but fighting, lying and stealing."

The city commissioners took his complaints seriously, and that was the end of the use of skilled slave laborers on the White House. In 1797, they "ordered that after the expiration of the present month no Negro Carpenters or apprentices be hired at either of the public buildings."

President Washington never got a chance to stay in the executive mansion, refusing to run for a third term in 1796, which led to the election of John Adams. The White House was still not completed for the majority of the time Adams was in office, with the new president residing in Philadelphia. But on November 1, 1800, Adams arrived in Washington and entered the White House at about one o'clock in the afternoon. On the next day he wrote his famous benediction on the White House: "I pray Heaven to bestow the best of blessings on this house, and on all that shall hereafter inhabit it. May none but honest and wise men ever rule under this roof!"

Adams was antislavery, and unlike many of his contemporaries did not own or use slaves in any form or fashion, although he acknowledged that his life would have been a lot easier if he had. "[My] opinion against it (slavery) has always been known . . . [Never] in my life did I own a slave," he would write later in life.

Joined in Washington by his wife, Abigail Adams, a couple of weeks after his arrival, they calculated that they could have easily used thirty people to run the castle, but the government did not pay for the president's domestic help. Adams was responsible for worker wages, so the first White House domestic staff consisted of four white servants, hired by the president and his wife to help them manage "The President's House," as the White House came to be known. But the new president and first lady had to have known who was used to get their new house to that point.

Abigail Adams, looking out the window of the White House one day, saw a white overseer driving a group of twelve slaves to carry away dirt from the road in front of the White House. First the slaves would fill up their wagons with dirt, and then while four slaves would haul the dirt to another location, the other eight would rest on their shovels until the four wagons returned. And then they would start filling the four wagons again. The first lady decided two New England men could have done a better and quicker job, but she clearly did not believe that was the slaves' fault. In a letter to one of her friends, she criticized their overseer as being one of an ilk "a grade below the negroes in point of intelligence and then below them in point of civility."

The refusal of President John Adams to use African slavery inside the White House would end a chapter of the African American relationship with the presidency for less than a year. Thomas Jefferson's victory in 1800 would start a whole new chapter, one that would stretch to the Civil War.

CHAPTER 6

THOMAS JEFFERSON AND THE FIRST WHITE HOUSE SLAVES

In 1801, the White House wasn't white.

Instead, it was a smoky gray, an unfinished stone mansion located square in the middle of an incomplete city in a still-uncleared swamp. The newly occupied President's Mansion was boxy and damp, it lacked servants, and its unfinished trappings of nobility did not impress the just-elected Thomas Jefferson, who before his presidency had ridiculed the largest house in the nation as "big enough for two emperors, one Pope and the grand Lama."

Swept in on a wave of populism, Jefferson tried his best to tear down any semblance of a burgeoning monarchy. There was nothing he could do about the size of the White House (he did tear down the presidential outhouse and install indoor toilets, as well as dig a White House well so he could take a bath indoors instead of swimming naked in the Potomac River like the White House's first occupant, John Adams), but Jefferson was determined to make a change to the way things operated on the inside.

The outgoing John Adams hosted elegant presidential parties called levees inside the mostly unfurnished White House, where he entertained the nation's greatest thinkers and dignitaries, all of whom were instructed to bow as they entered the second president's presence.

Jefferson did away with those events and the protocol, instead instituting the now-familiar White House receiving line, where the president shakes hands with his guests instead of forcing them to bow as if he were

European royalty. And instead of partying with the elite and the power-ful, Jefferson invited anyone and everyone worth hearing from to dinner.

This president conducted business and negotiated policy over mul-ticourse meals, with as many as a dozen people gathered around ornate place settings three nights a week with courses and courses of delicious food for all to consume. Only one type of cuisine and setting suited America's first gourmet president, who had traveled Europe and America tasting the best food colonial times had to offer. "French servants in livery, a French butler, a French cuisine and a buffet full of choice wine," was the description of one such dinner by John Adams's daughter-in-law and the future first lady, Louisa Adams.

To make all of this happen, Jefferson needed a chef de cuisine who would meet his demanding standards. The only occupant the White House had known at that point was Adams, and when he left in 1800, he took all of his servants with him. When Jefferson arrived, the White House's kitchen was empty. He had already planned to bring north some of his slaves from his Monticello plantation, but there was no one he owned that he could trust to immediately be prepared to create the culi-nary masterpieces he knew he needed to impress not only visiting digni-taries and royalty but also rough-hewn frontiersmen and country gentry.

Luckily, Jefferson knew just the right man to become the White House's first official chef. And so, five days after his election, he had Wil-liam Evans nose around the back kitchens of a Baltimore tavern. That was where the best chef the president ever knew worked—a man named James Hemings.

Jefferson was glad to find such a wonderful chef so underemployed. "You mentioned to me in conversation here that you sometimes saw my former servant James, & that he made his engagements such as to keep himself always free to come to me," he said in a letter. "Could I get the favor of you to send for him & to tell him I shall be glad to receive him as soon as he can come to me?"

The offer to become the personal chef to the American president and live inside the White House would be irresistible for most professional chefs, especially ones who are working inside a tavern instead of a four-star restaurant. And Hemings wasn't just any chef: He had traveled all

Thomas Jefferson, third president of the United States and first president to serve a full term inside the White House. LIBRARY OF CONGRESS

over Europe and the Americas, he spoke and wrote both fluent French and English, and he had trained in the kitchens of royalty off the Champs-Elysées in Paris.

At first glance, this seemed to be the perfect match: a Francophile president and an accomplished French chef de cuisine looking for work because he was cooking in an establishment that was beneath his station, something Jefferson acknowledged by his assumption that his offer of employment would be accepted. The president even wrote the French envoy, Philippe de Létombe, that his search for a new chef was over, saying "I have a good cook."

But there was one complicating factor: Hemings and Jefferson already knew each other. Not only was Hemings a former chef at Monticello, he was also the president's unofficial, unacknowledged brother-in-law, one of only two slaves Jefferson freed during his lifetime and, most famously, the brother of the president's alleged slave concubine, Sally Hemings.

While Hemings never set foot inside the White House as far as it is known, a study of his life shows the complicated and complex relationships between the presidents of the United States and their slaves. Just like many white masters and their slaves in colonial America, the presidents' personal, professional, legal, and familial relationships were entangled with that of their slaves. And there was no one more involved with his slaves than Thomas Jefferson, as shown by his relationship with James Hemings. The story of the Hemings family and the story of Jefferson's slaves inside the White House are closely intertwined, despite the fact that James Hemings never became White House chef.

To this day, the Jefferson and Hemings names are linked, not because of the president's desire to have James Hemings as the first White House chef but because of Jefferson's alleged sexual relationship with Hemings's younger sister, Sally, who is known around the world as the president's slave concubine.

An enemy of Jefferson's who had expected the politician's patronage—a job as postmaster in Richmond, Virginia—and never received it first exposed the alleged relationship publicly. So on September 1, 1802, almost a year after James Hemings's death, James Calendar wrote in the *Richmond Recorder*: "It is well known that the man, whom it delighteth the people to honor, keeps and for many years has kept, as his concubine, one of his slaves. Her name is SALLY."

Jefferson never acknowledged the rumors, although at least one of Sally Hemings's children, Madison, publicly claimed his parentage during his lifetime. The controversy has lasted until modern times, when the

1998 DNA testing of Jefferson and Hemings descendants has shown a clear link between the males of Jefferson's lineage and Sally Hemings.

However, the reported relationship between Sally Hemings and Thomas Jefferson was not the only connection between the two families. Jefferson and his family owned five generations of Hemings, with the third president even marrying the half-sister of one of the Hemings women, Martha Wayles.

James Hemings's mother, Elizabeth "Betty" Hemings, was the daughter of an African slave named Susannah and a white slave ship owner named John Hemings. Hemings actually tried to purchase Betty from her owner, Francis Eppes IV, but Eppes refused to sell. Instead, Eppes gave Betty Hemings to his daughter Martha and her new husband, John Wayles, as a wedding gift. The Wayles soon had a daughter they named Martha after her mother. This Martha would go on to become the future Mrs. Thomas Jefferson, but she would not be the only Wayles child to move to Monticello. After Martha was born, her father took Betty Hemings as his slave concubine and sired six more children, including James Hemings, who would eventually come under control of Thomas Jefferson as part of his wife's inheritance.

Perhaps as recognition of their relationship, the Hemings siblings and their mother were never treated by Jefferson the same as other slaves at Monticello. The male Hemings could come and go as they pleased within reason, as long as they were there when Thomas Jefferson needed them. And instead of being forced to endure manual labor in the Virginia heat, the Hemings were sheltered inside the main house and given only the lightest work to do inside and skilled artisan work to do outdoors. Betty Hemings's children became Monticello's butlers, seamstresses, weavers, carpenters, blacksmiths, gardeners, musicians, and travel companions.

James Hemings, for example, was taught how to cook. And when Jefferson was appointed minister to France in 1784, the future president took the nineteen-year-old Hemings along with him for schooling in French cuisine. The instructions given to Hemings from Jefferson once they arrived illustrate the easy relationship between the two men and the trust that Jefferson had in his black slave. When the two men arrived in

Le Havre on the French coast in July 1784, Jefferson wrote in one of his journals that he had given Hemings money to go ahead alone to secure lodging for them in Rouen, a city more than fifty miles away.

Hemings took the money and left on horseback. For the mulatto slave, this trip presented what was likely his best chance for freedom. In France, there was no slavery and the country operated under the Freedom Principle: the idea that every human being who set foot in that country was automatically free. The day Hemings arrived in France with Jefferson, he could have legally claimed his freedom, with Jefferson powerless to stop him. And Hemings now had unlimited time away from his master, money in his pockets, and a mode of transportation that could have taken him far away from Jefferson and any chance he would ever be forced back to the United States and into slavery.

As for Jefferson, he undoubtedly knew about France's Freedom Principle before bringing Hemings into the country. Only a few months after arriving in France, Jefferson felt comfortable enough with French law to advise a fellow slave owner on how to get around the nation's laws if he so desired. "I have made enquiries on the subject of the negro boy you have brought, and find that the laws of France give him freedom if he claims it, and that it will be difficult, if not impossible, to interrupt the course of the law," Jefferson told Paul Bentalou in a letter. "Nevertheless, I have known an instance where a person bringing in a slave, and saying nothing about it, has not been disturbed in his possession. I think it will be easier in your case to pursue the same plan, as the boy is so young that it is not probable he will think of claiming freedom."

There was no chance that plan would work with James Hemings. Jefferson knew that Hemings was intelligent enough to find out about the Freedom Principle on his own. Jefferson respected his mind enough to instruct him to traverse a foreign country and conduct a financial transaction of some importance without being able to speak or write in French. Regardless, Jefferson sent his slave off, trusting Hemings to go and return. And Hemings did, securing rooms for their entourage and returning to Jefferson to lead him to their temporary residence. He even brought back the change, with Jefferson writing that he had received "back from James of the money given him."

The men proceeded to Paris, where Hemings started his apprenticeship with the French chef Combeaux, whom Jefferson paid 150 francs to begin his training. Hemings would stay with Combeaux until 1786, learning the French style of cuisine that would shape his style of cooking for the rest of his life. But Hemings's early days in France were not easy. As he did not know French—though his teachers likely knew a few words of English—Hemings was undoubtedly expected to keep up the best he could until he learned the language. Apparently, it was slow going. In February 1786, Jefferson wrote a note home and instructed the gardener at Monticello to pass along a message to Hemings's mother Elizabeth: "James is well. He has forgotten how to speak English, and has not learnt to speak French."

But Hemings was trying. Learning the language must have been important to him, because in 1787, Hemings hired a local Parisian to instruct him in how to speak French. How the slave cook found Frenchman Perrault is unknown, but what is known is that Hemings worked on his French with him for at least twenty months. Perrault also was one of the victims of Hemings's quick temper. Apparently, there was a dispute between Perrault and Hemings over the payment for the French tutor, and Perrault showed up at Hemings and Jefferson's Paris residence in an attempt to collect what he saw as his due. But the welcome he received from Hemings was not pleasant, according to an angry letter Perrault sent to Jefferson describing their fight as if the Frenchman was watching it instead of participating.

"Gimme (James) then attacked him with kicks and punches, which forced him to take to his bed since that time, and tore an overcoat ("Redingotte") from him which is the only article of clothing he has against the rigors of the season, thus putting it out of his power to earn his living, since it is so cold and he daren't appear with his clothes in pieces," the January 1789 letter said. "Please help him recover his salary, he having always acted well in your respectable house. Your porter was a witness, as were others of this ignominious treatment I received at your hotel."

There is no indication that Jefferson ever responded, but the Perrault fight proved Jefferson must have known James Hemings had a very volatile and forceful personality long before their confrontation over the White House chef job.

After his apprenticeship with Combeaux was over, Hemings began learning specialized French pastry cooking. He had several instructors, but the most impressive was a chef in the household of the Prince de Conde, Louis-Joseph de Bourbon. He learned how to cook on a potager, a stew-holed stove, and he learned the art of saucing foods. Later that year, Hemings was ready to work on his own, and Jefferson made him chef de cuisine at his home on the Champs-Elysées, cooking for French dignitaries and aristocrats.

Hemings kept that status when he returned to America with Jefferson in 1789, becoming head chef at Monticello, and then following Jefferson and the federal government to New York City and then Philadelphia. After two years in Philadelphia, Jefferson made plans to return to Virginia. Reluctant to return to a slave state, Hemings negotiated a contract with Jefferson by which he would gain freedom after training a replacement chef at Monticello to take his place.

In the 1793 agreement, Jefferson wrote, "Having been at great expence in having James Hemings taught the art of cookery, desiring to befriend him, and to require from him as little in return as possible, I do hereby promise and declare, that if the said James shall go with me to Monticello in the course of the ensuing winter, when I go to reside there myself, and shall there continue until he shall have taught such person as I shall place under him for that purpose to be a good cook, this previous condition being performed, he shall be thereupon made free, and I will thereupon execute all proper instruments to make him free."

James agreed and trained his younger brother, Peter, to cook French cuisine. Jefferson kept his word, and freed James. Being chef had taken James Hemings around the country and overseas at Jefferson's side, but he was basically buying his freedom by ensuring his brother would serve Jefferson for years more. Regardless of what James Hemings thought about it, Peter Hemings would end up serving as head chef at Monticello from 1796 until 1809. Jefferson would never officially free him. But after being released by a Jefferson relative, Peter Hemings showed up in Charlottesville, Virginia, working as a free tailor in 1830.

In 1796, James Hemings left Monticello with thirty dollars and his free papers. He continued to travel the world, though he kept in contact with Jefferson. In a letter to his daughter, Jefferson wrote that James "tells me his next trip will be to Spain. I am afraid his journeys will end in the moon. I have endeavored to persuade him to stay where he is and lay up money."

By the time Jefferson moved into the White House, James Hemings was back in the United States and working in Baltimore. He was hard-drinking and quick-tempered at this point, and likely didn't take well to being summarily summoned by the same southerner who had kept him and his family in slavery for their entire lives. And especially from a man who wouldn't even bother to personally address the chef he wanted to run the kitchen at the White House.

But a direct request? Man to man, potential employer to potential employee and president to citizen? That Hemings was willing to consider, and he wrote to Jefferson through a mutual friend, Francis Say, to request just that. Jefferson had written to Hemings through a proxy. Hemings decided to respond in the same way, making his interest clear but also requesting the president address him directly instead of through subordinates. "I have spoke to James according to your Desire he has made mention again as he did before that he was willing to serve you before any other man in the Union but sence he understands that he would have to be among strange servants he would be very much obliged to you if you would send him a few lines of engagement and on what conditions and wages you would please to give him in your own hand," Say wrote back to Jefferson.

With those words, Hemings had thrown down a gauntlet.

Before this day, all of his official communication to Jefferson had been as slave to master. When Jefferson spoke, Hemings had to listen. When Jefferson called, Hemings came, no questions asked or conditions allowed. But that was while James Hemings was a slave. Now he was free, and with that letter he seemed to be showing Jefferson that if he wanted his services as White House chef, their relationship would have to change.

That was a transformation Jefferson apparently was not ready for. Hemings's only request was for Jefferson to write him personally and tell him in advance the conditions of his new job. Jefferson was not willing to give his former slave the respect of a personal reply. The president, who was understandably busy trying to put together the first administration following a political party transition, apparently felt Hemings wasn't worth the aggravation of negotiation after a couple of letters back and forth through colleagues.

"I supposed I saw in the difficulties raised by James an unwillingness to come here, arising wholly from some attachment he had formed in Baltimore; for I cannot suspect an indisposition towards me," Jefferson wrote the friend. "I concluded at once therefore not to urge him against inclination, and wrote to Philadelphia, where I have been successful in getting a cook equal to my wishes."

Consequently, James Hemings never set foot inside the White House. But he and Jefferson must have eventually made up, because Annette Gordon-Reed in her book, *The Hemingses of Monticello: An American Family*, reported that James Hemings returned to Monticello to work as a chef for twenty dollars a month sometime in August. Five days after Jefferson's relationship with Sally Hemings was first hinted at in William Rind's *Virginia Federalist* in 1801, James Hemings left Monticello for good. A few months later, Hemings committed suicide at age thirty-six. Jefferson's go-between, Evans, would eventually write the president and tell him Hemings had been "delirious for some days previous to his having committed the act, and it is as the General opinion that drinking too freely was the cause."

To the end, Hemings was a man of contradiction, but no more than Jefferson, a slave master who fought against slavery laws, including ones that would have led to the permanent enslavement of all Negros in his home state of Virginia. In 1769, as a member of the Virginia legislature, Jefferson had proposed legislation that would let slave owners free their slaves without legal restraints. The bill was quickly defeated, but Jefferson was undeterred. He then acted as attorney pro bono in two Virginia legal suits for freedom by enslaved mulatto children.

In one of the cases, in 1770 he helped a young mulatto man named Samuel Howell sue for his freedom based on his mother being a free Englishwoman. Jefferson argued, "under the law of nature, all men are born free." But he and Howell lost his case in the 1770 session of the General Court, and Howell ran away shortly after the verdict. In 1774, Jefferson had represented George Manly "to recover freedom," again charging nothing. Manly was, like Howell, a mulatto obliged to serve until age thirty-one, but he had attained the age of thirty-four by the time he went to court. He won his suit and became a hired employee at Monticello.

This is not to insinuate that Jefferson was a friend of Africans, dedicated to their freedom. He inherited fifty-two slaves from his father's estate when he turned twenty-one, none of which he freed during his lifetime. He also proposed laws as a Virginia legislator that would have banned or severely restricted free blacks from entering or living in Virginia, and wrote legislation that would have banished children whose father was of African origin and exiled any white woman who had a child with a black man. None of these laws passed, being too extreme even for colonial times.

Jefferson seemed to be of two minds about slavery as a young man. But his future path seemed to be cemented when Jefferson began courting his future wife, Martha Wayles, and committed himself to the life of a southern plantation owner. That is also how he met and came to own the Hemings.

When Jefferson entered the White House in 1801, he took no direct member of the Hemings family to live with him full time inside the executive mansion. Apparently Jefferson wasn't satisfied with Peter Hemings's talent or training as a French chef, because after trying to hire James Hemings, he ultimately contracted with Honoré Julien, a noted French chef and former chef to President George Washington in Philadelphia, to take the position. He then brought north several Monticello slaves to apprentice with Julien so that when his terms as president ended they could bring their talents back to his plantation and continue the tradition of French cuisine that had begun with James Hemings.

The first to make the 120-mile journey to the nation's capital in the fall of 1801 was fourteen-year-old Ursula Hughes, the wife of James Hemings's nephew, Monticello gardener Wormley Hughes. Jefferson's choice to bring Ursula with him to learn French cuisine might have been a sentimental one, since she was the granddaughter of the longtime

Monticello chef, Ursula, who held the position until James Hemings returned from Paris. But Ursula's stay in Washington was brief, and her skills in the kitchen apparently never developed the way Jefferson wanted. Part of Ursula's problems in the White House kitchen could have been caused by Julien's refusal to speak anything but his native language, French. This was not a barrier to Jefferson, who after his long stay in Paris was a fluent French speaker, but it is unclear how many of his slaves outside of James Hemings spoke French.

A second problem could have been the fact that Ursula was pregnant by Wormley Hughes, something that Jefferson likely did not know when he decided to bring her to work in the White House kitchen. It is unlikely he would have consciously decided to employ a first-time mother who had been separated from her husband in a high-pressure job like White House apprentice chef. Ursula gave birth on March 22, 1802, the first woman to give birth inside the President's Mansion. However, the unnamed infant did not live long, and soon thereafter Ursula was sent back to Monticello, where she led a double life, working in the kitchen when Jefferson was resident there and going back to the fields when he returned to Washington.

With Ursula's dismissal came the young fifteen-year-old Edith (Edy) Hern Fossett, who also had married a Hemings man from Monticello. Little is known about Edy before her trip to Washington, DC, for her instruction in French cuisine from Julien. She was born in 1787 on Monticello to David Hern, an enslaved carpenter, and Isabel, an enslaved domestic servant. (Ironically, Isabel was supposed to go to Paris with Jefferson but fell sick after giving birth to Edy. Sally Hemings took the trip to Paris instead, which is where her apparent relationship with Jefferson began.) As a teenager she married into the Hemings family by wedding Joseph Fossett, the son of James Hemings's sister Mary.

Together, Fossett and Edy had ten children in their lifetime, with Edy pregnant at fifteen when she left Monticello for Washington at the beginning of Jefferson's presidency. She was joined there in 1806 by her eighteen-year-old sister-in-law Frances "Fanny" Hern, who had married Edy's brother, David, a wagon driver from Monticello. These two slave women seemed to have worked out a lot better, with Jefferson's maître d'hôtel at the executive mansion, Etienne Lemaire, describing them as "two good girls," and by the time Jefferson's presidency was finished, telling him that "they will give you much satisfaction" as chefs at Monticello.

Jefferson had an extremely sophisticated kitchen installed for the women to work in and learn French-style cooking. There were numerous pots and pans, thirty-one casseroles, fish kettles, tin molds, pudding dishes, and the like. Especially rare for an American kitchen was the range, which was constructed inside one of the kitchen fireplaces. It burned coal, had spits, and was equipped with a crane to swing hot pots and pans on and off the hottest locations on the stove.

And Fanny and Edy had a good teacher in Julien. He had been in the country for almost a decade when Jefferson brought him down from Philadelphia, where Washington had employed him during the last four months of his presidency while Hercules was cooling his heels back at Mount Vernon.

Margaret Bayard Smith said everyone who ate at Jefferson's table acknowledged his "excellence and superior skills." Congressman Samuel Mitchell said Julien "understands the art of preparing and serving up food, to a nicety." Dinner guests raved about the food, especially a dessert of ice cream "inclosed in covers of warm pastries."

Guests to the White House were introduced to several new delicacies, all of which Fanny and Edy learned to prepare and use. They included macaroni and vermicelli, anchovies, olive oil, vanilla, citron, Parmesan cheese, and European nuts and figs. The ices and creams that Julien produced were also new and sensational to most of the company. The results can be seen by the reports of their meals. "Never before had such dinners been given in the President's House," said one Washington resident.

Fanny and Edy were likely never seen by the dinner guests visiting the White House. While Jefferson dressed his waiters and butlers in fine livery, knee britches, and gilt- or steel-buttoned blue coats with crimson trimmings and lace edging, the women only wore aprons for their work and were instructed to stay in the basement, where the slave quarters and the kitchen were located.

Jefferson was pleased with their work enough to give them a gratuity of two dollars a month, money they could spend on whatever they wanted since Jefferson supplied their basic necessities. He provided food and drink for Fanny and Edy, and supplied them with not only their clothes but also the clothes for their children as well. Noted in one of Jefferson's expense books was a mistake he had found, that the nightgowns for Edy's infants had been "twice charged."

He also took care of their medical needs. It was Jefferson who paid the midwife her three dollars when their children were born, and then paid for two weeks of nursing care for mother and child. Jefferson brought doctors and nurses to the White House to take care of his slaves, reporting in one journal that he had "quite a hospital, one half below and above stairs being sick."

For slaves, Fanny and Edy's lives must have seemed especially comfortable. But their time at the White House could not have been completely happy. There were long separations from their husbands. David Hern was only allowed to come to the White House with his mule cart twice a year to carry plants and supplies back and forth. The separation could have caused strains in the Herns' relationship. During one such visit, the Herns got into "a terrible quarrel" inside the White House.

"Davy was jealous of his wife, and I reckon, with good reason," former overseer Francis Bacon said. In his memoirs, Bacon recalled that Jefferson was so displeased with the Herns for their fight that the slave overseer was summoned to take the four-day journey to Washington. Once Bacon arrived, Jefferson ordered him to take the husband and wife across the Potomac to Alexandria, Virginia, and sell them down south. The Herns "wept, and begged, and made good promises, and made such an ado, that they begged the old gentleman out of it," Bacon said.

Edy saw her husband even less. Joseph Fossett was not allowed to see his wife once Jefferson took her away from Monticello and to the nation's capital. This led to a confrontation with Jefferson, and the only arrest of an escaped slave on White House grounds. Edy was pregnant with the first of her ten children when she arrived at the White House, one of three children she would bear while in the executive mansion. Only two would survive, however, leading to the belief that Edy and her children were ill during part of her stay in Washington. It would take word of something like that to make her husband, Joseph, do what he did.

Fossett was foreman of the Monticello blacksmith shop, a prestigious job on the plantation, and as a Hemings, he led a much more charmed life than most of the other plantation slaves. But word reached Monticello that Edy or their child, who was reaching its second birthday in 1808, was sick. Either Fossett asked for permission to come to Washington and was denied by Jefferson (a likely scenario, because records show the child had whooping cough and Jefferson likely did not want the contagious disease taken back to his plantation by an anxious father) or Fossett simply didn't ask. Either way, one day Fossett abandoned the blacksmith shop and disappeared, much to the consternation of the Monticello foreman and apparently Jefferson.

Jefferson knew where Fossett had gone, however. In a July 31 letter to Joseph Dougherty, his Washington agent, Jefferson described Fossett as a "young mulatto man . . . 26 years of age, who ran away from here the night of the 29th." To Jefferson, Fossett had no reason to run, saying he left "without the least word of difference with anybody, and indeed having never in his life received a blow from any one." Like many southern slave owners, Jefferson did not formally acknowledge slave marriages, but he knew about the slave relationships among his people.

"We know he has taken the road towards Washington," Jefferson said. "He may possibly trump up some story to be taken care of at the President's House till he can make up his mind which way to go, or perhaps he may make himself known to Edy only, as he was formerly associated with her."

On August 3, 1806, Fossett was arrested on the White House lawn, having made the 120-mile journey in four days. He was caught sneaking out of the White House after spending the night there with Edy. "I took him immediately & brot. him to Mr. Perry & has him now in jail. Mr. Perry will start with him tomorrow for Monticello," Dougherty reported to Jefferson. Fossett was jailed in a nearby prison for a few days, and then sent back to Monticello, where he would have to wait two years before seeing his wife again at the end of the Jefferson presidency.

Surprisingly, there was no punishment recorded for Fossett, likely because other members of the White House household interceded on his behalf after their baby died later that year. "The poor unhappy mulatto got [i.e., Joe] was not difficult to take. He well merits a pardon for this," Lemaire wrote.

Fanny, too, bore and lost a baby while she lived in the White House, with whooping cough carrying off her child in November 1808. Jefferson tried to get proper medical help for the infant, Margaret Bayard Smith said in her letters. "He wrote to a lady who resided at some distance from the city, requesting her to send him the receipt for a remedy, which he had heard her say had proved effectual in the case of her own children when labouring under this disease," she said.

It didn't work for Fanny's child. Jefferson watched every penny, and so recorded his expenses for the burial of Fanny's infant. A coffin, delivered together with a load of wood, cost $2.25; the grave digger charged $1.35; and the hearse was hired for $2.75 for the trip to the burying ground.

Of at least five children born to the Monticello cooks in Washington, only two, James and Maria Fossett, survived to adulthood.

The Monticello slaves were not the only ones to work inside the White House, with Jefferson purchasing others while in the District of Columbia. One was John Freeman, purchased by Jefferson from a Maryland doctor in 1804 for four hundred dollars after years of renting his services.

Freeman, described as "straight and well made" with a "pleasing countenance," was one of the few blacks in the house whom White House visitors saw every day. Like the other white servants upstairs, he wore the official White House uniform: blue broadcloth coats with crimson or scarlet collar and cuffs, plated buttons, and a decorative woven edging, in silver, called livery lace; red waistcoats; and velvet or corduroy pantaloons.

Freeman worked as a waiter during Jefferson's many dinners, and once the dinner was done, he also cleaned the hall and dining room, and then possibly served as a part-time personal servant for the president. This favored position did not seem to sit well with some of the white servants hired by Jefferson to work upstairs in the White House. Freeman would later write a letter to Jefferson complaining of being "treated with a great deal of hostilitie in your family," which is what the president called his domestic staff.

Footman Edward Maher was vocal with his complaints, saying Jefferson "gave preference to a negro rather than to him in following you." Even the steward, Rapid, heard Maher saying "he would not wear the same sort of outfit as a negro wore, in speaking of the livery." Jefferson apparently told Maher to keep his complaints to himself. "The negro whom he thinks so little of, is a most valuable servant," he said.

Jefferson thought enough of Freeman to take him on several trips with him to Monticello, where the slave fell in love with a Hemings woman. Melinda Colbert, a niece of James and Sally Hemings, was the domestic servant of Jefferson's daughter Maria Jefferson Eppes. During their many trips to Monticello, Freeman became more and more attached to Melinda and planned to ask for her hand in marriage. But just as Freeman was ready to ask for Melinda in April 1804, Eppes died. That placed Melinda in serious danger of being sold away from Monticello and Freeman. The slave hit upon a solution, and approached his patron Jefferson.

"I am sorye to trubel you with a thing of this kind," Freeman wrote, saying he felt obliged to do so because "I have been foolish anufe to in gage myself to Melindar."

Freeman asked that Jefferson buy both him and his fiancée, thereby keeping Melinda at Monticello and giving Freeman continued access to the plantation and his wife. But this was one request that Jefferson turned down. Jefferson did buy Freeman a few months later, but he refused to buy Melinda, explaining that he already had too many house servants "in idleness" at Monticello. Luckily for the two slaves, Eppes's husband allowed Colbert to stay at Monticello, hired out as a house servant to a resident free workman. Freeman and Colbert married and began having children. By 1809, Colbert had been freed from Monticello and moved to Washington to be with her husband inside the President's House, where she did odd jobs.

She became one of the first free black women to be employed inside the White House, but she wouldn't be the last. Sally Houseman and Biddy Boyle were free blacks who were the White House's resident washerwomen, with Boyle recorded as receiving seven dollars a month. There were other "negres" and "negresses" hired on by Lemaire for special duties around the executive mansion, including cleaning the bathrooms, sweeping the chimneys, taking care of the infants so Fanny and Edy could work, or even taking care of Jefferson's flock of sheep that he kept on the White House grounds. Jefferson also hired free black males, Sandy, Isaac, and Jack, to work as scullions, servants who do menial tasks in a kitchen like washing dishes and cleaning up after the cooks.

What happened to these men and women after Jefferson's presidency ended and he headed back to Monticello?

John Freeman didn't want to go back. Virginia law said free blacks could not live there, so he considered it unsafe for Melinda to return with him to Monticello. But Freeman knew he was Jefferson's property, having personally asked the president to buy him. That request must have laid heavily upon his heart, because he wrote a heartfelt letter to Jefferson explaining his solution, which was to separate himself from his family.

"Rather than disples you I will go and do the best I can. . . . I shall be oblige to leave [Melinda] and the children," Freeman wrote.

His devotion to his family must have touched Jefferson. To keep from having to split up the couple, Jefferson sold Freeman to his successor, President James Madison, who then employed Colbert as a paid seamstress for his family while in the White House.

A few years later, Madison freed Freeman and the couple continued to serve the president as hired workers at the White House. John and Melinda Freeman would go on to become antislavery activists in Washington, and successful enough to leave their children a house on K Street a few blocks away from the White House upon Freeman's death in 1839.

When Ursula Hughes was returned to Monticello after her brief year of training under Chef Julien, she worked in the kitchens when Jefferson was around, and went back to the fields to do manual labor when he was not, rejoining her husband, Wormley Hughes. He ended up being one of the most loyal of the Monticello slaves, digging the grave of his master in July 1826. Having been one of Jefferson's favorites, he was informally freed by Jefferson's daughter.

Ursula was not. At the January 1827 sale of Jefferson's estate, Ursula and eight of her children were sold to different slave owners and scattered across Virginia. Eventually, most of them were purchased back by

Jefferson's grandson Thomas J. Randolph, and they lived their lives out at Randolph's plantation, Edgehill.

Edy Fossett and Fanny Hern returned to Monticello with Jefferson in 1808 to become the head chefs. Before leaving Washington, Jefferson notified the white overseers of his wishes: "the two cooks which are here will take the place of Peter Hemings," who had been serving as the head cook since his brother James Hemings had left. (Peter Hemings became a brewer of beer, with Jefferson writing "Peter's brewing of the last season I am in hopes will prove excellent . . . the only cask of it we have tried proves so.")

For years afterward, visitors to Monticello raved about the food Fanny and Edy created, especially the vegetables, roasted meat, and ice cream, a favorite dessert at Monticello. Jefferson's guests continued to praise the meals, saying that "the dinner is always choice and served in the French style." But their gifts did not earn them their freedom after Jefferson's death. Fanny Hern and her husband, David, were purchased by University of Virginia professor Robley Dunglison, where they disappear into history.

Joseph Fossett was freed in Thomas Jefferson's will, but Edy and their ten children remained slaves. Joseph was able to buy into freedom Edy, five of their children, and four of their grandchildren before leaving Virginia forever for the free state of Ohio, where Edy died in 1854.

CHAPTER 7

THE GREAT AMERICAN MELTING POT

WHILE JAMES HEMINGS'S FAMOUS SISTER, SALLY HEMINGS, NEVER crossed the threshold of the White House as far as we know, the rumors of her relationship with Jefferson spread far and wide throughout the early United States and are still debated to this day. Perhaps one of the reasons it was so easy to believe was because racial mixing of white colonial Americans and African slaves and freedmen was a commonplace occurrence by the time the new nation had formed.

Despite laws meant to keep whites and blacks from consummating relationships in the early days of the colonies, the sexual commingling of the two races— sometimes willing and sometimes forced—was routine from the first days that Europeans landed on North America. By the time the colonies won the War of Independence and declared themselves to be the United States of America, quite a few slaves could claim part-European ancestry, and it was these slaves—sometimes light-skinned, well-educated and Caucasian-looking—who were used to work inside what we now call the "big house" as butlers, maids, and cooks, and subsequently were used by presidents as the public face of their slaves inside the White House and other executive mansions.

Take the first four most famous presidential slaves. While the parentage of William Lee, the companion of President Washington, was never recorded, it is relatively clear he was racially mixed. Lee was clearly described as a "mulatto" when Washington purchased him, because the future president had to pay more for the light-skinned boy than he would have for a "Negro." Oney Judge was the daughter of Betty, an enslaved seamstress, and Andrew Judge, a white English tailor who was an indentured servant at Mount Vernon. Paul Jennings was the son of a white merchant named Jennings and a slave on James Madison's plantation. James Hemings was the son of a slave owned by the Jefferson family and John Hemings, an English sea captain. (His half-sister, Sally, was the daughter of John Wayles, the father of Jefferson's wife Martha, making the slave the half-sister of Jefferson's deceased wife during the time of their supposed relationship.) Clearly, only a few generations after those first servants came into Jamestown and were converted into lifelong slaves, there was visible human proof of sexual relationships between whites and blacks in the English colonies. By the time of the American Revolution, somewhere between sixty thousand and one hundred twenty thousand people of "mixed" heritage resided in the colonies. But this should not be a surprise to anyone. One of the most famous stories of the settlement of the North American continent by English settlers involves a racially mixed marriage, the famous story of Pocahontas.

Pocahontas will always be remembered as one of the most famous women of early North American history because of her dalliances and alliances with the English colonists who were moving into the lands that were already settled by her father's people. Daughter of Powhatan, the paramount chief of Tsenacomoco, a political alliance of Algonquian-speaking Indians in tidewater Virginia, Pocahontas is largely known for saving the life of the Jamestown colonist John Smith and then romancing him, although both stories are considered to be more mythology than history thanks to fanciful storytelling by John Smith and embellishment by moviemaking companies such as Walt Disney.

But it is a fact that English colonists held Pocahontas hostage in 1613 in an attempt to bring her father to the negotiating table to stop a burgeoning war between the natives and the English colonists. During this hostage period she met and eventually married English widower John Rolfe. (This actually was Pocahontas's second marriage: She was married to a man named "Kocoum, a captainne of Powhatan" when the English captured her. But the local tribes had a tradition that if an enemy tribe captured a woman, her marriage was dissolved, making her single when she met and married Wolfe in 1614.)

This is where Pocahontas's life intersects with the story of African American slavery. After she married Rolfe, the colonists decided to send the couple back to England for a goodwill and public relations tour of the old country in hopes of raising money and supplies. The ship used to sail Pocahontas from Virginia to England in 1616, the *Treasurer*, was the same ship that would return in 1619 to Jamestown with some of the first African slaves to set foot on the American continent. And it's through Rolfe that we get some of our first descriptions of the African slaves' arrival in Virginia.

"About the latter end of August, a Dutch man of Warr of the burden of a 160 tons arrived at Point-Comfort, the Comandor name Capt Jope, his Pilott for the West Indies one Mr Marmaduke an Englishman," Rolfe said. "They mett wth the Trer in the West Indyes, and determyned to hold consort shipp hetherward, but in their passage lost one the other. He brought not any thing but 20. and odd Negroes, wth the Governor and Cape Marchant bought for vietualle (whereof he was in greate need as he p'tended) at the best and easyest rate they could."

Pocahontas never met any of these slaves. She died as she and Rolfe prepared to return to Virginia, and was buried in an English graveyard, never to see her family or native soil again. But the Indian maid's relationship with the foreigner would not be the last time the white colonists would mix with people of different skin color, away from the watchful eyes of Mother England.

Those first Africans to come into Jamestown initially mingled amongst themselves—two of them, Antonio and Isabella, gave birth to William Tucker, the first documented child of African descent born in America, in 1624—likely because of the language and cultural barriers. But as the years went by, proximity, opportunity, and attraction blossomed into romance in the colonies, and Africans and Europeans began to intermingle. Paul Heinegg noted several of these early relationships in his book, *Free African Americans of North Carolina, Virginia, and South Carolina from the Colonial Period to About 1820, Volume 1.* "Francis Payne was married to a white woman named Amy by September 1656 when he gave her a mare by deed of jointure," he wrote. "Elizabeth Key, a 'Mulatto' woman whose father had been free, successfully sued for her freedom in Northumberland County in 1656 and married her white attorney, William Greensted. Francis Skiper was married to Ann, an African American woman, before February 1667 when they sold land in Norfolk County. Peter Beckett, a Negro slave in Northampton County, married Sarah Dawson, a white servant."

Newspapers would carry notices of black and white servants running away together, like this one from the *American Weekly Mercury* of August 11, 1720: "Runaway in April last from Richard Tilghman, of Queen Anne County in Maryland, a mulatto slave, named Richard Molson, of middle stature, about forty years old and has had the small pox, he is in company with a white woman . . . who is supposed now goes for his wife." And in the *Pennsylvania Gazette* of June 1, 1746: "Runaway from the subscriber the second of last month, at the town of Potomac, Frederick County, Maryland, a mulatto servant named Isaac Cromwell, runaway at the same time, an English servant woman named Ann Greene."

But the most famous of these early interracial relationships was the August 1681 one between Nell Butler and "Negro Charles," the slave of Maj. William Boarman of St. Mary's County. Eleanor Butler, or "Irish Nell" as she came to be known, was an Irish indentured servant brought to the American continent in 1661 by Charles Calvert, the Lord Baltimore, to work for Boarman as a washerwoman. Charles, a native of the West Indies, was one of Boarman's slaves, a fact that didn't seem to matter to Nell.

In 1681, Nell had finished her term of service to Boarman, and announced that she intended to marry Charles. The ceremony was conducted by a Catholic priest on the Boarman plantation. But for Nell, the day would not be a completely happy one. Lord Baltimore showed up for the wedding with a warning. He said to her: "what a pity, likely a young girl as you should fling herself away to marry a negro" and warned her that if she did, she would be making her children slaves.

Apparently, Nell was not worried and a little bit insulted. "My lord asked her how she would like to go to bed to a Negro . . . and she answered that she would rather go to bed to Charles than his Lordship."

Butler was not just risking her children's future. She was also risking her own status as a free woman for love. In addition to requiring the children of a male slave to be automatically enslaved, a 1664 Maryland law required that when a "free borne woman shall inter marry with any slave . . . [she] shall Serve the master of such slave dureing the life of her husband." Nell, by marrying Charles, would also become property of her husband's owner.

Lord Baltimore, despite Nell's offense, took pity on the love-struck woman, and used his influence to petition the colony's government to change the law to guarantee that no white woman would ever be forced into slavery. The Assembly, swayed by Nell's story or simply unwilling to stomach any possible chance that a white woman could be forced into slavery through their laws, changed the law to say that any indentured servant woman who married an enslaved man would immediately become free. Her children would also be free. Lord Baltimore had saved Nell from a life of slavery, but there was no help coming for Charles, who remained a slave for the rest of his life. Nell, meanwhile, took in spinning and acted as a midwife.

Charles and Nell Butler had seven or eight children, but the new law declaring them to be free didn't matter to the Boarmans, who kept them enslaved anyway. One of the Butler's neighbors, Mrs. Elizabeth Warren, recounted that Nell's oldest son, Jack, escaped from his enslavement by fleeing to southern Virginia, and later purchased his freedom from one of the Boarman family. The other Butler descendants would eventually use the law that saved Nell Butler from slavery to obtain their own freedom. In October of 1770, Nell and Charles's grandchildren, Mary and William Butler, successfully sued to gain their freedom based on the fact that Irish Nell was a white woman.

Attitudes toward mixed marriages were changing. From the beginning, there were repercussions for some for crossing the color line, especially if the couple was not married. Punishment could be levied against both or either partner. For example, on September 17, 1630, Hugh Davis was sentenced "to be soundly whipped, before an assembly of Negroes and others for abusing himself to the dishonor of God and shame of Christians, by defiling his body in lying with a negro; which fault he is to acknowledge next Sabbath day."

Ten years later, it was the woman, not the man, who was punished. A white planter named Robert Sweat apparently fell in love with a married Negro servant girl named Margaret Cornish, who lived on a neighboring plantation with her husband, John Gowen, the servant of an Englishman named William Evans in Elizabeth City, Virginia. (Gowen is believed to be one of the original Angolan slaves to come into Jamestown.) Margaret became pregnant in 1640, exposing the affair and sending the two of them to court. Virginia court records contain the sentence handed down on October 17, 1640.

"Whereas Robert Sweat hath begotten with child a negro woman servant belonging unto Lieutenant Sheppard, the court hath therefore ordered that the said negro woman shall be whipt at the whipping post and the said Sweat shall tomorrow in the forenoon do public penance for his offence at James City church in the time of divine service according to the laws of England in that case provided."

Of course, not all racial intermingling was consensual. In August 1861, a multiracial gang of servants and slaves of Thomas Cocke were in his Virginia orchard cutting down weeds. They decided to take a break, and the white servants and black slaves shared some alcoholic cider. Along came some white visitors, who joined in the drinking, including one of whom "dranke cupp for cupp" with the "Negroes."

One of these new drinkers was Katherine Watkins, the wife of a Quaker, who apparently had one too many. Two different stories survive about what happened next, that of Watkins and that of John Long, a mulatto slave of Cocke's. Watkins's advocates later said in court that Long raped her: "John threw the said Katherine down (He starting from behind a tree) and stopped her Mouth with a handerkerchief, and tooke up the said Katherines Coates (ie petticoats), and putt his yard into her and ravished her."

Long and other white servants in the orchard told a different story, a story of drunken Watkins coming on sexually to the black slaves. Watkins had, for instance, raised the tail of Dirke's shirt, saying "he would have a good pricke," put her hand on mulatto Jack's codpiece, saying she "loved him for his Fathers sake for his Father was a very handsome young Man." According to the testimony of John Aust, one of the white servants, after drinking quite a few cups of cider, "And a while after she tooke Mingoe one of the said Cocke's Negroes about the Necke and fling on the bedd and Kissed him and putt her hand into his Codpeice, Awhile after Mulatto jacke went into the Fish roome and she followed him, but what they did there this deponent knoweth not for it being near night this deponent left her and the Negroes together, (He thinking her to be much in drinke)."

Long was exonerated. He was not prosecuted for being a black slave having sex with a white woman, but for being accused of forcing her. That's because interracial sex might have been frowned upon in the early days of the American colonies, but it wasn't illegal for the first Africans and the first Europeans to intermingle. But that would soon change.

No one knows exactly when the disapproval of interracial mixing changed into an outright ban. The first statute to this effect came about in 1661, when Virginia passed legislation prohibiting interracial marriage and then passed a law that prohibited ministers from marrying racially mixed couples. The fine was ten thousand pounds of tobacco. Maryland soon followed, passing a law saying a woman who married a Negro slave had to serve her husband's owner for the rest of her married life, a law that was repealed after Irish Nell Butler's wedding to Charles the slave. But a few years later, in 1715 and 1717, Maryland's legislature made cohabitation between any white person and a person of African descent unlawful. Massachusetts, North Carolina, South Carolina, and Pennsylvania adopted similar prohibitions during the next quarter-century and Georgia when Negroes were admitted to that colony in 1750. But even banning miscegenation through law wouldn't stop the sexual mixing of the two races.

Thomas Branagan, who visited Philadelphia in 1805, observed: "There are many, very many blacks who . . . begin to feel themselves consequential . . . will not be satisfied unless they get white women for wives, and are likewise exceedingly impertinent to white people in low circumstances . . . I solemnly swear, I have seen more white women married to, and deluded through the arts of seduction by Negroes in one year in Philadelphia, than for eight years I was visiting [West Indies and the Southern states]. . . . There are perhaps hundreds of white women thus fascinated by black men in this city and there are thousands of black children by them at present."

But as the indentured servitude of the early days of the American colonies changed into slavery, the voluntary attraction between blacks and whites would change into an uglier form of interracial sex between master and an often unwilling slave.

Slave narratives are filled with stories of white male masters forcing sex upon black female slaves, using their power of ownership over them to force them to share their bodies and bear children by them, children who then would belong to their fathers not as offspring but as property. The famous slave narratives of the colonial and antebellum American times are full of references to this, making the once-undercover relationships between master and slave a hotly debated topic in the public eye.

In his book, *Equiano's Travels: The Interesting Narrative of the Life of Olaudah Equiano: or Gustavus Vassa, the African*, Equiano describes rapes happening even before the slave ships arrived in North America. "It was almost a constant practice with our clerks, and other whites, to commit violent depredations on the chastity of the female slaves; and these I was, though with reluctance, obliged to submit to at all times, being unable to help them," he said. "When we have had some of these slaves on board my master's vessels, to carry them to other islands, or to America, I have known our mates to commit these acts most shamefully, to the disgrace, not of Christians only, but of men. I have even known them to gratify their brutal passion with females not ten years old."

Harriet Jacobs, a slave in Edenton, North Carolina, claimed in her book that when she reached the age of fifteen, her master, Dr. James Norcom, attempted to have sex with her: "My master, Dr. Norcom, began to whisper foul words in my ear. Young as I was, I could not remain ignorant of their import. I tried to treat them with indifference or contempt. The master's age, my extreme youth, and the fear that his conduct would be reported to my grandmother, made him bear this treatment for many months. He was a crafty man, and resorted to many means to accomplish his purposes. Sometimes he had stormy, terrific ways, that made his victims tremble; sometimes he assumed a gentleness that he thought must surely subdue. Of the two, I preferred his stormy moods, although they left me trembling."

Henry Bibb, author of *Narrative of the Life and Adventures of Henry Bibb, an American Slave, Written by Himself* (himself being the son of a slave woman and, according to his sources, state senator James Bibb of Kentucky), described how a slave trader attempted to force his light-skinned wife to work as a prostitute for white men or have sex with him. "She said that Garrison had taken her to a private house where he kept female slaves for the basest purposes. It was a resort for slave trading profligates and soul drivers, who were interested in the same business," he said. "Soon after she arrived at this place, Garrison gave her to understand what he brought her there for, and made a most disgraceful assault on her virtue, which she promptly repeled; and for which Garrison punished her with the lash, threatening her that if she did not submit that he would sell her child. The next day he made the same attempt, which she resisted, declaring that she would not submit to it; and again he tied her up and flogged her until her garments were stained with blood."

It wasn't just white men. White women on slave plantations also used their power over the male slaves to demand sexual favors. "The women went with colored men too. That's why so many women slave owners wouldn't marry, 'cause they was goin' with one of their slaves," one former slave recalled in an interview.

Some researchers argue that the sexual relationships between slaves and plantation masters and mistresses weren't always forced. By voluntarily sleeping with plantation masters, black female slaves could sometimes leverage better treatment for themselves and their families: work inside the house learning a craft or skill instead of the fields, maybe extra rations, less cruel treatment from overseers, possibly even freedom.

There were a large number of mulattos among manumitted slaves, likely because white slave masters wanted to free their progeny before death. The mothers of the mulatto children would often be manumitted, or freed for a reason, at the death of the master. The manumitted mulatto son or daughter would then become a part of the growing group of free African Americans. The 1860 census reported that a little more than one in ten slaves was a mulatto, while one in three of the free blacks was a mixed-race black.

For example, when Virginia planter Ralph Quarles freed his four mulatto slave children and one of his daughters married a slave, he purchased the son-in-law's freedom and gave the newlyweds a plantation and slaves. Quarles died in 1834 and left his property to his mulatto son.

The products of these willing and unwilling unions soon numbered in the thousands, a public reminder of what was going on behind closed doors on southern plantations. Alexis de Tocqueville observed after his visit in 1831 and 1832 that, "In some parts of America, the European and the negro races are so crossed by one another that it is rare to meet with a man who is entirely black, or entirely white."

In the South, however, most of these mulattos were condemned to slavery. By 1850, mulattoes represented 7.7 percent of the slaves and 10.4 percent in 1860, according to Robert William Fogel and Stanley L. Engerman in their book *Time on the Cross: The Economics of American Negro Slavery*.

"There are thousands upon thousands of mulattoes and quadroons, all children of slaveholders, in a state of slavery," they wrote. "Slavery is bad enough for the black, but it is worse, if worse can be, for the mulatto or the quadroon to be subjected to the utmost degradation and hardship, and to know that it is their own fathers who are treating them as brutes, especially when they contrast their usage with the pampered luxury in which they see his lawful children revel, who are not whiter, and very often not so good-looking as the quadroon."

As slaves, mulatto men and women were often as not used as house slaves: nanny to the slave owner's children, a cook, a seamstress, a butler, a carriage driver, or a valet. Slave owners believed the darker-skinned slaves were stronger and could tolerate the sun in the fields, while the lighter skin was related to the intelligence needed for jobs in the public eye instead of out in the fields. More often than dark-skinned slaves, mulattoes were provided some education, enjoyed good food, clothing, and shelter, and had opportunities to move about, both inside and outside the plantation. When it came time for the plantation master to move into the White House, those were the slaves they chose to take along with them.

CHAPTER 8

PAUL JENNINGS AND THE BURNING OF THE WHITE HOUSE

As he watched the light seep from James Madison's eyes, Paul Jennings probably could feel his privileged life dying right along with the ex-president. For most of his youth, Jennings had the best life a slave in antebellum Virginia could ask for. He was the manservant of one of the most influential men in the new United States, and as such, got to experience and see things few men of his race did at the time. But then, on June 28, 1836, Jennings found himself at Madison's bedside at his lavish Virginia plantation, watching the life slowly depart from the ex-president's body with the other slaves.

"That morning Sukey brought him his breakfast, as usual. He could not swallow," Jennings wrote in his book. "His niece, Mrs. Willis, said, 'What is the matter, uncle James?' 'Nothing more than a change of mind, my dear.' His head instantly dropped, and he ceased breathing as quietly as the snuff of a candle goes out."

Despite having been held in bondage by this man his entire life, Jennings had nothing but respect for his former master, calling him "one of the best men that ever lived." That respect apparently did not transfer to Madison's wife, Dolley. The faithful slave's relationship with the woman considered to be the first true first lady apparently was a prickly one after Madison's death, filled with financial woes, half-truths, and broken promises, that culminated with Jennings's sale to an insurance agent despite the former president's promise of his freedom. But even then, Jennings would prove to be faithful to the man who had brought him out of the slave quarters of the South and into the hub of activity for a growing nation.

Jennings worked for the Madisons for almost his entire life, and likely considered himself part of the family. Born on Madison's Montpelier plantation in 1799 to a slave mother descended from Native Americans and a white English trader named Benjamin Jennings, the ten-year-old Paul was a handsome boy who could read and write at an early age. Those skills, acquired by watching alongside as a white boy at Montpelier was being taught, likely made him a favorite of the Madisons, who promoted him out of the slave quarters and into the main house as the "body servant" of James Madison. Madison needed a quick replacement because he had earlier sold Billey, his former valet. Like Jennings would, Billey had followed the white politician everywhere taking care of his needs, including to the Continental Congress in Philadelphia.

But while there, Billey did more than take care of Madison's clothes and bring his dinner. Billey listened to the talk of revolution and freedom. And when it came time for Madison to return home to antebellum Virginia, he knew that his slave had learned too much from his time up North to return back to a docile, obedient slave at Montpelier. So Madison sold Billey, explaining his reasons to his father in a September 1783 letter.

"I am persuaded his mind is too thoroughly tainted to be a fit companion for fellow slaves in Virga. The laws here do not admit of his being sold for more than 7 years. I do not expect to get near the worth of him; but cannot think of punishing him by transportation merely for coveting that liberty for which we have paid the price of so much blood, and have proclaimed so often to be the right, and worthy pursuit, of every human being."

Billey ended up being freed when Pennsylvania declared all slaves free, and worked with people like Madison, Jefferson, and others, but died a few years later after falling into the ocean while on a voyage to New Orleans.

Despite holding more than one hundred slaves of his own, Madison seemed to understand the inherent hypocrisy of slavery in a country that had just fought and received its own freedom. And unlike many other southern whites of his time, he took care not to insult or belittle the slaves he kept in bondage or other Africans he met in public, Jennings said.

"One day riding home from court with old Tom Barbour (father of Governor Barbour), they met a colored man, who took off his hat. Mr. M. raised his, to the surprise of old Tom; to whom Mr. M. replied, 'I never allow a negro to excel me in politeness.'"

It was now Jennings's turn to follow this man, and the ten-year-old slave was packed up with the rest of James and Dolley Madison's belongings and shipped to Washington after Madison won the presidency in 1808. Jennings's first sight of Washington and the newly completed White House did not impress him, he remembered years later.

"The east room was not finished, and Pennsylvania Avenue was not paved, but was always in an awful condition from either mud or dust. The city was a dreary place," Jennings said.

But that "dreary place" would become Jennings's home for the duration of Madison's presidency, and Jennings would stay by the president's side as much as he could. Every other morning, he would shave Madison's face, and each day, he brought out the president's favorite suit, an easy chore for the slave because of the president's renowned austerity. Madison favored plain black suits that some of his colleagues said always made him look like he was going to a funeral. And he only kept one suit at a time, which made Jennings's task of choosing clothes for the president very easy. Madison had a simple reason for doing so, Jennings said later. "He had some poor relatives that he had to help, and wished to set them an example of economy in the matters of dress."

Dolley was different. Seventeen years Madison's junior, she never paid attention to Madison's example of austerity or modesty. She was tall, a full head over the five-foot-three Madison, and would show off her figure with imported French dresses with daringly low necklines and turbans covered with feathers at parties. While Madison was known as a scholar who was unfailingly bad at parlor chit-chat, at parties Dolley threw at the White House, writer Washington Irving said the first lady was "a fine, portly dame who has a smile and a pleasant word for everybody." Dolley Madison was always concerned with appearances, even during Madison's term as president. Thomas Jefferson had furnished the White House with furniture from his own home. The new first lady wasn't interested in doing that. Mrs. Madison worked with the architect Benjamin Henry Latrobe to make the White House as beautiful as possible, within a budget set by Congress. Dolley Madison began holding receptions every Wednesday at the White House to help boost her husband's popularity. Jennings and other White House slaves would serve the best wine and food to the Madisons' guests as politicians, royalty, and commoners mingled and talked about the news of the day.

Even throughout the War of 1812 and the burning of Washington, DC, by British troops, the Madisons—the shy James and the outgoing Dolley—stayed together and constructed one of the more successful presidencies of their time. When the Madisons left the District of Columbia to return to Montpelier for good, no one had a bad word to say about the two, not even the enslaved Paul.

"Mrs. Madison was a remarkably fine woman. She was beloved by everybody in Washington, white and colored," Jennings said. It was only after James Madison died that things changed.

While wealthy, the Madisons were not obscenely rich, and their sixteen years in Washington—eight while Madison was serving as Thomas Jefferson's secretary of state and eight as president—had severely depleted their funds. But the Madisons continued to entertain lavishly, because in retirement Madison stayed interested in politics, including the issue of what to do with the hundreds of thousands of slaves in the South. Madison felt that slaves could not be freed unless "they are permanently removed beyond the region occupied by, or allotted to a white population." With that in mind, in 1819 Madison founded the American Colonization Society dedicated to freeing slaves and transporting them to the west coast of Africa. But none of Madison's one hundred slaves ended up back in Africa. Instead, he kept Montpelier running with his slave labor planting and harvesting tobacco, corn, rye, wheat, and hemp while he worked on his memoir and papers. However, running Montpelier was not as financially lucrative as the Madisons had hoped, given that their time in Washington had allowed the plantation to become worn down and the fields fallow.

The Madisons also had another financial drain in the person of Dolley Madison's son from her previous marriage, Payne Todd. Todd was known for his recklessness, debauchery, drunkenness, and fiscal irresponsibility, and his stepfather and mother spent thousands of dollars regularly paying off his creditors, hoping in vain for the day when their son would finally marry, settle down, and assume responsibility. But it never happened, even after he moved into an estate next to his now-retired parents. The death of James Madison made everything worse. A year later, Dolley Madison returned to Washington, living in a house across Lafayette Square from the White House and leaving Payne Todd in charge of Montpelier. But in his mother's absence, Todd mismanaged Montpelier, leaving them with no income. That's when Dolley's relationship with Paul Jennings changed. As a favored slave, Jennings likely expected his freedom upon the deaths of the ex-president or his wife. But a destitute Dolley needed cash, and saw their slaves as a way to raise funds.

First, Dolley sold Montpelier and most of the slaves who lived there, keeping only a few, including Paul, with her in her Washington residence. This likely devastated Jennings, whose life under Madison had included pledges not to sell slaves without their permission. In his will, Madison had specifically said "none of them should be sold without his or her consent, or in case of their misbehaviour; except that infant children may be sold with their parent who consents for them to be sold with him or her, and who consents to be sold."

The sale of Montpelier was probably the first sign of bad days to come for Jennings. But he had another reason to be upset. The sale of the estate meant that Jennings would no longer have easy access to his wife and five children.

When Paul Jennings met her, Fanny Gordon was the maid to Mrs. Charles P. Howard, a neighbor of the Madisons in Virginia. They married in 1822, with Fanny's brother Edmund later remembering the Howards giving Fanny and her new husband "a marriage supper at her master's home." While they lived separately on plantations an hour's walk apart and likely only saw each other on Sundays, the traditional day off for slaves, Paul and Fanny Jennings ended up having five children: Felix,

William, Frances, John, and Franklin. During one of his last visits to Montpelier, Jennings discovered that Fanny was sick.

"Pore Fanney," he wrote to Sukey, a fellow slave, back in Washington, "I am looking every day to see the last of her." Fanny Jennings died on August 4, 1844, the same year Dolley sold Montpelier.

Back in Washington, things were looking grim for Dolley Madison. While she once was known as the epitome of American fashion, Dolley now was forced to wear the same black dress, and the same hat with the same pin and the same earrings, to public events like the laying of the cornerstone of the Washington Monument and her sending of the first private message by telegraph. People visiting the new presidents always made a stop to see Dolley Madison in her Lafayette Square house, and as word of her poverty began to spread, they made a habit of turning down her offers of wine, as they knew that she had an empty cellar in her house.

The sale of Montpelier didn't bring enough to sustain Dolley's lifestyle, so she began looking for alternative means of funding. One of the routes she took was to rent Paul Jennings out for work. This probably surprised Jennings, who was expecting his freedom once James Madison had died. In fact, Dolley Madison had said words to that effect to Jennings.

Immediately after the death of her husband, Mrs. Madison promised to set him free, as she knew it was the wish and expectation of Mr. Madison. But that didn't happen. On his return from Montpelier, Jennings was sent over to the White House to work for President James Polk as a butler and horseman. But Dolley Madison would be the only person to profit from this arrangement, according to the *Liberator*.

"After she brought him to the city, he worked for a year and a half or two years on wages, which she took to the last red cent, leaving him to get his clothes by presents, night-work or as he might," the newspaper reported.

But Jennings still had hope for freedom from Dolley. She had written as much in her will of 1841: "I give to my mulatto man Paul his freedom"—the only slave so treated. But things were getting worse and worse for Dolley financially, and the trust between her and Jennings seemed to fade.

Dolley Madison, wife of President James Madison. LIBRARY OF CONGRESS

Jennings, who was now forty-two, began to wonder if Mrs. Madison not only wouldn't free him, even upon her death, but would sell him to slave traders who might take him down to the fields of the South. Jennings figured his only option would be to set a price himself for his freedom.

"Fearing every day her wants might urge her to sell him to the traders, he insisted that she should fix the price, which he would have to contrive to pay, whatever it might be," the newspaper said.

His instincts proved correct. Dolley Madison sold Paul Jennings in September 1846 to Pollard Webb, an insurance agent in the city. Six months later, Jennings was purchased by Senator Daniel Webster of New Hampshire, who wrote up the following arrangement: "I have paid $120 for the freedom of Paul Jennings; he agrees to work out the same at $8/month, to be furnished with board, clothes, washing . . . his freedom papers I gave to him." The sale of Paul Jennings, and the likely hard feelings the slave had toward Dolley Madison for having to work for his freedom after years of service, likely led to one of the greatest controversies over the Madisons' time in the White House. Dolley Madison took care to craft the stories that made her beloved to Americans even today. One of those stories includes how she bravely saved the historic painting of George Washington by artist Gilbert Stuart from being burned by the British with the White House in the War of 1812, a story that Dolley Madison told herself in a letter after the hostilities had ended.

"Our kind friend, Mr. Carroll, has come to hasten my departure, and is in a very bad humor with me because I insist on waiting until the large picture of Gen. Washington is secured, and it requires to be unscrewed from the wall," she said. "This process was found too tedious for these perilous moments; I have ordered the frame to be broken, and the canvass taken out it is done, and the precious portrait placed in the hands of two gentlemen of New York, for safe keeping. And now, dear sister, I must leave this house, or the retreating army will make me a prisoner in it, by filling up the road I am directed to take."

While the words of Dolley Madison's letter have the fervor of a wartime correspondent, experts today do not believe she wrote this account in the midst of fleeing Washington, as has been believed. But the story of

Dolley Madison saving the painting of George Washington was repeated over and over in the newspapers of the day, making her into a national icon. Once freed, Paul Jennings heard about this, and immediately set the record straight.

"It has often been stated in print, that when Mrs. Madison escaped from the White House, she cut out from the frame the large portrait of Washington (now in one of the parlors there), and carried it off. This is totally false. She had no time for doing it. It would have required a ladder to get it down. All she carried off was the silver in her reticule, as the British were thought to be but a few squares off, and were expected every moment. John Susé (a Frenchman, then door-keeper, and still living) and Magraw, the President's gardener, took it down and sent it off on a wagon, with some large silver urns and such other valuables as could be hastily got hold of."

To this day, experts studying Dolley Madison and the War of 1812 are puzzled by the conflict in the two stories, with some saying Jennings's account was his revenge for her broken promises about setting him free and her treatment of some of her other slaves.

The destruction of the White House during the War of 1812 ended the first chapter of African American slavery under the US president. The Madisons, their slaves, and their servants would end up living in several different houses around the nation's capital while the White House was being reconstructed exactly as it was before the British soldiers burned it down. They finally settled into The Octagon, a three-story brick home in downtown Washington designed by William Thornton, the first architect of the Capitol. (The Octagon is not an octagon at all. It is an irregular hexagon house that was designed to fit an irregularly shaped lot. It survived the burning of Washington only because it was being leased to the French ambassador at the time, who smartly flew France's flag from the roof, leading redcoats to pass it by for buildings such as the White House and the Capitol.) It was in the Octagon's second-floor parlor on February 17, 1815—a room now appropriately known as the Treaty Room—where the Treaty of Ghent was signed, ending the war with Great Britain. The Madisons would leave the nation's capital without ever living inside the White House again.

Jennings wasn't the only slave Dolley Madison lied to. James Madison was close friends with his fellow president, Thomas Jefferson, and served as his secretary of state during the Jefferson Administration. The two men visited each other constantly, sharing tips on governance, farming, and philosophy as they traveled through state and national government. Jefferson even tried to get Madison to purchase a nearby plantation so they could be neighbors. Madison turned that idea aside, and bought Montpelier, thirty miles away. But their warm relationship meant each man spent as much time visiting his esteemed neighbor as he could, as noted by Jennings.

"While Mr. Jefferson was President, he and Mr. Madison (then his Secretary of State) were extremely intimate; in fact, two brothers could not have been more so. Mr. Jefferson always stopped over night at Mr. Madison's, in going and returning from Washington," Jennings said in his book.

A member of the Hemings family confirmed the friendship between Madison and Jefferson. Peter Fossett, the son of former White House assistant chef Edy Fossett, ended up being the last living slave of Jefferson's, and he was interviewed about his time at Monticello by the *New York World*, for an article published on January 30, 1898. "Mr. Madison used to come and stay for days with Mr. Jefferson. He was a very learned man, as was also Mr. Jefferson," Fossett said. "He was a kindly looking old gentleman, and his coming looked for with pleasure by the older servants for he never left without leaving each of them a substantial reminder of his visit."

These encounters make it likely that Jennings and the famous Hemings family also knew each other, considering Jennings's attachment with the Madisons and the Hemings family's positions with Jefferson. But there is also a direct link between the Madisons and the Hemings family, one recorded as another lie from Dolley Madison to a slave family, although not as serious as the one she told to Jennings.

Sally Hemings had several children at Monticello during the time the Madisons were visiting Jefferson, and for some reason, Dolley Madison took interest in one of them, as the child would record later in his life.

"As to myself, I was named Madison by the wife of James Madison, who was afterwards President of the United States," Madison Hemings said. "Mrs. Madison happened to be at Monticello at the time of my birth and begged the privilege of naming me, promising my mother a fine present for the honor. She consented, and Mrs. Madison dubbed me by the name I now acknowledge, but like many promises of white folks to the slaves she never gave my mother anything."

Obviously, that promise must have been one related to Madison Hemings later in his life, most likely by his mother, Sally, since it supposedly happened soon after he was born. It stuck with Hemings for the rest of his life, and he repeated the story in his memoir, as told to S. F. Wetmore, in the *Ohio's Pike County Republican* in 1873.

It turns out the story that Madison Hemings told was not entirely true. Dolley Madison wasn't at Monticello on the day of his birth, January 19, 1805, but historians have discovered that the Madisons were at Monticello during Sally Hemings's pregnancy with him the year before. The conversation between Sally Hemings and Dolley Madison, and the future first lady's promise, must have happened during that time, which was about six months into Sally Hemings's pregnancy. Sally Hemings must have been reminded of Dolley Madison's broken promise every time she called her son's name, and she must have reminded him of that so many times he remembered it all the way to adulthood.

This is still not the last lie Dolley Madison would tell a slave.

While working for Webster, Jennings played a key role in the greatest mass escape attempt by African American slaves in American history. Jennings, despite being owned his entire life by kindly masters like the Madisons and Webster, felt that slavery was wrong for both him and the other enslaved African Americans in and around Washington. Meeting up with a ship captain named Daniel Drayton of Philadelphia in 1848, the two of them hatched a plot to spirit as many African American slaves away from the nation's capital as possible. Aided by free black families in the area, Jennings, Drayton, and another sea captain named Edmund Sayres spread the news that freedom was available if slaves were courageous enough to try to seek it.

While plans were being made for the great escape, Dolley Madison was making plans of her own. With money getting more and more tight, Mrs. Madison hatched a plan to betray another one of her longtime slaves.

Just as Paul Jennings was James Madison's personal slave, Susan, or Sukey as she was better known, served as Dolley Madison's personal maid and slave. Almost nothing is known about Sukey's personal life: where she was born, how old she was, what she looked like, or when she died. But what is known is that she trained from an early age to be a maid to Dolley Madison, a demanding woman who was very concerned about what she and her clothes looked like.

While Jennings was only ten when he came to the White House with the Madisons, it is believed that Sukey was older, with some sources saying she was around the same age as James Madison, who was fifty-eight when he became president. Perhaps her age explains why Dolley Madison called Sukey their "most Efficient house servant." But just because Sukey was good at her job didn't mean that she and Mrs. Madison always got along, a situation that would come back to haunt the slave maid in the future.

One disagreement between the two women meant that Sukey was punished by being banished from the main house at Montpelier to one of the outer farms owned by the Madisons. Dolley Madison recorded this punishment, saying Sukey "has made so many depridations on every thing, in every part of the house that I sent her to Black Meadow last week but find it terribly inconvenient to do without her, & suppose I shall take her again, as I feel too old to bring up another—so I must let her steal from me, to keep from labour myself." In 1833, Mrs. Madison reported "my most efficient House servant Sucky lies very ill with bilious fever."

What did Sukey do to be banished from Dolley Madison's sight and why did Mrs. Madison even care that she was sick? Slaves were known to steal from their masters as a form of rebellion, but usually most were smart enough, or fearful enough of a potential punishment, not to get caught. Mrs. Madison's statement makes it seem that she knew Sukey was stealing but also made it clear that she was so dependent on Sukey to bathe, dress, and prepare her for her daily tasks that she was prepared to forgive just about anything to keep from having to take care of herself.

Sukey was brought to the White House along with Paul Jennings, and apparently, it was Sukey who first saw the man hurrying toward the executive mansion to warn them the British were coming.

The White House after its burning by the British in the War of 1812. It was this fire in which Paul Jennings and Dolley Madison disagreed over who exactly saved the famous painting of George Washington. LIBRARY OF CONGRESS

"While waiting, at just about 3, as Sukey, the house-servant, was lolling out of a chamber window, James Smith, a free colored man who had accompanied Mr. Madison to Bladensburg, gallopped up to the house, waving his hat, and cried out, 'Clear out, clear out! General Armstrong has ordered a retreat!'" Jennings wrote in his book.

It is also because of Sukey, through Paul Jennings, that we find out that not every American supported Madison's desire to go to war with Britain in the War of 1812. Sukey evacuated the White House at the side of Dolley Madison in their carriage, becoming nomads on the lands of the nation's capital after the burning of the executive mansion. Sukey and Mrs. Madison stayed at several different places during wartime, but that first night was especially difficult.

The president and the first lady were somewhat prepared for the British to march on the District of Columbia, because they had prepared a meeting site outside of Washington, where Sukey and Dolley Madison headed toward with all possible speed, according to Jennings.

"Mrs. Madison slept that night at Mrs. Love's, two or three miles over the river. After leaving that place she called in at a house, and went up stairs. The lady of the house learning who she was, became furious, and went to the stairs and screamed out, 'Miss Madison! if that's you, come down and go out! Your husband has got mine out fighting, and d--you, you shan't stay in my house; so get out!' Mrs. Madison complied, and went to Mrs. Minor's, a few miles further, where she stayed a day or two, and then returned to Washington, where she found Mr. Madison at her brother-in-law's, Richard Cutts, on F street. All the facts about Mrs. M. I learned from her servant Sukey."

Sukey returned to Montpelier with the Madisons, and after James Madison's death, returned to Washington to live in the Lafayette Square townhouse with Mrs. Madison. Sometime between the Madisons' stay in the White House and Dolley Madison's return to Washington, Sukey found time for romance, and ended up having five children, one of which Mrs. Madison brought to Washington with Sukey. (Sukey's other children, whose names have been lost to history, were sold off one by one with the Montpelier estate by Payne Todd.)

Sukey and her last child, Mary Ellen Stewart, waited on Mrs. Madison in her townhouse, but money was getting tighter and tighter. Finally, Dolley Madison decided that there was one expendable slave in her household that she could sell: Mary Ellen Stewart. But Mrs. Madison had a problem: Sukey. Her longtime maid would be expected to stay and continue to work with her after Mary Ellen was sold away, despite Madison's directive that no slave was to be sold away without his or her consent. And there was no way Sukey or Mary Ellen would give their consent, or stay silent once slave traders came to inspect Mary Ellen. So Dolley Madison decided to have the inspection done on the sly.

Dolley Madison "owned a mother, fifty odd years of age and a daughter of fifteen. About three months ago, the old lady called this girl into the parlor, one day, nominally to bring her some water, but really to show her to a Georgian, as the colored people call the slave-drivers," according to a March 31, 1848, newspaper article in *The Liberator*.

"The girl was quick on the scent, and at a glance perceived she was to be sold. Her mistress, (Mrs. Madison) agreed with the purchaser to send the unprotected child to the pump (in the street of course) at a certain hour on a day fixed upon, when he could conveniently seize her and carry her off!"

No fool, Mary Ellen quickly escaped from Dolley Madison's house and fled into the city. Having escaped the slave purchasers and Dolley Madison, she hid among the freed blacks in Washington for six months, waiting for her chance to get out of town. It was lucky that it was just at this time Paul Jennings and other blacks around the District were planning an escape of their own, and they let Mary Ellen in on their plans. During the dark of night, more than seventy men, women, and children snuck aboard the New Jersey–registered *Pearl*, a borrowed schooner sitting in a Washington wharf. In addition to the slaves aboard the ship, several free black families came along to help their enslaved relatives and brethren.

Before heading for the ship, Jennings took the time to write a letter to Senator Webster and leave it for the out-of-town politician to find.

"A deep desire to be of help to my poor people has determined me to take a decided step in that direction," Jennings wrote. "My only regret is that I shall appear ungrateful, in thus leaving with so little ceremony, one who has been uniformly kind and considerate and had rendered each moment of service a benefaction as well as pleasure. From the daily contact with your great personality which it has been mine to enjoy, has been imbibed a respect for moral obligations and the claims of duty. Both of these draw me towards the path I have chosen."

But just before the *Pearl* set sail, Jennings changed his mind. He had entered an agreement with Webster and felt his honor was at stake if he broke his word by escaping to freedom. He said his goodbyes to his friends aboard the *Pearl* and returned to Webster's house, where he retrieved his letter.

Jennings was lucky he stayed ashore.

The *Pearl* headed down the Potomac, and made it as far as Point Lookout, Maryland, where the Potomac meets the Chesapeake Bay. But there the winds died, leaving the schooner dead in the water less than 150 miles away from the nation's capital. Meanwhile, the angry slave masters were on the hunt, but the escape was so well planned that they didn't know which way the slaves went. In the end the slaves were betrayed by one of their own. A black man who drove a horse and carriage named Judson Diggs supposedly gave the plan up because one of the escaped slaves did not pay the cab fare to the ship, according to John Paynter, author of *Fugitives of the* Pearl.

"Judson Diggs, one of their own people, a man who in all reason might have been expected to sympathize with their effort, took upon himself the role of Judas," Paynter said. "Judson was a drayman and had hauled some packages to the wharf for one of the slaves, who was without funds to pay the charge, and although he was solemnly promised that the money should be sent him, he proceeded at once to wreak vengeance through a betrayal of the entire party."

Diggs apparently informed some of the slave owners whose slaves were missing, and they jumped on a steamer and raced after the *Pearl*, still adrift in windless water.

Returned to Washington in chains, most of the African Americans on the ship, whether escaped slave or free black families, were immediately put up on auction block for sale to the Deep South. The whites onboard were jailed, with Drayton not getting out of jail until he received a presidential pardon in 1852, four years later.

Jennings, meanwhile, escaped blame in the escape. He made it back to Webster's house and retrieved the letter he had written describing his planned escape without anyone connecting him to the *Pearl*. He didn't forget the people he had tried to help, however. He was one of the main fundraisers who worked to save at least one of the families on board the ship from being sold south into slavery.

One of the people he tried to save was Mary Ellen Stewart. Once the *Pearl* was dragged back to Washington, Stewart, who was just fifteen, was thrown in jail with the rest of the free and slave families who were aboard the ship. Mrs. Madison, who was informed about her slave's escape, never bothered to go see her and didn't want Mary Ellen back.

Mrs. Madison sold Mary Ellen to a Baltimore slave dealer for four hundred dollars, and the girl was shipped off away from Washington and Sukey, who was still enslaved inside Dolley Madison's household. One hundred dollars of the money Dolley Madison got for Mary Ellen immediately went to Payne Todd to help with his debts.

"If you can wait for a few days I hope to send you $100 which will put your clothes in order—by the sale of Ellen at $400—who is kept quietly in jail until she recovers from her 6 months dissipation," she said. "You have seen perhaps in the N. papers that she was taken in the vessel freighted for the North by Abolitionists—I have not seen her, but hear a bad acct. of her morals & conduct—I wait as you suggest a quieter time for the Bill & sale of the girl."

Several people tried to help Mary Ellen, including Congressman John G. Palfrey of Massachusetts. Mrs. Madison had no idea what Palfrey was up to, and invited him over to her house for tea. Palfrey politely declined, knowing what she had done. "The thought of the poor fugitive child, whom she had been selling and buying, was in the way, and Mrs. M. had to take her tea without me."

Finally, Mary Ellen's supporters raised enough money to free her, and Baltimore physician and abolitionist Joseph E. Snodgrass went to the Baltimore slave pen in June 1848 and paid out the money for her freedom. The *Rochester North Star* confirmed that "Dr. Snodgrass, with the aid of some kind friends has purchased Mrs. Madison's slave who attempted to escape on the *Pearl* and has set her at liberty." By the time Palfrey came to call on Mrs. Madison, Sukey was gone—not because she tried to escape to freedom, but because Dolley Madison put Sukey up on the sales block as well.

"Immediately after this event, Mrs. Madison either piqued a little by the loss of the daughter or by her necessities, offered the mother for sale. By great good luck she found a family in the city in want of a capable woman like herself," the Rochester newspaper said.

Jennings' anger with Mrs. Madison over her lies to him didn't last, considering his actions later in life. Dolley Madison sank further and further into poverty, eventually becoming dependent on charity, some of which her former slave provided.

"In the last days of her life, before Congress purchased her husband's papers, she was in a state of absolute poverty, and I think sometimes suffered for the necessaries of life," Jennings wrote. "While I was a servant to Mr. Webster, he often sent me to her with a market-basket full of provisions, and told me whenever I saw anything in the house that I thought she was in need of, to take it to her. I often did this, and occasionally gave her small sums from my own pocket, though I had years before bought my freedom of her."

Jennings, once freed from Webster, went on to lead a comfortable life in Washington. He married again, a mulatto woman named Desdemona Brooks, and reunited with his now-freed children. Webster, even though Jennings was no longer a slave, continued to employ him. And when he had no further need for his services, Webster wrote his former dining room servant a recommendation to take to the government as part of his application for a job. Calling Jennings "honest, faithful, and sober," Webster likely helped the former slave get a job as a laborer with the Pension Office in the Department of the Interior, where he would stay for the rest of his working life.

It was there that he met John Brooks Russell, a writer for *The Historical Magazine and Notes and Queries Concerning the Antiquities, History and Biography of America.* In 1863, the first version of "A Colored Man's Reminiscences of James Madison" appeared in its pages, the first time someone from inside the White House had written about the people who lived there. A few years later, the article was collected in book form, and Paul Jennings's name would be forever linked with the Madisons.

CHAPTER 9

SLAVERY, INDENTURED SERVITUDE, AND THE LAW

WHEN SLAVERY BEGAN IN THE THIRTEEN COLONIES, AFRICAN SLAVES brought into New York and Virginia in the early 1600s were treated mostly as indentured servants, and as such, the English law the colonies operated under provided them with some rights. Their masters had to sign a contract requiring them to feed, clothe, and house indentured servants, and at the end of the contract, were required to give their servants provisions: money, tools, and rights to a few acres of land. In addition, indentured servants were under the protection of the court system, which kept rich plantation owners from abusing the system.

Maryland became the first colony to protect indentured servants in 1637 by legally limiting their term of work to a maximum of fourteen years, and in 1643, Virginia authorized indentured servants to legally complain and ask for relief from harsh masters.

Granted, the form that indentured servitude took in the early colonies seemed eerily similar to the future slave trade: An enterprising captain would recruit servants in England, and upon arrival in Jamestown, the recruits would be auctioned off at dockside by the captain to wealthy colonists looking for cheap labor.

The legal categorization of Africans as indentured servants lasted only until the 1640s, when the inevitable changeover from expensive servants to cheap but profitable slaves occurred.

In June 1640, Nathaniell Littleton, the so-called gentleman justice of Accomack-Northampton County, Virginia, wrote that a Negro named John had been sold by him to Garrett Andrews for twelve hundred pounds of tobacco. In 1642, there's Thomas Jacob writing that he has sold his "negro Woman Susan" to Mrs. Bridgett Seaverne. Besides Susan, Jacob sold her the right to "their heyres and Assignes Freely forever."

By the 1650s, African slavery is commonplace. In a 1649 legal case, three Virginia servants, two white and one black, ran away and were recaptured in Maryland. In returning the three to Virginia, the Maryland court punished the two whites by ordering them to serve additional time as indentured servants. But no additional time could be added to the Negro as punishment, the court said, because he was already condemned to a lifetime of servitude.

Ironically, partial responsibility for rulings like that has to go to one of the first Africans to immigrate to the New World. Anthony Johnson was one of the original indentured servants brought into Jamestown. Originally known as "Antonio the Negro," he changed his name to Anthony Johnson and by 1623 had worked out his period of indenture and obtained his freedom.

Johnson became a successful tobacco planter and, in turn, employed five Africans as indentured servants, including John Casor. But when Casor completed his term of seven years and requested his freedom, Johnson turned him down. A white colonist, Robert Parker, threatened to testify for Casor in court if he was not released, and Johnson released Casor, who then immediately became an indentured servant of Parker's.

Johnson sued them both, claiming to the court that "hee had ye Negro for his life," a declaration that Casor was not a servant, but a slave who had no choice but to work for him forever. The court accepted Johnson's claim, ruling that "said John Casor Negro forthwith returne unto the service of the said master Anthony Johnson." Casor was duly returned to Johnson and worked as a slave for the rest of his life, becoming the first man in the North American colonies to be legally classified as a permanent slave. Lifelong slavery had its first legal precedent.

His wealth did not exempt Johnson from the oncoming racism of the South. When Johnson died in 1670, his thirteen hundred acres of land passed, not to his children, but by court ruling, to a white colonist. The courts declared that "as a black man, Anthony Johnson was not a citizen of the colony."

African slaves did have some success in court. A woman named Elizabeth Key Grinstead became the first woman of African ancestry in the North American colonies to sue for her freedom from slavery and win. She had been promised by her father, a white Englishman named Thomas Key, to her godfather Humphrey Higginson at age six as an indentured servant under the conditions that he release her at fifteen. Higginson, however, left for England never to return and transferred his assets to a friend named John Mottrom. But Mottrom decided to treat Grinstead as a slave instead of an indentured servant, and refused to let her go. By the time Mottrom died in 1655, Grinstead was twenty-five and had an infant son, John. The overseers of Mottrom's plantation then classified Grinstead and her son as Mottrom's property and listed them to be sold to pay off the plantation owner's debts.

Grinstead sued, arguing that she was the daughter of a free Englishman, and therefore inherited his status. Also, she and her attorney and common-law husband, William Grinstead, argued that as a baptized practicing Christian, she could not be held in servitude for life.

Grinstead's case against the Mottrom estate was heard before a jury in the Northumberland County Court in Maryland on January 20, 1655. After hearing all the evidence, the county court jury ruled that Elizabeth's father was a free Englishman. Based on the jury's factual findings, the County Court judge ruled that Elizabeth ought to be freed. Mottrom's estate appealed to the highest authority at that time, the General Assembly of Maryland, but they upheld Grinstead's freedom.

"Elizabeth ought to bee free and that her last Master should give her Corne and Cloathes and give her satisfaction for the time shee hath served longer then Shee ought to have done," the lawmakers said.

Grinstead's victory would not stem the tide of slavery. In response to that decision, the first statutory provision on whether a Negro's status followed his mother or father was adopted in Virginia in 1662: "All children borne in this country shall be held bond or free only according to the condition of the mother." But that wasn't enough, because sometimes a free white mother would have a child by a slave, who would then be free.

To take care of that, a few years later, in 1691, an amendment was added saying a free white woman who had a child by a Negro or mulatto man had to pay fifteen pounds after delivery. If she didn't have enough money of her own to pay, she would be forced into indentured servitude for five years. The mulatto child would become an indentured servant for thirty years, regardless of what happened to the mother.

In 1664, a few years after Elizabeth's suit, Maryland slave owners succeeded in getting a law enacted saying that Christian baptism had no effect on a slave's status. A few years later, they went even further: all "negros and other slaves, shall be slaves during their natural lives."

Other colonies soon joined in, with South Carolina in 1712 stating that "all negroes, mulatoes, mustizoes or Indians, which at any time heretofore have been sold, or now are held or taken to be, or hereafter shall be bought and sold for slaves, are hereby declared slaves; and they, and their children, are hereby made and declared slaves, to all intents and purposes."

By 1770, Georgia had adopted South Carolina's slavery code and African slavery was the law of the land.

Some of these new laws could have been a reaction to slaves attempting to regain their freedom through violence. While some of the most famous slave rebellions took place in the 1800s—Denmark Vessey's plan to take over Charleston, South Carolina, in 1822, John Brown's raid on Harpers Ferry, West Virginia, in 1859, Nat Turner's 1831 rebellion in Southampton County, Virginia—they were far from the first. The insurrections had begun even before slavery took permanent hold in the United States and even before the British set foot on the North American continent.

The very first African slaves in America were not owned by the British, but by Spanish explorers who were looking to settle what is now Georgia. And these slaves were not only the first African slaves in America, they were also the first to successfully revolt against their European masters and escape to freedom.

Inspired by the reports of the successful exploration of Florida by Ponce de Leon, Lucas Vazquez De Ayllon, a Spanish judge living in Hispaniola (modern-day Haiti and the Dominican Republic), left the island in 1526 with six ships, five hundred colonists, and over one hundred African slaves to settle North America and claim its lands for the Spanish empire. De Ayllon's plan would be remembered as one of the worst colonization attempts in American history. He followed the instructions of a captive Native American, who instead of leading the would-be conquerors to fertile ground filled with gold, jewels, and precious metals, led them to his home soil near the Pee Dee River in South Carolina, where he promptly escaped, leaving the Spanish behind to fend for themselves. De Ayllon moved his settlement south to modern-day Georgia, where the colonists began to die of disease and starvation. A desperate De Ayllon led them on a futile attack on the local Indian tribes in hopes of taking over and living in their towns so that they would have shelter from the oncoming winter. That maneuver failed miserably. The Guale Indians repelled their cowardly attacks and killed even more colonists.

The attacks did prompt an alliance between the indigenous people and the African slaves who had been dragged into the wilderness by the Spaniards. The African slaves rebelled against De Ayllon, leading to even more colonist deaths before they escaped to live with the same tribes the Spanish had attacked. Soon afterward, De Ayllon and the remaining Spanish colonists abandoned North America and fled back to the Caribbean with only 150 of the original six hundred colonists still alive after less than a year on the North American continent. The African slaves stayed and blended into the Indian community in coastal South Carolina and Georgia, becoming some of the first non-native Americans to settle into life in the new world.

The first rebellion against British colonists came more than one hundred years later, when white indentured servants joined up with black slaves in a plan "to destroy their masters and afterwards to set up for themselves" in 1663, in Gloucester County along the coastal shores of Virginia not far from the Jamestown settlement. Colonist Robert Beverley wrote that the uprising was led by followers of Oliver Cromwell, the Puritan who conquered England and had King Charles I executed in 1649. But after Cromwell's death, his son was forced to abdicate, and King Charles II was restored to the throne in 1660. The indentured servants who took part in the Gloucester rebellion in the Poropotank River and Purtan Bay region, Beverley said, were "soldiers that were sent thither as servants" after the English monarchy was restored.

The insurrectionists apparently had planned out their attack well but failed to maintain secrecy. Their plot was discovered by an unsympathetic servant named John Berkenhead, who informed the colonists that the attack was coming. An unknown number of rebels were executed, and their bloody heads placed on chimney tops. For his efforts, Berkenhead—who has been described by historians as both a black indentured servant and a white indentured servant—received a reward of five thousand pounds of tobacco plus his freedom from John Smith of Purton.

The fact that indentured white servants, who had a possibility of freedom in the New World, were willing to risk their lives to overthrow their masters showed that life as an indentured servant in colonial America was not easy and can be considered only a few steps above being a slave. But African slaves would be on their own in most future rebellions, including the New York City slave rebellion in 1712, which can be credited with helping bring about the end of legal slavery in the North.

In 1712, twenty-five or thirty African slaves, enraged by how they were treated by their white masters, decided to take revenge by destroying the city and killing every European who lived there. They set fire to a building and waited for the whites to come to battle the blaze. When they did, the slaves set upon them with knives, guns, and axes. Jill Lepore described what happened next in her book, *New York Burning: Liberty, Slavery, and Conspiracy in Eighteenth-Century Manhattan.* "Adrian Hoghlant's slave Robin stabbed him in the back. Nicholas Roosevelt's slave Tom shot Andries Beekman in the chest," she wrote. "Peter the Porter, owned by Andries Marschalk, killed young Joris Marschalk with a dagger blow to his chest. Before the butchery ended, nine whites had been killed and six more wounded."

The next day, Governor Robert Hunter ordered the militia to "drive the Island," where troops captured nearly all of the rebels. Twenty-one of the conspirators were executed, some burned alive, others hanged, and at least one "broke on the wheele," a torture method where a person would be lashed to a wagon wheel and beaten to death with an iron hammer or cudgel.

Unfortunately, New Yorkers would not forget what had nearly happened in their city, and even the rumor of a slave rebellion was enough to cause panic and sometimes death. In 1741, rampant rumors of a soon-to-happen rebellion caused soldiers and citizens to round up slaves and whites in New York City in hopes of staving off an attack. It is unknown to this day whether these rumors were based on fact or were part of a larger paranoia over slave uprisings. What is known, however, is that 154 Negros were imprisoned, thirteen burned at the stake, eighteen hanged, and seventy banished from Manhattan. Twenty whites were jailed, four hanged, and eight banished.

The only good thing to come out of this rebellion for slaves was the fact that other northern colonies took notice, leading some to make radical changes in their laws. The 1712 New York City slave rebellion was one of the events that incited Massachusetts legislators to adopt a ban on the further importation of slaves, and Pennsylvania lawmakers to place a high duty on Negro slaves, effectively discouraging their importation into their state. It would take another few decades for an American territory, Vermont—during their attempt to free themselves from New York State and become their own country—to legally ban slavery in its lands in 1777. In the first chapter of its new constitution, Vermont made clear where it stood on the issue of slavery with a section subtitled "A Declaration Of The Rights Of The Inhabitants Of The State Of Vermont":

THAT all men are born equally free and independent, and have certain natural, inherent and unalienable rights, amongst which are the enjoying and defending life and liberty; acquiring, possessing and protecting property, and pursuing and obtaining happiness and safety. Therefore, no male person, born in this country, or brought from over sea, ought to be holden by law, to serve any person, as a servant, slave or apprentice, after he arrives to the age of twenty-one Years, nor female, in like manner, after she arrives to the age of eighteen years, unless they are bound by their own consent, after they arrive to such age, or bound by law, for the payment of debts, damages, fines, costs, or the like.

CHAPTER 10

ANDREW JACKSON'S STABLES

THE MASTER BEDROOM OF THE WHITE HOUSE WAS INFINITELY MORE comfortable than the many military tents President Andrew Jackson had slept in during his long military career, but his advancing age and illnesses made rising from even the softest bed more and more difficult. But deeply ingrained military discipline demanded he rise with the sun, so the now white-haired man known affectionately by his admirers as "Old Hickory" or just "The General" rose at first light. Rolling over in his canopy bed, Jackson watched the pre-dawn sun leak into his bedroom, illuminating his slave George quietly preparing his clothes for the day.

An unusually tall and lanky man, Jackson slung his legs over the side of the bed and stepped over George's pallet on the floor next to his bed. Shucking off his nightgown, George handed the general his usual black mourning suit in the memory of his late wife. Slowly dressing, with his body servant's assistance, Jackson would gather up his cane and then amble down the White House stairs—likely feeling the toll of the life-time of hard choices—and out the front door into the sunlight.

Every morning, soft whinnying would inexorably draw him out into the grass and east toward the rising sun, toward the stables he had built onto the White House and the beautiful chargers he had imported from his Hermitage plantation. His horses were the only thing that made Andrew Jackson feel like the dashing southern general America remem-bered and elected, instead of the doddering elderly politician his time in Washington had turned him into.

By the time Jackson made it to the stables each morning, his slave jockeys were already hard at work. While the house slaves kept Jackson and his family clothed and fed, and the field slaves kept the Hermitage fields productive, Jackson's favored slaves were the jockeys and the trainers, the slaves who kept his precious horses fed, watered, exercised, and ready to triumph on the racetrack.

"Old Hickory" loved horses, and when he left from his plantation in Tennessee for the nation's capital, he brought along some of his most prized thoroughbreds and created out of the White House what was then one of the largest racing operations on the East Coast. There were so many horses, trainers, and jockeys at the President's House there wasn't quite enough space for them or the slaves needed for their proper care and training. So likely unknowing, Congress likely for the first time paid for a dwelling specifically for slaves in Washington, DC, as Jackson spent public money to expand existing White House stables for his beloved racehorses and the men who took care of them and rode them to victory at nearby racetracks.

With Jackson's administration, slavery moved out of the White House and onto the grounds, with enslaved black men living in some of the first stables built for horses in the presidential complex.

Today, people are used to seeing only the President's House as the main building on the White House grounds flanked by the Treasury Department and the Eisenhower Executive Office Building. But over the years there have been several other buildings that have been part of the presidential complex.

Before the modern era, many of the luxuries that people today take for granted had to be provided for the presidents and their families outside the White House walls. And so there needed to be places near the presidential mansion for the presidential cooks, butchers, and other domestic staff to access things needed for the daily operations.

For example, when John Adams moved into the presidential mansion, there was no indoor plumbing. So the president, his family, their guests, and the entire White House staff had to make use of a wooden outhouse that stood next to the White House for the world to see. Thomas Jefferson had the outhouse knocked down when he moved in and replaced with "water closets"—as indoor bathrooms were known in those days—but he found more ingenious uses for the other structures on the grounds he inherited from his defeated predecessor.

The White House grounds were originally dotted with shacks for the workers who helped construct the President's House, some of whom were slaves. And after the construction was finished, Thomas Jefferson used those shacks for another purpose. He turned the shacks that had housed construction workers into sheds for sheep, cows, horses, and chickens and also built an external wine vault and added wings that contained a coal house, meat house, and milk house. He also ordered an icehouse built, which records show was built just to the west of the White House in 1801. Several years later in 1805, Jefferson covered the icehouse with the first West Wing addition that housed domestic quarters for White House staff.

Many of Jefferson's external additions to the White House were lost during the War of 1812, but his decision to build on the White House grounds was repeatedly copied by other presidential residents. John Whitcomb and Claire Whitcomb wrote in *Real Life at the White House: 200 Years of Daily Life at America's Most Famous Residence*: "When Ike Hoover, a longtime White House usher, first came to the mansion in 1891 to help wire it for electricity, he was surprised to find that a wine vault, meat house and smokehouse were still out back."

Those weren't all of the extra buildings on the White House grounds. Horses had always been a major part of the presidency, with almost all of the first presidents being great riders. George Washington, John Adams, Thomas Jefferson, and James Monroe were all known for their equine skills, so the first presidents of course needed somewhere to keep their horses nearby.

Although it is difficult to envision the executive mansion's grounds today with horse stables, the fact that horse-drawn carriages and horseback were the major forms of transportation for the majority of the early days of the United States made it necessary to house the horses of the president and the First Family nearby. So after John Adams moved into the President's House, stables had to be built somewhere nearby.

So Adams requested stables for his team of horses and carriages when it came time to move in. By August 1800, a presidential stable to house twelve horses, a carriage house for three carriages, and a small grain room had been substantially finished two blocks east of President's Park on a city lot at F and G and Thirteenth and Fourteenth Streets at a cost of sixteen hundred dollars. That Georgian-style brick building, which was never popular with its city neighbors, lasted until 1806, but with its unpopularity, the presidents decided to move their horses even closer to the presidential mansion. So Jefferson, who was not shy about making changes to the President's House, decided to add a coach house and tack room to the West Wing and a stable and a cowshed to the East Wing.

People would be aghast at the idea of stables and barns at the White House now, but the founding presidents were all plantation owners and knew how important it was to keep animals within reach for eggs, milk, and meat. So visitors to the White House of the past were just as likely to encounter a curious cow or chicken wandering around the executive mansion as they were a presidential aide. There were so many animals at the White House, Jefferson in 1801 even built a "ha-ha" at the southern end of the South Lawn, which was an eight-foot wall with a sunken ditch meant to keep the livestock from grazing in his garden.

For foreign visitors expecting the grandeur of Europe, the smells of the horses and cows wafting through the executive mansion must have been a sobering reminder of the rough-and-tumble nature of the new country under construction. But even though he rejected the luxury items that John Adams left behind—he sold the secondhand coaches, horses, and silver-mounted harnesses left behind by his predecessor, keeping only a one-horse market cart—Jefferson knew the value of keeping his horses nearby.

As said earlier, the British destroyed many of the buildings left behind from the original construction of the White House and those added by Jefferson in 1814 when they burned the White House. But having access to their horses was important enough that James Monroe had a temporary frame stable appended to the end of the rebuilt East Wing. He then had constructed by James Hoban a sixty-foot stable near the West Wing in 1819 for greater convenience to a coach house. The addition was built off the West Wing but stretched to the south, producing the "L" shape at the end of which stands the Oval Office.

None of this was good enough for Jackson, who brought his prized racehorses and slave stablehands and jockeys with him to Washington, DC, after he won the presidency. The president had been a gambling and

Andrew Jackson, on horseback with another horse in tow, arriving at the White House. LIBRARY OF CONGRESS

sporting man his entire life, from his birth in South Carolina to his life in Tennessee. But horse racing was his particular passion, and to be successful in that sport in the South required great horses, a gambling spirit, and ready-made access to wealth or enslaved men willing to work for free as jockeys and trainers. And with his slaves at The Hermitage, Jackson had a stable of horses and slave jockeys and trainers he could use to pursue his pastime.

Jackson was very comfortable with slavery, having lived with it and profited from it all of his life, just like the rest of the southern-born presidents. He bought his first slave in 1794, and over his lifetime his family would own more than three hundred slaves (the maximum they owned at any one time would be 150). Most of Jackson's slaves worked at his home, The Hermitage plantation outside of Nashville, Tennessee, in the fields growing and harvesting crops, or in the "big house" as servants, butlers, maids, and cooks. His first purchase in Tennessee was "a Negro woman named Nancy" on November 17, 1788, shortly after arriving there as a young man. But he soon pivoted to training his slaves to take care of horses and race as jockeys on tracks around the South.

For some slaves, that was a good opportunity. Working with horses and excelling at horse racing and training was a blessing because they then would be excused from the drudgery of field or housework and be valued by white masters in ways few of their companions were at that time.

For blacks, racing provided a false sense of freedom. They were allowed to travel the racing circuit, and some even managed their owners' racing operation. They competed alongside whites. When black riders were cheered to the finish line, the only colors that mattered were the colors of their silk jackets, representing their stables. Horse racing was entertaining for white owners and slaves alike and one of the few ways for slaves to achieve social status.

A good slave jockey was worth his weight, with stars like Lynch's Dick or Colonel George Elliott's hunchback Monkey Simon commanding on the block a price equal to that of a first-class racehorse. Jackson owned slave jockeys himself, although most of their names have been lost to history. One of them may have been Jane's Jack, who author Elbridge

Streeter Brooks called "the general's best jockey" in the book *A Son Of The Revolution: Being The Story Of Young Tom Edwards, Adventurer, and How He Labored for Liberty and Fought It Out With His Conscience In The Days Of Burr's Conspiracy.*

In this book, which reads like an adventure novel, Jane's Jack is supposed to be racing Jackson's best horse, Truxton, in a race at Jackson's home course near The Hermitage, Clover Bottoms. But a dispute between jockeys had forced Jane's Jack out of the race. "For Jane's Jack disputing with a rival jockey had been laid *hors de combat* in a 'gouge,' and could neither see nor stand nor ride," Brooks said. The hero of Brooks's book, Tom Edwards, steps in for Jane's Jack, and rides Truxton to victory, earning Jackson's everlasting friendship. Nothing else is said about Jane's Jack.

Being slaves, the Jackson jockeys were not as important to the historians and racehorse owners as their horses were, so while we can easily find out the names of Jackson's horses—Indian Queen, Greyhound, Bolivar, and Truxton, just to name a few—finding the names of the slave jockeys who sometimes rode those horses to victory and won Jackson thousands of dollars in winnings is near impossible. But they did exist, and are mentioned repeatedly in the annals of the day. There's one story about how Jackson sold one of his slave jockeys, and then found himself facing the jockey in a race.

Jackson "had a heavy bet upon a certain race, and the jockey who was to ride the competing horse was a mulatto boy whom he had owned himself, but with whom he had become discontented," a magazine wrote. "He had sold him to a neighbor, and it was this neighbor's horse that was now running against Jackson's. Before the race came off, Jackson was overheard giving instructions to the little mulatto. He was heard to say: "You black rascal, I want you to know that I understand you, and I don't want you to play any of your old tricks upon me. If I catch you squirting your tobacco juice in my boy's eyes, I will cut your heart out."

Of course, if that unnamed jockey worked for Jackson, he had pulled the same tricks against Jackson's competitors with the general's tacit, if not outspoken, approval. But that was Jackson at heart: an implacable foe to his enemies whether in or out of uniform, and a man who didn't take losing gracefully in any arena.

This Jacksonian trait can be best illustrated by the general's years-long rivalry with a famous horse and its black jockey. A chestnut mare named Maria and her rider, a slave named Monkey Simon, clearly outclassed anything or anyone The Hermitage would produce or that Jackson could buy, and yet the Tennessee general almost spent himself into the poorhouse trying to prove his superiority to the celebrated horse and rider. An examination of Simon's life as a jockey also gives us insight into the advantages slaves, including those at The Hermitage and the ones Jackson brought to the White House, could gain by participating and succeeding at horse racing.

For years, Simon was Jackson's biggest nemesis and kept defeating the general's best horses on Maria. Before Simon and Maria, Jackson basically ruled horse racing in Tennessee, the United States's western border at that time. "Gen. Jackson may be considered the first patron of the turf in Tennessee, and he stood at the head of it for twenty years," said the *Chicago Tribune* on December 8, 1895.

But then Jackson met his match with Maria and "the unbeaten Monkey Simon, said to be the king of all riders," the Muhammad Ali and Michael Jordan of his time. "If tradition be true he was the greatest rider of race horses who ever lived," the *Tribune* said. Another writer called Simon "the greatest of living jockeys, known from New Orleans to Richmond; the rider of the unbeaten Maria; the victor of a hundred turf battles; a prince in his African country, stolen and sold into slavery; the dwarf whose negro wit was as famous as his riding: who took no man's rebuke, who feared no one."

Today, "Monkey" would be considered a derogatory term for a black man, though back then it was apparently a common term for the diminutive black jockeys. But his white admirers said with Simon, his nickname "conveys a forcible idea of his appearance."

He was a native African and was brought with his parents when quite young to South Carolina, before the prohibition of the slave trade took effect. In height he was 4 feet 6 inches and weighed 100 pounds. He was a hunchback with very short body and remarkably long arms and legs. His color and hair were African, but his features were not.

He had a long head and face, a high and delicate nose, a narrow but prominent forehead and a mouth indicative of humor and firmness. It was rumored that Simon was a prince in his native country. I asked Uncle Berry the other day if he thought it was true. He replied, "I don't know; they said so and if the princes there had more sense than the rest he must have been one of 'em, for he was the smartest negro I ever saw."

His small stature, common for jockeys then and now, belied his grace, skill, and determination to triumph once on the back of a horse. Simon was described by the *Spirit of the Times* sporting weekly as someone who "was not only able to hold a steady reign and maintain a graceful easy seat, but no emergency ever came upon him so suddenly, so unexpectedly, as to cause him to lose his presence of mind or disturb his equanimity. No danger, no peril was too great for his courage to encounter, and he moved with steady nerve in the face of the most appalling and threatening conflicts. His integrity was as pure as his courage was firm. To conquer, was the motto emblazoned by nature upon his mind and heart."

Owned by Col. George Elliott, Simon traveled around the South riding horses to victory after victory on tracks from Louisiana to Tennessee. "If he had a weakness it was in being too eager for success in a close contest," one commentator said.

Simon's skills were such that Elliott made money by renting him out to other stables at auctions for important races, commanding as much as one hundred dollars a race, which he shared with his master. Elliott even rented Simon out on contracts for as long as a year, and then hired him back during that time period for important races. The jockey was of enough importance that he was allowed to watch these sales, and even comment on them. As said by an earlier observer, Simon was known for a sarcastic wit and a mouth ready to comment on anything around him, secure in the knowledge that his fame made him immune to reprisals from even the harshest slave master. "There was no rider in all the West more nearly idolized among horsemen than Monkey Simon," and because of that he was willing to take liberties that other slaves would not have dreamed of. One such incident was witnessed by Col. Bailie Peyton, a close friend of Jackson's, who saw the bidding for Simon run up to thirty dollars by Col. Robert C. Foster, "the then price of a good field hand."

"I concluded to drop Simon on the Colonel's hands and take the chance of hiring him privately. Simon watched the bidding with the deepest interest, as he was most anxious to remain in the stable and enjoy the fame and emoluments of riding Haynie's Maria and other distinguished winners," Peyton said. "When I indicated that I would bid no more, Simon turned to the Colonel and said in his peculiarly sarcastic manner, with his head laid back and one eye closed, 'Colonel Foster, by God, I am not a-selling, but a-hirin' for only one year.' The Colonel, who was a man of high spirit and great dignity replied, shaking his cane at Simon, 'You impudent scoundrel, do you know who you are talking to?' Simon with the most aggravating coolness, replied, 'I think I do, and if I am not mistaken you are the same gentleman who made a small 'speriment for Governor once' alluding to a race the Colonel had made for Governor under very unfavorable circumstances, in which he was badly beaten."

Simon's smart mouth got him into trouble at another race at Clover Bottoms. A white boy wanted to enter the race with a nag, and the renowned black jockey said he wouldn't be running his horse Bompard against "them two scrubs—them two woods colts." And then, "Something leaped like a wild cat from the back of Paddy Whack to the back of Bompard. Monkey Simon was in its path and Monkey Simon went off, hitting the ground until the breath went out of him. But the thing was at his throat and shook him as a terrier would a rat." Spectators tried to break up the fight, but Jackson wouldn't hear it. "Don't touch him, Baker. By God—it's a fair fight and my money's on the Red Head! Go it, Ireland, give it to the negro, Red Head," Jackson shouted.

Simon's employer was frantic. "My God, General, he will kill the greatest jockey alive—worth ten thousand dollars a year to me—never beaten in a race."

"Never beaten, hey? By the Eternal, he's getting it now, and the man that touches him is my enemy. Go it, Ireland, I am that stock myself," and the General smiled grimly at the shout of applause from the crowd now cheering the boy they had but a minute before jeered and hooted.

"You've licked me," wept Monkey Simon after they had pulled the white boy off, "but I'll ride you to hell in this race—see if I don't."

Simon lost that race, one of the few recorded in which the black jockey did not triumph.

Simon didn't just sass turfmen and jockeys; he went after Jackson as well. In fact, Jackson, and his obsession at beating Simon and Maria, made him a favorite target of the banjo-playing jockey. And Jackson respected Simon—"the smartest, meanest, gamest, boldest rider that ever threw a leg over a sheepskin," he called him—enough not to retaliate against him for saying things for which he would have tried to kill a white man, much less a black slave. One time, Jackson confronted Simon before a race at his home track, Clover Bottoms, maybe hoping to throw the jockey off his game.

> *The General said to Simon on one occasion just before the horses started in a very important race, "Now, Simon, when my horse comes up and is about to pass you, don't spit your tobacco juice in his eyes, and in the eyes of his rider, as you sometimes do"; to which Simon replied, "Well, Gineral, I've rode a good deal agin your horses, but (with an oath) none were ever near enough to catch my spit." The old General flushed and reached for his riding whip. "Pardon him General; it's Monkey Simon, you know." The General fingered his whip, then smiled grimly and sat down.*

And this apparently wasn't the only time Simon mouthed off to Jackson. Known for his skills with a banjo, Simon often made up little ditties about his opponents to tease them, much as Muhammad Ali did during his reign as boxing's heavyweight champion. "Simon was an inimitable banjo-player, and improvised his songs, making humorous hits at every body and everything—even General Jackson did not escape him—and no man was his superior in repartee," according to one racing magazine.

The *Atlanta Constitution* said in its January 30, 1873, issue that Simon may even have been the author of the ditty: "Such a gittin' up stairs, I met General Jackson at the corner of the street. Says I 'General Jackson, ain't you gwine for a treat?'"

Keep in mind this was the feared Jackson, who only a short time before had killed the owner of the horse Ploughboy in a duel for failing to pay the forfeiture fee after withdrawing from a race against Jackson's famed racehorse Truxton. But Simon was so confident of his skills that he kept after Jackson again and again verbally and on the track.

On another occasion, after Maria had beaten the general's favorite, Pacolet, and when no friend dared to take a liberty with him, Simon, meeting him in a large crowd, said: "Gineral, you were always ugly, but now you're a show. I could make a fortune by showing you as you now look, if I had you in a cage where you could not hurt the people who came to look at you."

Not a man to give up easily, especially with a slave jockey making fun of him, Jackson was intent on finding someone or something to beat Simon and Maria. This is how we know Jackson wasn't averse to renting other slave jockeys to ride his horses, because he imported a famous one known only as Dick to take on Simon in a rough and tumble race for high stakes, someone with a little something extra besides riding skills: his reputation among fellow jockeys as a conjurer.

Whether true, or just a trick to make other jockeys fear him, Dick decided to use his reputation as an advantage against Simon and Maria. If he could make sure that he and his horse had the lead at a mile and a half, he would win the race.

So he sought Simon, and told him, in the strictest confidence, and with a most earnest and confidential air, that he had been communicating with some unknown and fanciful being, who told him that if Simon undertook to pass him before he came to the half-mile pole on the second mile, that he would trip Maria, and cause her to throw him and kill him.

This greatly affected the superstitious Simon, who had no choice but to go ahead and run the much-anticipated race. Unusually silent, Simon listened to instructions from Maria's trainer, Green Berry Williams to get out front from the start and never let Dick get anywhere close to the lead.

To Williams's amazement Maria started leisurely, and the DeWett mare passed the stands at the end of the first mile a good hundred and twenty yards ahead. Williams yelled to his rider to give her the spur, but Maria kept on at the same speed until she struck the back stretch. Then the spectators saw a sight that taxed the credulity of their senses. The chestnut mare leaped forward like lightning. Such a burst of speed had never been seen on a Tennessee track. The hundred-and-twenty-yard lead diminished, vanished. Maria went ahead and thundered home the winner by one hundred and eighty yards.

When Williams demanded an explanation afterward, Simon told him that the other rider had threatened him if he didn't let him take the lead for most of the race. "I wasn't going ahead of dat nigger," said Simon, "till he got by the half-mile pole on the second mile, 'cause he done told me 'fore I start dat if I did I was a dead nigger; and I know'd 'twas so, 'cause he done trick Maria, and she would 'a fell down and killed me, and lost the race too." Williams wisely let it go.

Jackson also would eventually let go his hopes of beating the Negro jockey and his filly. In the end, Simon beat Jackson's horses with Maria nine times from 1811 to 1815. So, since he couldn't beat him, Jackson tried to join in with Simon after his last defeat. Simon and Maria had just trounced another of Jackson's horses, but some Virginia horsemen weren't impressed. They with their arrogance said that there were horses in their state that would easily beat the famed Maria. So Maria's owner, Jesse Haynie, told them to put their money where their mouths were, and told them he'd match Simon and Maria against any horse in the world at any race between one to four miles with his five thousand dollars at stake. Jackson, when told about this conversation by Haynie, had one slight modification for him and the Virginians. "Make the race for $50,000 and consider me in with you. She can beat any animal in God's whole creation," said Jackson, confident in his words after the years of trouncing he had taken.

How much did those losses affect Jackson? Jackson couldn't find a horse or jockey to beat Simon and Maria, so he quit the sport of racing after his last defeat. He sold off all of his horses except some of his favorite mares and colts by Truxton. It would not be until Andrew Jackson had reached the White House that he resumed horse racing by creating the largest horse racing operation in the capital city.

In an ultimate compliment to Simon, Jackson apparently remembered his defeats for the rest of his life. "It is a well-authenticated anecdote of Gen. Jackson that when, in the evening of his life he was asked by an old friend if he had ever undertaken anything heartily which he did not accomplish, he reflected for a moment and replied, 'Nothing that I remember, except Hanie's Maria—I could not beat her,'" said author Josephus Conn Guild.

Was Maria just a special horse, with Simon along for the ride? It doesn't seem so, because Maria's successes ended when she was separated from Simon. Maria was sold in South Carolina in 1816 as a nine-year-old filly, and she was soundly beaten again and again. In fact, she never won again.

Various were the opinions concerning her sudden failures. But the best reason given was that she had lost the careful nursing of Green Berry Williams and the masterly horsemanship on the track of her old jockey, Monkey Simon, who rode every race she made in Tennessee, and she was never beaten until she left the state.

Later authors place Maria's failures solely on the fact that Simon was no longer working with her. "The most plausible reason for this is that she had lost the masterly horsemanship of her old jockey, Monkey Simon, who rode every race she ever won," said the *Courier Journal* of Louisville, Kentucky, on May 6, 1894.

Simon apparently ended up becoming part of Jackson's stable of jockeys, either as a hired-out rider or purchased as a slave jockey. "Monkey Simon, Jackson's famous Negro jockey," one author called him. And several authors placed the two together at The Hermitage several times—including the moment when the health of Jackson's beloved wife, Rachel, took a turn for the worse.

Mary Cornelia Francis—who called Monkey Simon "Jackson's favorite jockey"—described the scene in which Mrs. Jackson began her inevitable decline in her book, *A Son of Destiny: The Story of Andrew Jackson*:

"Jackson and Monkey Simon were inspecting the horses in an open field near the stables when they were startled by one of the young blacks, Peter, a half-grown cub, who came rushing up to them, his eyes rolling and his tongue hanging out," she said. "'Come! Come quick!' he gasped.

'Missus done took awful! Hurry, Mass' Jackson!' He blubbered and wrung his hands."

Rachel Jackson would die before Jackson made it to Washington. Simon would die during Jackson's presidency, but it is not beyond the pale to envision the president inviting the celebrated jockey to come to Washington or to the White House. Simon "never did anything but ride, and when overtaken by age he was welcomed everywhere," according to the *Cincinnati Enquirer* on July 3, 1909.

Historian Edward Hotaling discovered while writing his book, *The Great Black Jockeys*, that Simon died during a cholera epidemic in Tennessee in 1833, and more importantly, Simon died a free man. "Interestingly, the list did not identify him as a slave, suggesting that, even if he had not been formerly emancipated, he perhaps no longer lived as a slave—perhaps his technical status as a slave had become irrelevant, and he had simply become a town character, long since on his own," Hotaling said.

Jackson also had slaves as trainers for his thoroughbreds. His reputation as a horse breeder was helped in part by those slaves.

In the first organized race in the state, at Gallatin in 1804, Jackson entered his mare Indian Queen and lost. He was not deterred. He acquired the renowned Truxton, sired by the English champion Diomed. Jackson also acquired the champion Greyhound and an interest in the Clover Bottoms racetrack, where he organized races involving Truxton. Also using Truxton to stud, Jackson, with the help of his slave Dinwiddie, became the top horse breeder in Tennessee.

Called Dinwiddie because of the name of the Virginia county on the bill of sale where his old owner lived, Jackson and his family nicknamed him "Dunwoody" and used both names interchangeably. Dunwoody soon became one of the most trusted slaves that Jackson ever owned.

He was in his early thirties when his owner, John Verrell, sold him to Jackson for eight hundred dollars. Dinwiddie was a noted horse trainer and caretaker to whom Jackson entrusted his stables for the next four decades.

Being one of Jackson's favorites, and essential to his pastime of running horses, Dunwoody likely enjoyed a life better than his compatriots working the fields or even cooking and cleaning inside The Hermitage.

He was good at his task, one that Jackson appreciated him for, and his fame as a horse trainer brought him the kind of protection from other whites that other slaves couldn't dream of. For example, Jackson leaped to his defense once when a neighbor for whom Dunwoody had been working complained about his horses.

In 1810 Dr. William Purnell, one of the original white settlers of the Cumberland region, accused Dinwiddie of poisoning one of his horses. Jackson wanted to know in exact detail how the horse had acted before it died, what it ate, and the conclusions of the doctor who examined its corpse. "If the horse was poisioned" he wrote, "the villain that did it ought to & and must be punished. If Dinwiddie had been falsely blamed, however, the accuser 'deserves punishment.'" Purnell denied accusing Dinwiddie of the act, even enclosing an affidavit from an alleged witness to his statements that supported his claim. Jackson let the matter drop.

It wasn't as if Dunwoody was perfect with horses. Jackson had some complaints about him as well. When he was president, Jackson attacked Dun in a letter about his horse Bolivar: "if his breathing had not been injured, he was one of the first runners ever owned in America. Dunwoody by neglect destroyed him as a runner & ruined my Oscar filly also a runner."

But it was not worth it for Purnell to pursue his complaint against the black trainer, knowing how Jackson felt about Dunwoody, whether he truly believed the slave had poisoned his horses or not. Because of the exalted position that Dunwoody held, and the fact that Jackson already was known for having a temper and a willingness to go to extremes like dueling over honor, by pressing the issue Purnell might have risked his life.

Regardless of the complaints, Dunwoody's fame for working with racehorses grew. Others in the racing world also had heard of his skills, and his services were seemingly requested often. Jackson must have let Dunwoody work on other plantations with other stables, given the number of times he got requests for his slave's skills.

"Where (is) Dunwoody, he is the only man I wish to assist me in preparing the horses this next session," John M. Garrard wrote to Jackson on July 2, 1805.

A few years later, there came a second entreaty from a neighbor, Anthony Butler. "As you have Mr. Hutchings with you Dinwiddie might be spared to come over, and the Horses should be here to rest a few days previous to the Races which commence tomorrow week," he wrote. "I shall expect Decatur and at least one more that can be counted on, we have a much better show of Nags over here than last year, and they have been so bantering and jeering me that I must beat them if possible."

But no matter how much others wanted Dunwoody for his skills, Jackson never sold him, keeping him at The Hermitage for the rest of his life, to consult about his prized horses. Jackson's granddaughter, Rachel Jackson Lawrence, after his death remembered riding around The Hermitage with him on his favored horse, Sam Patch, who had at one point lived in Washington, DC, with the former president. "It was on this old horse, after our return from Washington, that my grandfather took me, every morning after breakfast, and rode around the farm to see the stock. He would stop and talk awhile with old Dunwoody, at the negro's cabin, about the colts," she said.

Jackson's passions for his horses and the slaves who cared for them meant that the Monroe stables were not going to be big enough, or good enough for his thoroughbreds and their caretakers, which he had sent for from The Hermitage. "In April, 1832, Major Eaton and his wife, stopping at The Hermitage, learned that on the day before, Steele, the overseer, had started on the road to Washington three horses and three colored jockeys. Behaving with the promptness that had once characterized his actions in larger concerns, the Major directed Steele to call back the horses. Then he wrote to Jackson. With a campaign coming on, further display of the President's sporting proclivities would be inadvisable; and to run the horses under Donelson's name would deceive no one. Old Hickory did not criticize the well-intentioned action of his friend. But he ordered the colts and jockeys sent on to Washington."

Having his horses and their jockeys and caretakers in Washington was a great comfort to Jackson, who made sure he checked on them first thing every day. "President Jackson used to visit his stable every morning, until he became too feeble, and he paid special attention to the manner in which his horses were shod," reported the *Estherville Daily News* of Estherville, Iowa, in December 1892. Watching them run in races in nearby tracks was a great comfort to the general, though apparently it was a little inappropriate for a sitting president to have an active stable competing from the White House. So, Jackson had his secretary, Andrew Jackson "A.J." Donelson, pretend to be the person in charge, but it doesn't seem like the charade fooled anyone because several onlookers documented the true ownership of the horses.

"For the past year he had kept a number of colts in the White House stable," wrote Marquis James in *Andrew Jackson, Portrait of a President.* "They were entered at the National City and other nearby tracks under the name of A. J. Donelson, but it was no secret to whom they actually belonged. Though none of them won an important race, the supervision of their care and training proved a wholesome relaxation for the President."

While that author makes it seem like Jackson didn't care whether his horses won any races—treating it more like a hobby than the passion it really was—another horse owner made clear that Jackson intended to win and was willing to bet substantial amounts of cash on his horses and jockeys to back up his beliefs. In 1836, Jackson entered a filly from The Hermitage in a race in Washington under Donelson's name. Bringing a horse from Tennessee to Washington was no easy feat, and while the racer isn't named, what is known is that Jackson had the utmost confidence in both horse and jockey, because he bet nearly one thousand dollars on his horse to win. (Today, that amount would be equivalent to more than twenty-five thousand dollars.) Not only did the president bet his own money, his confidence inspired many of his friends to also bet their own money on the general's horse to win the race. But it was not to be.

Jackson found it hard to "conceal his chagrin when the filly was beaten by an imported Irish colt named Langford, owned by Captain Stockton, of the navy, and he had to pay lost wagers amounting to nearly a thousand dollars, while Mr. Van Buren and other devoted adherents who had bet on the filly were also losers."

Needless to say, "Captain Stockton" was a bit more expressive describing his victory in his memoirs. Commodore Robert Field Stockton, future US senator from New Jersey and one of the architects of California's entry into the Union through the American victory in the Mexican-American

War, was also quite the sporting man. He raced horses as well, and saw quite the success in Washington, DC. His victory showed how much Jackson cared about winning, and how much other people cared about what Jackson thought about horses.

In one race, Stockton's favorite horse, Langford, won more than $250,000 in today's money because of the confidence that people had in Jackson and his stable skills. Jackson was confident of victory, so everyone else was as well in this particular race. And then things got worse for Stockton.

A few days before the race, Captain Stockton's trainer fell sick, and, unable to supply his place, the captain came on himself and took the place of the trainer, superintending minutely the grooming of his horse until the day of the race. A day or two before the race, Langford had the ill luck to fall lame suddenly while galloping around the course. These incidents inspired the friends of his competitors with additional confidence; and, though the lameness disappeared immediately after its cause was ascertained, (a piece of gravel,) and was removed, the jockeys pretty generally bet on the General's horse. An immense concourse of people assembled on the race-course on the day of trial. The President's horse was the general favourite, and odds were freely given by those who bet on the field. So confident were those who bet on the General's horse of his success, that the floor of the ballroom, where the annual ball of the season was given, was ornamented with a full-length portrait of the horse. To the astonishment of the crowd, however, Captain Stockton's horse proved to be the winner.

That doesn't sound like Jackson was running his horses just as a hobby. But was Dunwoody sent for to help get these horses ready for the race? It would make sense, but there is no documentation that the horse trainer left The Hermitage for the White House. It seems unlikely that Jackson would have been serious about running and winning races in Washington and left the best trainer in Tennessee behind. But it has never been proven that Dunwoody lived at the White House, or stayed at the stables Jackson eventually had built for his horses and crew.

Perhaps Jackson brought along one of the enslaved grooms, Ephraim, to take care of the horses. The designated groom for Truxton, Jackson was fiercely protective of Ephraim or Ephraham as the general called him, and was willing to throw blows to anyone who attempted to hurt his favored groom. "Ephraham" complained to Jackson one day that he had been attacked by a white man named Grayson in Lebanon, Tennessee. This man, the slave said, had struck him with a riding whip. Jackson retaliated in his normal way: overwhelmingly. "Jackson forthwith went to Lebanon, beat up Grayson and beat him with a heavy cane so severly that he was laid up for four or five weeks and then warned him if he ever touched 'Ephraham' again—or any other 'servant' of his—he would shoot him at sight. 'Ephraham' was not molested any more," author Charles Anthony Shriner said.

Regardless of which ones made the trip, once he had moved all of his horses and black support crews to Washington, Jackson quickly found out that there wasn't enough room in the stables that Monroe left behind. So he directed the construction of a "freestanding neoclassical brick stable trimmed with Aquia sandstone about 100 yards east of the East Wing of the White House at a cost of about $3,600."

A show-place carriage house and stable, with stalls for ten horses, had supplanted the barn and sheds of wartime construction. Built of brick and stone with stucco covering, the tall, wide building was sheltered behind a brick fence positioned in its own grassless yard. Stalls, feed room, tack room, and accommodations for two coaches and several smaller vehicles flanked this hall. On the second level was a hayloft and quarters for grooms and the coachman. This was where Jackson would shelter his prized thoroughbreds—and the jockeys that rode them.

It was no secret in Washington what Jackson was doing, running a major racing operation out of the White House. According to one report, "The stable, with its complement of colored jockeys, was as much a part of the White House establishment as the East Room, and as frequently honored by eminence and fashion. With Jackson in the White House, the black horsemen enjoyed a freedom unlike any before them. One writer called them a "corps of jockeys and hustlers and horse-wise hangers-on who had slept wherever they could spread a blanket and foraged victuals from the presidential kitchen."

The White House stables that replaced the ones built by President Andrew Jackson. LIBRARY OF CONGRESS

And once again, everyone knew the jockeys and trainers were there. "Sporting congressmen and major generals had used to seek them out as authorities on the points and performances of horses," one author pointed out. Peyton, who was also a congressman from Tennessee, was even invited to the White House to see the horses train, which led to the most famous presidential horse race story.

Peyton was invited by Donelson to see the White House stable, which included "Busiris, by Eclipse, owned by General C. Irvine; Emily, by Rattler, and Lady Nashville, by Stockholder, belonging to Major Donelson, and Bolivia, by Tennessee Oscar, owned by General Jackson." Helping out with their time trials, Peyton then was invited to come out to the track the next morning for the last run and was informed that Jackson and his vice president, Martin Van Buren, would be there at the racetrack.

While Jackson was getting on in years by the time he made it to the White House, he still had a commander's attitude and the perspective of a Tennessee turfman. He didn't suffer fools—or willful horses—gladly and was quick with advice or scorn for either, Peyton noticed. "On our arrival the horses were brought out, stripped, and saddled for the gallop. Busiris, an immense animal in size, and of prodigious muscular power, became furious and unmanageable, requiring two men to hold him for Jesse, Major D.'s colored boy, to mount," Peyton said.

Jackson leapt to the occasion, towering over the group with his high fur hat with a broad band of black crape. "Why don't you break him of those tricks? I could do it in an hour," Jackson shouted at the White House jockey.

Not getting the results he wanted, Jackson got madder and madder as the nervous horse was forced toward the starting gate. "Hold him, Jesse. Don't let him break down the fence; now bring 'em up and give 'em a fair start," he bellowed in his high-pitched voice. But by this point, Van Buren had gotten so interested in the battle with the enraged horse, he neglected to notice exactly where he and his horse were as Busiris got ready to leap out of the starting gate.

Mr. Van Buren had left his safe position in the rear and ridden almost into the track below the stand. Jackson stormed out, "Get behind me, Mr. Van Buren, they will run over you, sir." Mr. Van Buren obeyed orders promptly.

Jackson's comment to Van Buren would be used against Jackson's heir apparent when it came time for him to run for president himself, inspiring a cartoon that still exists to this day.

Lest we forget, the jockeys and the horsemen were not the only slaves brought from The Hermitage to the White House. Jackson, like his predecessors, brought a full set of slaves to work inside the President's House as the domestic staff.

One of them was George, his faithful body servant. He had been with Jackson for years, the son of longtime Hermitage slave "Old" Hannah. Born in 1800, he was one of Jackson's most trusted slaves, accompanying Andrew Jackson Donelson to Transylvania University as his body servant and eventually being promoted to serving as the general's postwar body servant, the man who dressed the president, helped him get ready for bed and get dressed each morning. As such, George probably knew the president's secrets in ways no other human being did during his time in the White House, and watched his decline as the days in the capital passed by slowly. George knew of his pain and his sadness, and was a constant

companion who gave the old president comfort in his loneliness and sadness after his wife's death. At night, one of the things that would stay near
Jackson would be a picture of his beloved wife.

"At night after the General's mulatto body-servant, George, had
assisted his master into a long white nightgown, Jackson would remove
the picture and prop it up on a bedside table so that it might be the first
thing to meet his eyes on awakening," James said. "In bed the General
would open the worn Bible which had belonged to Rachel, and read a
chapter before George snuffed the candle and stretched out to take his
own sleep on a pallet on the floor beside the bed of his master."

George was a good example of how kind Jackson could be to his
slaves while keeping them in human bondage. Jackson allowed his slaves
to form official family units, getting married (and divorced) and never
separated families by selling them apart unless asked to by the slaves
themselves. (While this could be seen as a kindness by Jackson, it could
also be seen as a clever way to keep slaves from wanting to run away
from The Hermitage or the White House by giving them a wife, child,
or mother who perhaps would be left behind to the tender mercies of a
spurned and upset slave master.)

Regardless, George is an example of a Hermitage slave who was
allowed to get married. After Jackson returned home from the presidency,
George married a slave from another nearby plantation, Manthis, who
was owned by Albert Ward. And to help out his newly married slave,
Jackson bought Manthis from his neighbor for one thousand dollars.
George would spend the rest of Jackson's days as a driver for the Jackson
family, including Sarah Jackson.

George would also be a good example of the limits of the love even
"good" masters had for their slaves. Despite their closeness, Jackson never
released any of his slaves even after he died. He bequeathed The Hermitage to his adopted son, Donelson, along with all of his slaves, except for
two boys whom he gave to his grandsons and four female slaves whom
he left to Sarah.

And the younger Jackson was not a good manager of his estate. The
promises and practices the slaves had grown accustomed to with the
elderly president fell to the wayside.

For example, after the elderly Jackson's death, Donelson began to sell off his slaves to pay his ever-growing debts, including Manthis, George's wife, who was sold to a Presbyterian minister named Carr. Carr then handed her over to a slave dealer named Nathan Bedford Forrest, who would soon become a famous southern Civil War general. Luckily for George and Mathis, George was hired out or sold to a man named Dr. John Donelson Martin of Memphis, the same city in which Manthis had been located. Whether out of the kindness of his heart, or because of pleading and negotiating by George and Manthis, Martin ended up buying Manthis from Forrest, and reuniting the couple at his plantation in Alabama, "where they both died during the last year of the War Between The States."

Charles also made the trip from The Hermitage to the President's House. Charles, like George, had been with Jackson for years—including while he was in the military. Charles also worked with Dunwoody with the racing colts and drove the carriage while Jackson was in Washington, something that almost got him into trouble.

Despite his reputation as a kind master, Jackson could be tough on his slaves and would threaten to send them back to the fields of Tennessee if he wasn't pleased. Charles faced his wrath one time at the White House.

Jackson's love affair with his wife was well known. As a token of his affection, he bought for her what was then considered the finest horse carriage in Tennessee, paying for it twenty-five hundred dollars, and he highly prized this coach in the after-years. He had it with him in Washington, and would ride in no other. Therefore he was quite angry one day when Charles allowed it to be hurt.

His horses ran away with it and it was brought back considerably damaged. Jackson was very angry, and his private secretary heard him say to his black coachman: "Charles, you know why I value that carriage. This is the second time such an accident has happened, and if it ever occurs again I will send you back to Tennessee."

This wasn't the only cherished carriage in Jackson's collection. He also was presented a carriage made from the frigate *Constitution*, and this was the carriage he traveled to the White House in with his successor, Martin Van Buren. While no one knows what happened to Rachel's prized carriage, the *Constitution* carriage was lost in a fire at one of his descendants' houses in Clifton, Ohio. According to *Publications of the Southern History Association*, Volume I, "On April 12, 1897, the dwelling in Clifton, Ohio, occupied by James Jackson, a relative of Andrew Jackson and an inheritor of relics of the deceased President, was greatly damaged by fire. Among them was Gen. Jackson's carriage, the wheels of which were made from timber taken from the old war frigate *Constitution*. This carriage was stored in the garret and was nearly destroyed, together with some other relics in the shape of furniture."

Charles was also one of those slaves who got married, and then wanted to get divorced. While at the White House, Jackson sent a letter to his neighbor, Robert Chester, letting him know about the unhappy separation and proposing a solution that would make everyone happy: "I received a letter from Mr. Steel, my overseer, informing me that Charlotte had applied to you to purchase her, being discontented where she is now. I bought her, being the wife of Charles, at his request. He now appears desirous that she with her children be sold. I have therefore come to the resolution to part with her."

So for eight hundred dollars, the plan was for Charles and Charlotte to be separated and work on neighboring plantation. Jackson lamented the fact that his actions would break up a family, but wanted Chester to know that it was the family's choice. "I think I have placed Charlotte & her children as low as they could be bought now here, & sent to my farm, but I do it that she may be contented," Jackson wrote.

There must have been a reconciliation after that breakup, or the deal fell through, because Charles and Charlotte were back together again at The Hermitage a couple of years later. Were they a couple again, or were they just sharing custody of their children on the Jackson plantation? No one knows, but we do know that Charlotte at least was ready to make her way away from her spouse and children again two years later. In 1832, Andrew Donelson wrote a friend of his, Samuel Hays, to ask him if he was willing to take Charlotte on as a slave as payment of a debt. Hays was willing, and Charlotte was half ready to go: "I immediately called up Charlotte to ascertain whether she was willing to leave Charles and her children and I find she is half willing to leave them and Charles. I had just taken her into the house and also as a washer. She is certainly a valuable servant and I hardly know how I can well spare her—and separate her from her children and Charles . . ."

What was the final result between Charlotte and Charles? No one knows. They fade into history with Jackson's death and the breakup of the Hermitage slave families.

Those slave families expanded during Jackson's time as president, and because Jackson was in Washington. In fact, Jackson is one of the only presidents we know definitely purchased more slaves while living inside the White House. One of those purchases came about because of Jackson's decision to not only have Hermitage slaves working as White House domestics, but free blacks as well.

The White House of Andrew Jackson was one of the most diversified of its time, with white employees like the Belgian stewards Joseph Boulanger and Antoine Michel Giusta, Irish doorkeeper Jemmy O'Neil, Hermitage slaves like Charles, George, and jockey Jesse, and black freedmen like Augustus Price all working together.

Price was only one of the freedmen working inside the White House, but he may have been the most important. He was described as being "of mixed African, Indian and white descent, and some evidence suggests that his father may have been a Revolutionary War officer and statesman."

Price may have been a freedman, but he had Hermitage roots as well. Born, raised, and educated under the future president's direction, Price ended up coming to Washington with the president to serve as his "trusted servant and private secretary" as a freedman, not a slave like George or Charles. But just because he wasn't a slave and held an important job—one book called him "the doorkeeper of the White House"—doesn't mean that his life in Washington was idyllic. Price, who would go on to become active as an abolitionist and a doctor although he "could not secure the necessary permit or license," had to run for his life during the first major race riot in the nation's capital.

The Snow Riot erupted behind an inebriated slave who threatened a white woman. Arthur Bowen, an eighteen-year-old slave in the house of Mrs. Anna Maria Thornton, was fond of his liquor and desiring of freedom. So one evening, he got drunk and found an axe. When Mrs. Thornton woke, Bowen was standing in her room drunk and with an axe.

Thornton slipped past the slave and fled for help. Bowen's mother, likely knowing what her son was like when drunk, pushed him out of the house and locked the door, making Bowen even angrier. "I'll have my freedom. I'll have my freedom, you hear me? I've got just as much right to freedom as you," he shouted at the white people and his mother on the other side of the door. A few minutes later, Bowen stumbled into the night, not knowing what he had started.

Bowen was soon arrested, and a lynch mob formed. But since he was in prison, the angry young white men's intentions were frustrated. So since they couldn't get to Bowen, they decided to go after other blacks in the city and their establishments. White mobs attacked schoolhouses and other structures associated with the free black population. The riot takes its name after one of those other blacks, Beverly Snow, who had his restaurant, the Epicurean Eating House, trashed by the rioters. Snow may also have been a target because it was alleged that he spoke disrespectfully about the wives and daughters of white Navy Yard mechanics. Snow escaped, so the crowd went looking after some more "uppity" Negroes to take their frustration out on, and the White House and Augustus Price was a good target.

Jackson was out of town when the riot started, leaving the people who worked for him vulnerable to the mob, especially those blacks who were doing well for themselves, and therefore perhaps striking jealousy in the hearts of poor and middle-class whites who wanted the lives those blacks had. This caused Price's life to be put in danger, according to one author. "The mob, as I learned, had manifested intense exasperation against, and had been very anxious to get hold of, a certain Augustus, a remarkably fine looking mulatto, who was one of the President's hired domestics, in the capacity of waiter on his office. As the story ran, Augustus had disappeared, and no trace of him could be found so long as the General was away; but the moment the latter had got back, there was Augustus also."

Why would a "remarkably fine looking mulatto" like Augustus Price return when Jackson did? With his heritage he may have been able to pass in other cities or at least have a better life. So why stay? It may have been safer as a black man to be close to Andrew Jackson than farther away.

While harsh to his enemies and even sometimes to his friends, Jackson had paternalistic protective feelings toward those under his command, in his employ and under his wings, and never once allowed those outside of his command to unfairly attack or malign those on his side. So Augustus Price likely knew that if he returned to work, Jackson with the power of the presidency and the power of his own personality would be the best protector he could find. And that's exactly what happened.

Some whites, still intent on taking their frustrations out on well-to-do blacks, came to Jackson and demanded that Price be banished from the White House and Jackson's patronage be withdrawn. Jackson wouldn't hear of it, when an acquaintance asked about it. "My servants are amenable to the law if they offend against the law, and if guilty of misconduct which the law does not take cognizance of, they are amenable to me," Jackson replied. "But, I would have all to understand distinctly that they are amenable to me alone, and to no one else. They are entitled to protection at my hands, and this they shall receive." And as far as we can tell, Price was left alone and continued to work inside the White House.

This public loyalty to blacks in his employ and his enslaved workers was nothing new for Jackson. He frequently stood up for his slaves publicly and privately to ensure that they had at least a decent quality of life while under his employ. He told his overseer at The Hermitage once to ensure that he was not to abuse any of his slaves after hearing of the death of slave James—who Jackson feared died because of "ill treatment of the overseer"—and that if he heard of anything to the contrary, the overseer would be fired. "I hope Mr. Steel will treat my negroes with humanity as I have requested him," Jackson said. "I have confidence in him, have no wish to remove him, if he will only treat my slaves with humanity."

And Jackson spent a good deal of money and time after leaving the presidency defending his slaves, including White House slave George, from a murder charge. George, Squire, Jacob, and Alfred Jackson were attending a large party at a neighboring plantation when Alfred got a little wild, or as Jackson wrote to a friend, "Alfred cryed out he was the best man in the House and altercation ensued." The fight ended with the death of a male slave, Frank, owned by Jackson's nephew, Stockley Donelson. Jackson had shaky relations with Donelson, so Donelson decided that out of all of the slaves who were there, he would have four of his uncle's charged with Frank's murder. Jackson did not take to that well, and demanded that his slaves get due process. "Now being arrested the magistrate was bound to hear their defence, that it was a constitutional right, that all men by law presumed to be innocent until guilt was proven," Jackson said.

Jackson went as far as to hire three Nashville lawyers for his slaves, and to ridicule the testimony against them. "The ransaked, the drunken hords of Negroes, worthless Whig Scamps, & worthless fishermen" had "swore too much—contradicted each other, and their credit was blown sky high," he said to James K. Polk. Jackson believed the testimony of other slaves, Raina and Nathan, who said the fight happened but none of Jackson's slaves were involved in the fatal blow.

"Nathan says, that Alfred and Cancer was fighting, Frank came up seized Alfred by the collar and jerked him off Cancer, that as soon as Alfred was on his feet and saw Frank, they both stooped down and picked up stones, when Frank cursed him and told him fire away," Jackson said. "Alfred threw, struck Frank in the breast, he stooped, when Jack struck him on the head with a rock, knocked out his brains and killed him, but swears positively that Squire did not touch Frank at all."

That was the story that the jury believed. The charges against George were dismissed by the grand jury and Squire, Alfred, and Jack were acquitted "in two minutes," Jackson said.

All of the stories about Jackson's loyalty and kindness to his slaves may leave the impression that everyone—the slaves and their masters—was one big happy family at The Hermitage and during Jackson's time in Washington, DC, but that would be false. Even Jackson's most loyal slaves were still slaves, and they desired freedom just as much as anyone else in their situation. Alfred Jackson, the slave who caused the fight during the slaves' holiday party, was one of the most loyal of Jackson's people. He stayed at The Hermitage for his entire life, even after Jackson's death, and was known to repeatedly praise Jackson as one of the greatest men who ever lived. But even Alfred wanted to be free. One day, a tutor hired to work at The Hermitage decided to quiz Alfred about his life, considering that "he had the easiest and most honorable position possible for a slave" as Jackson's favored slave. Roeliff Brinkerhoff thought he would explain to Alfred how well he had it.

"You have a kind master, have you not?"

"Yes, Massa Andrew is always very kind."

"You have a wife and children and a pleasant home, have you not?"

"Yes, but who knows how long Massa Andrew will live?"

I saw that the shadow of possible separation darkened his thought, and I took another tack. I showed him how freedom had its burdens as well as slavery; that God had so constituted human life that every one in every station had a load to carry, and that he was the wisest and the happiest who contentedly did his duty, and looked to a world beyond, where all inequalities would be made even. Alfred did not seem disposed to argue the question with me, or to combat my logic, but he quietly looked up into my face and popped this question at me, "How would you like to be a slave?"

It is needless to say I backed out as gracefully as I could, but I have never yet found an answer to the argument embodied in that question.

Alfred Jackson was one of the most loyal of all of Jackson's slaves, and he yearned to be free. And despite having it as well as a slave could possibly expect—respect, family, shelter and food—he still wanted freedom. Not just freedom for himself, but freedom for his wife, Gracy Bradley, as well. With Gracy's purchase in Washington, DC, Jackson became the first president we know of to buy slaves in the District of Columbia while working as America's chief executive.

The fact that Jackson was buying slaves did not go unnoticed by the antislavery crowd in the United States, who ascribed the worst motives they could to the president's actions. In the *Liberator*, an antislavery newspaper in Boston, they called slave owners "monsters in human shape" and in an article written by the anonymous "Am. Citizen," accused Jackson of using the White House as a slave-fattening pen.

"A gentleman who has spent most of his winters, for the last five years, at Washington, states that Gen. Jackson, during the term of his Presidency, was in the habit of buying debilitated slaves, as well as those low in flesh, who are generally sold at comparatively small prices, and of fattening them in his kitchen; after which they were sent to his plantation in Tennessee, where the best of them were sold to other planters—thus converting the President's, or rather the People's house, into a stall for fattening of 'human cattle!'" the newspaper said.

The *Liberator* went on to editorialize that they were sorry to bring this accusation out against "a man who stands high in the affections of the American people" but they "feel the more deeply on the subject, because we are far from supposing the case to be a singular one." While the newspaper was right in that Jackson purchased several slaves while president, and did send some of them down to The Hermitage, his motive was actually better than they suppose. In fact, Jackson's purchase helped keep a family together, instead of breaking them apart. Gracy Bradley would go on to become the seamstress at The Hermitage, and one of the longest-tenured slaves there, but there is little information about her early life in Virginia. What is known is that her sister, like Augustus Price, was a free black woman working inside the White House for President Jackson. (Some records name her sister as a "Nellie Richards," but that has not been confirmed.) The sister, who happened to be a pastry cook inside the White House, knew that her enslaved family's master was looking for someone to sell them to. And it just so happened that the white master, a Colonel Hebb of Virginia, was similar to Jackson in that he didn't want to separate families unnecessarily. Therefore, "he gave them permission to select homes and purchasers for themselves." This is when Gracy's sister jumped into action.

> *A woman named Gracey was sent for by a sister, a freedwoman living in Washington City. The latter had been employed as pastry cook at the White House and knew Mrs. Sarah Jackson. This sister sent Gracey to Mrs. Jackson, who was so favorably impressed with her and interested in the situation that she took her in to see the President and laid the matter before him. Without a moment's hesitation he purchased the whole family, consisting of the old mother, three daughters, and one son. The mother, one daughter, and the son were sent on to the Hermitage; but Gracey and her sister Louisa remained at the White House as nurses to Mrs. Sarah Jackson's two children, Rachel and Andrew.*

Gracy (whose name is spelled Gracy, Gracey, and Gracie interchangeably by writers during her time) and Louisa become two of the only slaves purchased by a sitting US president in Washington, DC. Gracy was around fifteen when bought by the president, and her new life working for the Jacksons began in Washington, where she worked inside the White House as a nurse and personal maid for Sarah Jackson, the president's daughter-in-law. But being a nurse wasn't her calling. Soon, the Jacksons discovered that Gracy was an excellent seamstress, and she was put in charge of designing and creating clothes for the family. Was she responsible for the clothing that the slaves wore inside the White House? Unlikely, but it is likely that she repaired, and perhaps even modified some of the uniforms that the public saw, which were "blue coats with brass buttons, white shirts, and yellow or white breeches. Maids, who did not appear in the public rooms, used a long white apron, reaching to hems at the floor."

Sleeping with the rest of the slaves in bedrooms on the second floor and in the attic, Gracy soon made herself invaluable to the Jacksons. She became especially close to Sarah Yorke Jackson, with whom she worked the closest. Between the two, "a warm friendship sprung up between them which lasted until death." Gracy became one of the most loyal and popular slaves for the Jacksons, who heaped praise upon her during her lifetime.

"Gracey did not disappoint the expectation of her mistress, for she relieved her of most of the household cares, supervised the other servants, nursed the children, and was an expert seamstress," said Mary C. Currey Dorris, author of *Preservation of the Hermitage, 1889–1915: Annals, History, and Stories*. "She was invaluable in illness, and nothing could soothe the mistress as did the ministrations of Gracey.'. . . . This excellent servant won not only the esteem but the affection of the family, and even now she is spoken of gratefully. She had no superiors, few equals, and her life was a chapter in the old slave days full of beauty and interest."

When the Jacksons left Washington after the general's presidency, Gracy went along with them back to The Hermitage to rejoin her family, continue her servitude, and become the master seamstress at The Hermitage. It was also there where she found love.

Alfred Jackson, the Jackson body servant who declared himself "the best man" at the slave Christmas party and caused the ruckus that ended with Jackson having to defend his slaves from murder charges, fell in love with the seamstress, who returned his affections. With the blessings of the Jacksons, Alfred and Gracy got married at The Hermitage in 1837.

Sarah Jackson, in honor of her favorite slaves, made it an affair to remember. Instead of having a slave celebration, which would have included likely jumping a broom and a feast at the slave cabins, she moved the entire affair to inside The Hermitage, where Sarah Jackson "had the couple stand in the large hall while they were married and gave them a fine wedding supper. These two favorite servants were given a cabin very near the house."

For the rest of her life, Sarah Jackson would praise Gracy. "I don't know what I would do without Gracey," Sarah Jackson said in the *Greensboro Patriot* in the February 25, 1880, edition. "She knows my ways and my needs, she anticipates my every want. She is stout and well, and I do hope that her life will last longer than mine."

It would be close. Gracy and Alfred would go on to become the longest tenured slaves at The Hermitage, staying there throughout Jackson's retirement from the presidency and becoming the greatest defenders of his family and reputation. They, along with other slaves, were at his bedside when the former president finally died.

Just like many of his predecessors, family and friends surrounded Jackson as he died. Already gaunt and tired from his years as president, and suffering from lead poisoning from the many bullets lodged in his body from years of dueling, Jackson was bedridden at the conclusion of his life, and began to call his allies and family to his side.

A slave, Old Hannah, said George was one of the last people Jackson would speak to.

"'Richard hand me my specs,' Jackson said. 'He wet them with his tongue and wiped them on the sheet, looked around and said here's poor George and Hannah, I have [arranged] it that you shall be well taken care of' . . . He then turned to us all and said 'I want all to prepare to meet me in Heaven; I have a right to the Tree of Life. My conversation is for you all. Christ has no respect to color. I am in God and Gods in me. He dwelleth in me and I dwell in him.'"

Hannah said Jackson was propped up on three pillows, and asked George to take some of them away.

"Missus cried 'don't George don't.' Just then Master gave one breath hunched up his shoulders and all was over," Hannah said. "There was no struggle. Missus fainted and we had to carry her to her room, strip her and bathe her in camphor before she come too. 'Our master, or father is gone.' The darkees would not be driven out. They looked on him as if they had as much right to him as Massa Andrew."

Jackson did not consider taking care of George to mean giving him his freedom. He did not free any of his slaves in his will, instead doling them out to his surviving relatives. He made special mention of Gracy, however, cementing her fate to that of Sarah Jackson. "I hereby recognise, by this bequest, the gift I made her on her marriage, of the negro girl Gracy, which I bought for her, and gave her to my daughter Sarah as her maid and seamstress, with her increase, with my house-servant Hanna and her two daughters, namely, Charlotte and Mary, to her and her heirs for ever," Jackson said in his will.

Forever wouldn't be long. The Civil War started about two decades after Jackson's death in 1845, but Alfred and Gracy would not leave with the rest of the Hermitage slaves, instead choosing to stay in the cabins given to them by the Jacksons. According to a newspaper article, "When the Civil War broke out he and his wife, Gracey, alone of all the servants stayed with their mistress, never leaving the place for an hour." Eventually, they became the true caretakers of The Hermitage. "In a measure they reversed the old order of things, particularly after the death of the adopted son, and became the protectors of Mrs. Sarah Jackson and her sister, Mrs. Adams, all that were left of the once sunny household," author Mary C. Currey Dorris said in her book, *Preservation of the Hermitage*. "It was Gracey who prepared the now frugal meals, and it was Alfred who did the man's work of the household."

After the former president's death, Alfred Jackson and Gracy Bradley (they chose separate last names after becoming free) became the caretakers of the reputation and history of The Hermitage and Jackson, and conducted tours of the land and property for curious onlookers wanting to know what life was like for the president and the people who lived with him in his heyday. And by the way, they got remarried on April 29, 1866, since their first marriage was a slave wedding.

In their caretaker positions, Alfred and Gracy profusely praised Jackson to anyone who would listen on their tours. A tourist who wrote about his tour of The Hermitage described his experience with Gracy in this way: "That Gen. Jackson was the greatest man who ever lived is as fixed in her mind as the eyes in her head, and she feels that his lightest word has a value demanding caution and dignity in her repetition. She took us through the house, showing us her master's books and sword and favorite chair, this last comfortably facing Washington's arm-chair, so that neither need be moved if ever the two great ghosts want to talk together in the dim old room."

Joined by Alfred, the two would continue to extol Jackson's greatness, with Gracy saying at The Hermitage, "it was Christmas all de year round." Finally, Gracy summed up their feelings by saying, "He didn't have a servant but would 'a' died for him."

Gracy and Alfred would live out their lives at The Hermitage, with Gracy dying in 1887, the same year as Sarah Yorke Jackson. Alfred would go on living at The Hermitage, outlasting the existence of the land as a plantation. It was eventually turned into a memorial to Jackson run by the Ladies' Hermitage Association. Alfred came along with the place, and continued to uphold the virtues of Jackson even to future presidents.

When Rutherford B. Hayes came to Nashville to attend the National Convention of the Prison Association, he was invited to The Hermitage by the Ladies' Hermitage Association. They then called for Alfred.

He was introduced with the remark: "'Uncle Alfred, this is President Hayes. Come and shake hands with him,'" one author wrote in a Hermitage history. "He grasped the ex-President's hand and said: 'If you'd been as great a man as General Jackson was, I could a'most er shook yer han' off.'"

As far as we can tell, Alfred Jackson never lived permanently at the White House, but some members of his now-extended family say he drove the Jacksons to Washington several times, meaning that he must have at least stayed overnight.

After the Ladies' Hermitage Association was organized to preserve The Hermitage, Alfred Jackson just came along with the plantation, and spent the rest of his days entertaining tourists with the stories of the days of Jackson and The Hermitage.

Like many other presidential slaves, Alfred was at the ex-president's side at his death, along with other members of the former president's family. Rachel Jackson Lawrence recalled the time of her grandfather's death in an article "Andrew Jackson at Home."

Jackson died on Sunday, a little after six o'clock in the afternoon. My father, his adopted son, stood at the head of his bed, old Alfred, my grandfather's body servant, was near him, and my mother and her sister, Mrs. Adams. . . . I was standing at the foot of the bed, with my hands on the bed, looking directly into my grandfather's face; some of the younger children and Mrs. Adams' three children, had gone to the Hermitage Church, and they were sent for. My grandfather became very faint for a while and could not see. The negro servants crowded at the windows and on the porch, and it was necessary to move them in order to get air.

Alfred would live at The Hermitage entertaining guests with his stories until his death at ninety-nine in 1901.

With Alfred Jackson's death, the last link to the plantation days of the president and his family was severed. Newspapers around the nation reported the death of Jackson's favorite slave and the guardian of The Hermitage: "For fifty years he never spent a night away from the old cabin in which he was born. His last night was spent there, and his relatives and friends held a prayer meeting in the old cabin. The next day the body was carried to the house and placed in the great hall, where the funeral services were held under the direction of The Hermitage association. Then the faithful darky was buried back of the house, within a few feet of the grave of his beloved master."

According to The Hermitage, Alfred Jackson's funeral was the only known burial of a formerly enslaved person at The Hermitage. "By having the LHA host such a lavish funeral for Alfred illustrates his ability to cross class lines during his lifetime," Hermitage historians said.

Alfred Jackson is buried directly to the right of Andrew Jackson's tomb, with the inscriptions on his tombstone reading "Uncle Alfred" and "Faithful Servant of Andrew Jackson." In the end, it was the latter title he was the proudest of.

CHAPTER 11

THE REST

Washington, Jefferson, Madison and Jackson weren't the only presidents to own slaves, not by far. The institution of slavery was prevalent among the first chief executives, with ten of the first twelve presidents being slaveholders at some point in their lives (John Adams and his son, John Quincy Adams, were the only ones of the first twelve presidents not to own slaves at some point). Twelve presidents held slaves at one point or the other in their lifetimes.

Monroe, Tyler, Polk, and Taylor also owned slaves during their times as president in Washington, DC. However, the stories told so far are the only ones we've been able to find in detail about the slaves who actually lived on the White House grounds with the presidents. There are likely many other stories out there, but they have yet to be discovered in hidden papers, buried manuscripts, or whispered family lore.

For example, we know that James Monroe brought some of his slaves to the White House with him. Elected president in 1814 after serving stints as James Madison's secretary of war, Thomas Jefferson's ambassador to England, and George Washington's ambassador to France, Monroe was the last of the Virginia slave-holding presidential dynasty. The last president of the Founding Fathers, Monroe was raised on his family's five-hundred-acre tobacco plantation and inherited the land and a slave named Ralph after his father died. He then purchased the plantation Highland in Albemarle County, Virginia, where he owned thirty to forty slaves. At least one of those slaves would go to Washington with him.

We know one was named Datcher, but we don't know much more about him. We do know that after being freed from Monroe Datcher ended up working at the War Department, because he's mentioned as being there in a biography of James Monroe:

When William L. Marcy was taking leave of the clerks in the War Department, "he shook hands with an elderly colored employee named Datcher, who had formerly been a body servant to President Monroe and said: 'Good-bye, Datcher; if I had had your manners, I should have left more friends behind me.'"

But who were Monroe's slaves? What were the stories behind their lives? What did they think about their master's opposition to slavery, while being held in bondage by him? Did they want to be repatriated back to Africa, which Monroe was a proponent of during his lifetime? We don't know, and we don't even yet have enough information about Monroe and slavery at his plantations to even read between the lines to find out.

We do know Monroe was the first president who publicly advocated an end to slavery, even while holding slaves. Perhaps part of the reason was because a slave conspiracy in his home state of Virginia targeted him directly. A slave blacksmith named Gabriel organized a rebellion against Virginia slaveholders, with slaves planning to enter Richmond with force, capture the Capitol and the Virginia State Armory, and hold then-Governor Monroe hostage to bargain for freedom for Virginia's slaves. However, on August 30, 1800, a thunderstorm poured over Virginia, delaying the slaves' planned gathering, and a few nervous slaves told their masters of the plot.

While no whites were killed in the revolt that never really got started, the state of Virginia executed twenty-seven blacks, including Gabriel, by public hanging. Whites then tightened legal restrictions on slaves. In a letter to Thomas Jefferson, Monroe explained how seriously they took the planned rebellion.

We have had much trouble with the negroes here. The plan of an insur-rection has been clearly proved, & appears to have been of consider-able extent. 10. have been condemned & executed, and there are at least twenty perhaps 40. more to be tried, of whose guilt no doubt is entertained. It is unquestionably the most serious and formidable conspiracy we have ever known of the kind: tho' indeed to call it so is to give no idea of the thing itself.

While he never acknowledged equal rights for the slave population, Monroe sought a gradual end to slavery and advocated resettling freed slaves in the Caribbean or Africa. Monroe was part of the American Colonization Society formed in 1816, whose members included Henry Clay and Andrew Jackson. They found common ground with some abolitionists in supporting colonization, and helped send several thousand freed slaves to the new colony of Liberia in Africa from 1820 to 1840. Liberia would rename its capital Monrovia after Monroe because he was a prominent supporter of the colony in sending freed black slaves to Liberia, seeing it as preferable to emancipation in America, where free blacks could encourage slaves in the South to rebel.

It was during Monroe's terms as president that the reconstruction of the White House after its burning in the War of 1812 would be completed. Rushed by Monroe, who wanted to be inside the presidential mansion before 1818, the federal government rehired James Hoban and ordered him to rebuild the President's House exactly as it was. But there would be some changes, according to William Seale: "One hundred ninety men, sixty of them probably hired slaves, labored hard through the summer of 1817. The exterior of the house was scrubbed down for painting, this time with an actual white lead paint in a linseed oil base, not whitewash."

Monroe would move into the executive mansion in October of 1817 even though it was still incomplete. By New Year's Day, the presidential mansion had opened to the public again with a midday open house for Washingtonians. In three years, Hoban and his workers had rebuilt a mansion that had taken almost a decade to construct. It was a brand-new building but some things would not change, with Monroe moving some of his slaves into the White House basement to serve him and his family during their time in the presidential mansion. But we still don't know the names of those slaves, just that they were there.

Like Monroe, we also don't know much about the White House slaves of President Zachary Taylor, although we know for sure he had some there with him from his first day. Taylor, when elected, was known as old "Rough and Ready," the hero of numerous military battles and the most popular man in America. Born in Virginia in 1784 and raised on a Kentucky plantation, Taylor was a lifelong Army officer who wanted to be a landed cotton plantation owner upon retirement.

He married Margaret, the daughter of a prosperous Maryland planter, while still a lieutenant, and the Taylors moved about the frontier as he advanced up the ranks fighting in Indian encounters and against Santa Anna and the Mexican forces in border skirmishes. After bouncing around several frontier forts, he settled in Baton Rouge, Louisiana, with some eighty slaves and bought a plantation in Mississippi, which included another eighty-or-so slaves. Called back into service, in February 1847, Taylor scored a stunning victory over Santa Anna's army in the Battle of Buena Vista with only five thousand men, three times smaller than the Mexican army. This made Taylor a national hero and a presidential candidate. (In an interesting side note, future president of the Confederacy Jefferson Davis eloped with Taylor's daughter in 1835, causing a rift between the then-young lieutenant and his commanding general. Sarah Taylor Davis would die a few months after marrying Davis.)

The country was already dividing up into factions before the Civil War, and both sides thought Taylor would support them: the South because of his ownership of slaves and the North because of his lifelong allegiance to the armed forces. Taylor actually played both sides for a while during the election. When a slave owner wrote him in 1848 to suss out Taylor's positions, the general responded with the skill of a lifelong politician. "Sir: I have worked hard and been frugal all my life, and the results of my industry have mainly taken the form of slaves, of whom I own about a hundred," the slave owner wrote. "Before I vote for President, I want to be sure that the candidate I support will not so act as to divest me of my property."

Not giving an inch, Taylor replied: "Sir: I have the honor to inform you that I, too, have been all my life industrious and frugal, and that the fruits thereof are mainly invested in slaves, of whom I own three hundred."

Elected president in 1849, the Taylors headed toward Washington and the capital circuit. They packed everything they might need, including a slave, William Oldham, "a faithful colored man, who had been the body-servant of General Taylor for many years."

Once in the White House, Taylor was a hard-liner on southern talks of secession. Having moved about his entire life, he did not have that strong link to a state like Robert E. Lee had for Virginia. And as a strong nationalist who saw the country as being inviolable as a whole, he opposed the extension of slavery into the territories newly acquired from Mexico and threatened to use military force against secessionists to preserve the Union. In February 1850, Taylor warned secessionist southerners if they were "taken in rebellion against the Union, he would hang them with less reluctance than he had hung deserters and spies in Mexico."

We might not know as much about Taylor's White House slaves because of his short time inside the White House. Having only been elected the year before, Taylor stood in the hot sun at the foot of the Washington Monument on July 4, 1850, listening to patriotic speeches celebrating Independence Day. That night he had an attack of cholera morbus, or acute indigestion, and he died five days later. His last words were, "I regret nothing, but I am sorry to leave my friends."

Some historians speculate that if Taylor had not died and been replaced by Millard Fillmore, who was more conciliatory with the South, the Civil War might have been averted. What that would have meant for slavery, however, is unknown.

Another president we know kept at least three slaves inside the White House was Taylor's predecessor, James K. Polk. Considered the first "dark horse" winner of a presidential election, Polk led the United States into its most aggressive western expansion. Under him, the United States added territory that now composes the states of Arizona, Utah, Nevada, California, Oregon, Idaho, Washington, much of New Mexico, and portions of Wyoming, Montana, and Colorado. An ally of Andrew Jackson, Polk obtained the nickname "Young Hickory" and as Speaker of the House, no one ever expected him to become president. "Who is James K. Polk?" asked skeptical opponents, but Polk soon adopted a platform of "Manifest Destiny"—and a promise of serving only one term—and the country swept him into office.

Polk brought to Washington the slave Henry Carter, who was the namesake and son of Henry Carter, the highest-earning slave on Polk's plantations and Mariah, the personal maid of Polk's wife Sarah.

What did Henry Carter do at the White House? Did he serve as a doorkeeper and a butler? Did he screen visitors for the president? Was it Carter whom the Rev. Dr. Dixon of the English Methodist Church wrote about when he visited the White House? "On our arrival we met with a black man, the only servant of the President we saw; and on asking whether it would be possible to obtain an interview, he said he saw no difficulty in the case, but would inquire," Dixon wrote later. "He went, with Mr. Slicer's compliments, and soon returned with a message that the President would be very happy to see us."

Or was this the famous Elias Polk, a longtime body servant who by his close proximity to a president transitioned from slave to politician to pauper all during his lifetime? "Used to luxury and patronage, and for a long time a mogul in the White House, his declining years were shrouded in the deepest poverty and he died a pauper," one obituary said.

Because of his popularity after Polk's death, we know a little more about Elias Polk's life outside the White House. He was born in Mecklenburg, North Carolina, in 1805 and moved to Tennessee when he was just a baby. Polk would brag for the rest of his life that he encountered every president from John Quincy Adams through Grover Cleveland, including Tennessee celebrity Andrew Jackson, who made a great impression on the young slave. "It was his delight all his life to tell how the famous soldier noticed him. Gen. Jackson stopped at Col. Polk's house," newspapers wrote in his later life. "When he was ready to leave, Elias was sent around for his horse, a big, gray, magnificent animal. Old Hickory, after he had mounted, reared back in his majestic way, and, putting his hand in his pocket, pulled out a six-and-four-pence, which he gave the little 7-year-old fellow."

Polk was given to the future president when he was a twelve-year-old child and James Polk was headed to college. After serving as a valet and body servant for Polk, Elias Polk began a tradition of driving his master to Washington, DC, during his political career and staying in the capital with him. Having spent his entire adult life with Polk, Elias Polk became very attached to his master and wouldn't leave even when given the chance. While on their way to Washington for the first time as president, the Polks were riding aboard the steamboat *China* when it docked in Cincinnati and a group of abolitionists boarded. The men and women demanded to know whether Polk had any slaves aboard, because their intent was to free them. A friend of Polk's went to tell the president-elect what was happening, and Polk sent back this message: "Mr. Polk wishes you to know that his coachman and his coachman's wife are at present, he thinks, eating their dinner. He says that you are at perfect liberty to interview them and offer whatever inducements you like. He says, furthermore, that, should his servants wish to go with you, they are free to do so."

But according to author Romeo B. Garrett, the slaves were not ready to go. "Expecting to be hailed as delivering angels and thanked with shouts of 'Hallelujah! Praise de Lawd!' the abolitionists were first bewildered, then irate. They could not persuade the pair to leave their master," he said in his book *The Presidents and the Negro*.

In today's parlance, Elias Polk would have been a complete "Uncle Tom," a black man who was more in love with his own captors than he was with the idea of freedom. Elias Polk proved over and over where his loyalties were, even when given a chance to be free.

It was Elias's custom to drive his master in his carriage to Washington. The first journey was made in 1826, when James K. Polk was elected member of Congress. On one of these trips, after the Tennessean had become President, a night was spent in Wilkes-Barre, Pa. The next morning, while Elias was in the stable getting his horses ready, several white men approached him and asked him if he didn't know he was free. They told him that he was in a State where a man could not hold slaves, and all he had to do was to leave and his master couldn't do a thing.

"Do you think I would go back on de President dat way? No, sir. You don't know me. I'd sooner die than run off."

The President happened to be near and heard this. He was greatly pleased, and the next day surprised his faithful valet by speaking of it, and told him whenever he wanted his freedom he could have it.

But Elias Polk wouldn't hear of it, and stayed with Polk for the president's entire life. "He was always a trusted and faithful servant," said Sarah Polk.

When James K. Polk was dying from cholera on June 15, 1849, Elias stood faithfully outside the bedroom door until his master called him and charged Elias to take care of "Miss Sarah." She lived in the house on Polk Place until her death in 1891. Elias, Milly, and the other slave servants lived behind the Polks' big house in frame structures. Elias Polk, who addressed Mrs. Polk as "Yassum, Miss Sarah," maintained a post-Emancipation alliance with the local white elite.

Polk rewarded his faithfulness by stipulating that all his slaves were to be freed upon the death of his wife. In his first will, he called Elias Polk one of his three favored slaves, and dictated that he was never to be sold outside the family. The Emancipation Proclamation of 1863 and the Thirteenth Amendment to the US Constitution approved in 1865 had freed all slaves long before her death, but Elias Polk stayed on to take care of "Miss Sarah."

During the Civil War, when Union forces took Nashville, the Federal general in charge came by to pay his respects to Sarah Polk, who had refused to leave her home and President Polk's gravesite. After eating dinner, the Union leaders encountered Elias Polk, who again proved that his loyalties lay with the South and his former slavers.

"One of the generals, as he passed out, said, 'Well, my colored friend, what do you think of the situation?' 'I'm for the rights of the South in the territories,' promptly replied Elias," Sarah Polk remembered later. "This unexpected answer raised the hearty laughter of the whole party as they went down the gravel walk, and one of them said, 'You'd better not ask another darkey his political opinions in this section of the country.'"

Elias Polk would stay true to himself after emancipation, defending the southern Democratic Party of the local white elite class despite the majority of the newly freed African Americans joining the Republican Party of the assassinated President Abraham Lincoln. He was not popular among some of his own people because of that choice. "In spite of the great odium in which it brought him with the people of his own race he was out-spoken in his adherence to Democracy, the party to which that master to whose memory he was so devoted belonged," reported one newspaper. "In several campaigns he made speeches for his side and so enraged the colored people that they threatened, and once or twice tried, to kill him."

But that didn't stop Elias Polk, who was considered at one point to become a Conservative candidate for the Tennessee legislature. He was one of the leaders chosen to meet with then-military governor and future US president Andrew Johnson's train as it approached Nashville. By 1869, Polk along with other conservative blacks had helped local southern whites take over the government of Tennessee from the out-of-state Republicans, leading more radical blacks to call them "old house slaves" allying with their former masters to put whites back in power. Polk was one of those who even formed "Colored Democratic Clubs" and cooperated with white locals to oppose "carpetbaggers" sent in by the government to rebuild the Tennessee government after the war. When leaving the White House at the end of the Polks' presidential term, Elias Polk is reputed to have said, "Ah sho' hates to leave dis place." And he wouldn't stay gone. Polk would return to Washington repeatedly just to meet the president and keep his streak alive.

Elias Polk, a colored man, the old body-servant of the late President Polk, shook hands with President Cleveland at one of his recent public receptions. The old man is eighty-one years old, and lives with the venerable widow of the late President at Nashville, Tenn. His boast is that he has personally seen every President since John Quincy Adams, the latter included, and is determined to see them all while he lives.

Elias Polk eventually would move to Washington, DC, and get work. In 1875, he would go to work for the clerk of the US House with a patronage job, which he lost when Republicans took over the House in 1881. He returned to Tennessee, and married for the fourth time to a woman forty-one years younger than himself. But he returned to the Washington area again, settling in Alexandria, Virginia, and taking employment at the Post Office, "but resigned on account of his feeble health." That's where he would die, according to newspapers.

James K. Polk was rare among presidents in that he didn't just inherit slaves. Polk, like Jackson, actively—but secretly—bought slaves while president. Unlike Jackson, however, Polk didn't buy them in Washington, DC, but secretly back down south. Why the secrecy? Because during his career, Polk straddled the lines between slaveholders and abolitionists, never completely joining either side.

Polk was already a major slave owner when he became president but was very cautious about letting people know about his ownership of other people. Perhaps he was afraid of the American people—especially abolitionists—finding out that he was buying children. "Of the nineteen slaves Polk bought during his presidency, one was ten years old, two were eleven, two were twelve, two were thirteen, two were fifteen, two were sixteen, and two were seventeen," said William Dusinberre, author of the great *Slavemaster President: The Double Career of James Polk.* "Each of these children was bought apart from his or her parents and from every sibling. One or two of these thirteen children may possibly have been orphans, but it would strain credulity to suggest many of them were."

So Polk, who needed more labor for his plantation, did what most rich politicians would do in his situation: found a way to increase his personal wealth without his constituents finding out about it. He set up agents to buy the slaves in their names and then transferred them to his possession at home.

> *These purchases took place just before and soon after the introduction into Congress of the Wilmot Proviso, which—had it been enacted—would have barred the extension of slavery into any new territory acquired from Mexico. The president uttered dire warnings that his purchases must be kept secret. No one must learn that he was buying slaves. Polk's knowledge of the law assured him that nothing required the slaves to be registered in his name, even though his agents (who ostensibly bought the slaves for themselves) immediately remade them over to Polk. The president had discussed his plans with his brother-in-law John Childress in March 1846, and he soon spelled out the legal niceties: "You can take the title in your own name and make a quit-claim conveyance without warranty to me."*

He even made sure he had plausible deniability. Dusinberre noted that Polk—living in a pre–Civil War America—made sure that while he bought slaves in the White House, he never used his presidential salary.

"He used his savings from his salary to pay campaign debts, to buy and refurbish a mansion in Nashville, and to buy U.S. Treasury certificates, but never to buy slaves," Dusinberre said. "Evidently he distinguished his private income—from the plantation—the public salary he received from government revenues. Thus, if the public had ever learned of his buying young slaves, he could always have truthfully denied that he had spent his presidential salary for that purpose."

Polk may have been careful about how he bought his slaves because he knew slavery was an evil institution. But Polk kept his slaves throughout his life and didn't even free them upon death, leaving that for his wife.

John Tyler also in his mind separated his work as president of the United States and his work as a plantation slave owner. Tyler's opinion was that "he held no Slaves as President of the United States, & as John Tyler it was nobody's business."

Tyler was the first vice president to ascend to the position by death of the president, William Henry Harrison. (A popular campaign song, "Tippecanoe and Tyler Too," referred to their presidential ticket.) On the day of his inaugural, Harrison talked for two hours outside in freezing weather. About three weeks later, he developed a cold, which turned into pneumonia. Unable to rest partly because of a steady stream of visitors at the White House, he died a scant month after his inauguration.

Tyler, who had returned to his Virginia plantation after the election, rushed back to Washington. Although many politicians considered Tyler to be just an interim president, Tyler insisted that he had the full power of the office and had himself sworn in immediately and took residence inside the White House with his slaves, only two of whom we know by name, James Hambleton Christian and Armistead (who in some places is also called Henry). The firsts continued for Tyler, who also was the first president to be kicked out of his political party (the Whigs kicked him out because he refused to go along with their intention to create a Bank of the United States), and the first and so far only US president to join an enemy government. Tyler became a member of the government of the

Confederate States of America once the Civil War broke out, planning to serve in the Confederate House of Representatives. He died before opening sessions, and was buried under the Confederate flag and reviled as a traitor in the United States.

Armistead, a body servant of Tyler's, was killed in an explosion on a warship that was being toured by President Tyler. The naval warship the *Princeton* was the pride of the pre–Civil War navy, the first steam-powered ship with screw propellers instead of a paddlewheel. The seven-hundred-ton sloop was captained by Robert Stockton and named after his hometown of Princeton, New Jersey. Intended to be the first in a series of new frigates, the full-rigged sailing vessel was designed by Swedish-born John Ericsson, who went on later to design the Union's first iron-clad, the *Monitor*. The screw propellers weren't the only new thing on the *Princeton*. She also sported "the two largest guns in the U.S. Navy: the 'Oregon' fired 12-inch cannonballs and had been built in England to Ericsson's design. An even larger 12-inch cannon called the 'Peacemaker' weighed more than 27,000 pounds and had been cast in the United States under Stockton's supervision."

To show off the new ship, and to inspire new funding from the Congress and president, Stockton sailed his new ship up the Potomac to the District of Columbia so he could give tours of the vessel. Although several members of Congress had already been on board, the tour of February 28, 1844, was to be the crowning achievement of his goodwill trip. Showing up this time would be a White House contingent: the president himself, John Tyler, and Armistead, a longtime slave and body servant; the president's young fiancée, Julia Gardiner; her father, Colonel David Gardiner; two members of Tyler's Cabinet: Abel P. Upshur, secretary of state, and Thomas W. Gilmer, secretary of the navy; and even the venerable Dolley Madison, widow of former president James Madison. More than two hundred other dignitaries, including several members of Congress, had boarded the *Princeton* to sail down the river to celebrate the new ship.

Tyler, who was a widower by this point, had been courting Miss Gardiner, who had been given the name of "the Belle of Long Island" since her father was a former New York state senator and hailed from that state. After boarding the ship, and watching the sailors fire several of the ship's big guns, the president and his entourage went below decks to enjoy a sumptuous meal and champagne, which was one of Tyler's favorite drinks. Before beginning his toasts, Tyler noticed that Julia Gardiner and her father were still above decks, and sent a messenger to get them. Was this Armistead? The identity of the messenger was never made clear, but what is known is that Julia and her father came below decks to join the party. Toasts were made, and champagne was consumed until someone noted that the *Princeton* was passing Mount Vernon, the home of George Washington. Despite the fact that the guns, including the Peacemaker, had been fired several times already, it was suggested by Gilmer over Stockton's objections that they be fired again to honor the father of the country. The elder Gardiner, Upshur, Gilmer, and Stockton headed upstairs to watch the last barrage from the largest naval gun in the world, but Tyler hesitated because his son-in-law from his first marriage, William Waller, had just broken into song about 1776. That song may have saved his life, but not that of Armistead, who had requested permission to see the gun as it was fired. He either had been sent above decks to fetch Miss Gardiner and stayed, or went up with the dignitaries to see it being fired in honor of George Washington. Either way, it was his last act.

> *Just as the young man came to the word "Washington" in the lyrics, the great gun exploded, hurling fiery iron in all directions. The ship trembled, and a dense cloud of white smoke smothered the deck, making it almost impossible to see or breathe. According to the editor of the* Boston Times, *an eyewitness, when the smoke cleared, dead bodies and detached arms and legs littered the deck. The blast had killed Secretary of State Upshur; Secretary of the Navy Gilmer; Virgil Maxcy, the American chargé d'affaires to Belgium; Julia Gardiner's father; Beverly Kennon, the Navy's chief of construction; and the president's personal valet, a slave named Armistead.*

Several newspapers detailed the gruesome scene aboard the ship, which included several limbs, blood and brains splattered everywhere, decapitation and crushed skulls, and wailing from the survivors. It seems that Armistead was severely injured, struck by flying metal, living for only ten minutes after the explosion. The *Public Ledger* of Philadelphia, Pennsylvania, also reported in its March 1, 1844, edition "the President's mulatto servant, who was also badly wounded, has died since."

Armistead may have been the last death caused by the gun's explosion. "No death has occurred, in consequence of the terrible accident, besides those mentioned yesterday, except that of a servant of the president (a colored man) who was near the gun at the time of its exploding," reported the *National Intelligencer* a few days later.

John Tyler's son anonymously described the accident to the *Washington Times* in its April 14, 1895, edition and detailed how Armistead died. "They lay upon the deck, a Union flag having been hastily thrown over them in accordance with the naval regulations," the now-elderly president's son said. "My body servant, a negro boy of about twenty-three years of age, had been leaning against another gun which was hit by the flying metal and the jar killed him on the spot." Unless there was a second Tyler slave aboard, that was Armistead (it was not unknown for relatives to share possession of slaves and body servants).

Another eyewitness, George Sykes of Burlington County, New Jersey, also saw what happened to Armistead, and also didn't see him struck by any of the flying metal. "The president's servant was leaning against a cannon which was struck by a piece of the exploded gun," Sykes said in a letter to his sister. "He was a stout black man about 23 or 24 years old and lived about an hour after when they came to examine him and lay him out neither the surgeon of the *Princeton* nor any other person could discover the slightest wound or injury about him."

In death, Armistead was treated differently than the other men who were killed. Reports of the disaster have Tyler weeping over the deaths of the members of his Cabinet, and comforting his fiancée who also lost her father in the explosion, but there is no mention of Tyler ever even expressing disappointment at the loss of his slave and body servant, who likely spent more time with him than any other human being. When it came time to remove the bodies from the *Princeton* "they were all placed in magnificent mahogany caskets, except for Armistead, who was placed in one made from cherry."

The carriages carrying the bodies of the dignitaries and Armistead left the Washington Naval Yard and headed to the White House to lie in state in the East Room, but there was one last indignity for Armistead. His carriage would not make the trip to the White House where he worked.

The crowds parted to make way as the horse-drawn hearses began their unhappy journey across town. More than sixty carriages pulled into line and followed the cortege to the White House, where Tyler ordered that the bodies lie in state until the funeral Saturday morning. Somewhere along the route, the hearse bearing Armistead's coffin had peeled off and delivered the slave's remains to his family.

There was no details published of Armistead's funeral. "The president's servant was buried by the coloured persons—and his relations—the next day after the accident," Sykes said in his letter.

Armistead's death left behind other slaves at the White House to work for Tyler, including James Hambleton Christian. However, Christian was one of those slaves who apparently didn't like his master that well, despite his fortune at being a house slave. Interviewed after obtaining his freedom, Christian said he was very young when first brought to the president's house. According to him, he was fathered by a slave master named Major Robert Christian in Virginia on the Cedar Grove Plantation. When asked later whether he was related to the Christians of Cedar Grove, he replied candidly, "I am Christian's son." He was very clearly mixed race in appearance, with "about fifty percent of Anglo-Saxon blood . . . visible in his features and his hair, which gave him no inconsiderable claim to sympathy and care." His half-brother took possession of him upon their father's death, and passed him along to their sister, Letitia, who ended up becoming Mrs. John Tyler.

That means that the Tylers brought to Washington the first lady's half-brother to serve as their slave. "He became a member of the President's domestic household, was at the White House, under the President, from 1841 to 1845," said biographer William Still. "Though but very young at that time, James was only fit for training in the arts, science, and mystery of waiting, in which profession, much pains were taken to qualify him completely for his calling."

Christian didn't like Tyler as a master at all, and like many house slaves, conflated his own sense of self-worth with the fortune of his slave masters, who were rich. "Mr. Tyler was a poor man. I never did like poor people. I didn't like his marrying into our family, who were considered very far Tyler's superiors," Christian said.

Tyler also was not a kind man, he said. "On the plantation," Christian said, "Tyler was a very cross man, and treated the servants very cruelly; but the house servants were treated much better, owing to their having belonged to his wife, who protected them from persecution, as they had been favorite servants in her father's family."

He likely also got protection because of his close familial relationship with the president's wife. But his half-sister died in 1842, leaving Tyler a widower, and willed Christian and his mother to her nephew, Virginia merchant William H. Christian.

It was at the merchant's home in Richmond where James Christian decided he had enough of being a slave. It wasn't because of how he was being treated—"I have always been treated well; if I only have half as good times in the North as I have had in the South, I shall be perfectly satisfied," he said—and it wasn't because he was being starved or beaten or uneducated: "With regard to apparel and jewelry, he had worn the best, as an every-day adornment. With regard to food also, he had fared as well as heart could wish, with abundance of leisure time at his command," Still said. Christian had also picked up some schooling at the College of William and Mary while attending with one of his father's children. So why did he run?

What prompted James to leave such pleasant quarters? It was this: He had become enamored of a young and respectable free girl in Richmond, with whom he could not be united in marriage solely because he was a slave, and did not own himself. The frequent sad separations of such married couples (where one or the other was a slave) could not be overlooked; consequently, the poor fellow concluded that he would stand a better chance of gaining his object in Canada than by remaining in Virginia. So he began to feel that he might himself be sold some day, and thus the resolution came home to him very forcibly to make tracks for Canada.

Christian, like many other slaves, vanishes into history at this point. But the fact that Tyler held slaves while president wasn't overlooked by abolitionists and journalists of his day, who took the president to task every chance they got, whether truthfully or not. One account came during the celebration of the Bunker Hill Monument in Massachusetts. Tyler traveled there to help dedicate the monument at the location of the first full-scale action between American militia and British regulars in the Revolution, but he apparently didn't go alone.

"'The Liberator' says that President Tyler brought with him on his pilgrimage to Bunker Hill ONE OF HIS SLAVES," trumpeted the *Liberator* on July 21, 1843, repeating an article from the *Woonsocket Patriot*. "If this be true, it was an act of indignity which ought not to be allowed to pass unnoticed."

An unnamed author—"a colored man" who wrote for the *United States Clarion*—wrote in the same newspaper that he had watched the dedication ceremony, and noticed something strange. "Three strange looking colored men were seen on the common; there were other colored men present, but those three looked very strange, and they acted very strangely," he said. "It was observed that while others were forcing their way towards the President, they kept as far from him as possible."

The ceremony continued, with Tyler taking the podium to give his blessing to the dedication. He was then followed by Daniel Webster, the great orator and secretary of state under Tyler. Considered one of the best speakers of his time, Webster captivated the crowd extolling the virtues of liberty and courage. And then:

A tremendous commotion took place—the ladies screamed, and every body was thrown into the greatest excitement. Presently these three strange looking men whom we saw on the common, rushed by, pursued by as many constables, all dressed up in Liberty's ribands.—"Stop them! stop them!" they cried; and the poor fellows being followed so closely, they took shelter behind the monument. Webster was compelled to stop speaking. The constables came up, and dragged them out, while they clung to the consecrated stone and wept, and pointed to the American Constitution that was hung to it, and begged to be protected. It was all in vain. They were three of the thirty slaves of John Tyler, who had taken the advantage of their masters' absence, and ran away. They were chained, and hurried away from the ground and the Constitution . . .

A dramatic tale, and one you would think would have been repeated over and over in the media of that day. It wasn't, and the reason why is likely because it never happened. The unnamed writer, having plucked at the heartstrings of his readers, caps his story off with one line that makes clear his intention: "All of this might have happened, though it did not."

While those are the only slave-holding presidents to have slaves inside the White House, there were other presidents who owned slaves at times during their lives. They include the aforementioned Harrison, who inherited around a dozen slaves from his father. He took at least seven with him when he went to the Northwest Territory in 1800, but there slavery was illegal. So to get around that, Harrison converted the terms of slavery into indentured servitude, which would last about a decade. He even sought out slaves to convert into indentured servants. "The woman should be of such a character as will promise fidelity in the performance of her engagements," he said in a letter. "I will agree that she shall be free at from 6 to 8 years in proportion to the price she may cost." How many of these "indentured servants" ended up working inside the White House for the month he was there?

And then there was Martin Van Buren, who was from one of those northern slave-holding families, a situation that may not have been as rare as some people like to think.

Van Buren's father, who lived in Kinderhook, New York, kept six slaves during his life, and Van Buren himself owned a slave named Tom, who ran away around 1814. When he was discovered ten years later by A. G. Hammond, Van Buren agreed to sell Tom for fifty dollars if Hammond could "get him without violence." Van Buren did not have any slaves inside the White House with him, as far as we can tell.

James Buchanan briefly became a slave master in order to free two slaves and protect his political career. While running for Senate in Pennsylvania, he decided to go visit his sister Harriet, whose husband owned two slaves. So in 1835, Buchanan decided to buy the twenty-two-year-old Daphne Cook, and her five-year-old daughter Ann, but didn't free them. Instead, Buchanan arranged to indenture Daphne and Ann Cook under the gradual emancipation laws of Pennsylvania.

"Daphne should give service to Buchanan for seven years and then become free, as provided in Pennsylvania law; and that Ann should be bound until the age of 28, seven years past the age of maturity," the agreement said. The Cooks performed household work at his Lancaster home.

Lastly, people are always surprised at the fact that Grant, the Union's general during the Civil War, was also a slaveholder. Grant owned at least one slave during his time as a Missouri farmer, acquiring William Jones from his father-in-law Col. Frederick Dent. Grant married Julia Dent in 1848, and the Grants lived on the White Haven plantation and were active in managing the place, which included more than two dozen slaves.

He then borrowed a slave from his father-in-law, one William Jones. Jones was about thirty-five and five-foot-seven, and was said to resemble "Grant in both age and build," according to William S. McFeely, author of the seminal book, *Grant*.

His wife can lay claim to slaves as well: Eliza, Julia, John, and Dan. Mrs. Grant brought Julia along on her visits to the then-General Grant's headquarters, causing not a little amount of trouble for the Union leader, who had opponents report back to Washington, DC, that his wife had her "little slaves" with her.

Grant personally freed William Jones on March 29, 1859. "I Ulysses S. Grant ... do hereby manumit, emancipate and set free from Slavery my Negro man William, sometimes called William Jones ... forever," he said in Jones's manumission papers. The rest of the slaves walked off of White Haven during the Civil War, and Missouri's new constitution ended slavery in January 1865, freeing anyone else left behind.

While his presidency preceded that of General Grant's, it is the slaves of Andrew Johnson who provide the final link from the enslaved slaves of the President's House to the domestic workers of the White House today.

Johnson, who inherited the White House after the assassination of President Abraham Lincoln, likely wouldn't have been anyone's choice in the North to lead the reconstruction of the country after the beaten Confederate states finally surrendered. Like Lincoln, Johnson was born in a log cabin, only for the seventeenth president it was in the wilds of North Carolina instead of Illinois. Illiterate for most of his childhood and teenage years, Johnson did not understand basic reading, grammar, or math until he met his wife at the age of seventeen.

Surprisingly for a southern slave master, Johnson knew personally about trying to run away to find freedom and a better life. As a child, Johnson's family was so poor his mother and his stepfather apprenticed a then-fourteen-year-old Johnson and an older brother to a local tailor named James Selby. But Johnson wasn't satisfied with the life of an apprentice (he was contractually obligated to stay with Selby until his twenty-first birthday), and ran away. Johnson's escape inspired the tailor to post reward posters for the future president and his brother that were very similar to slave escape posters, down to the warning against people helping the escaped apprentices.

RAN AWAY from the Subscriber, on the night of the 15th instant, two apprentice boys, legally bound, named WILLIAM and ANDREW JOHNSON. The former is of a dark complexion, black hair, eyes, and habits. They are much of a height, about 5 feet 4 or 5 inches. The latter is very fleshy, freckled face, light hair, and fair complexion. . . . They were well clad—blue cloth coats, light colored homespun coats, and new hats, the maker's name in the crown of the hats, is Theodore Clark. I will pay the above reward to any person who will deliver said apprentices to me in Raleigh, or I will give the above Reward for Andrew Johnson alone. All persons are cautioned against harboring or employing said apprentices, on pain of being prosecuted.

After staying away for a few years, Johnson returned to fulfill his contract but Selby had moved on and would not forgive him or re-employ him. Seeking his fortune, the future president left the state and headed west to Tennessee. Moving his parents to Greeneville, Tennessee, Johnson opened his own successful tailor shop, and met and married his wife, Eliza, the daughter of a shoemaker. He quickly pivoted into politics, serving in succession as a local alderman, in the state legislature, in the US House of Representatives, as Tennessee governor, and then as US senator, where he caught the North's attention by refusing to go along with Tennessee when it defected from the Union to join the Confederacy. He was the only member of the Senate from a Confederate state to remain at his post.

In a speech made March 2, 1861, *Harper's Weekly* recorded him saying: "Show me those who make war on the Government and fire on its vessels, and I will show you a traitor. If I were President of the United States I would have all such arrested, and, if convicted, by the Eternal God I would have them hung!"

After US forces captured Tennessee, Lincoln sent Johnson down to run the state as a military governor, which left Johnson extremely unpopular within his own state's people (his property was confiscated and his wife and two daughters were driven from the state) but a hero to the North. Because of his loyalty to the United States, Tennessee was exempted from the Emancipation Proclamation. Why did Andrew Johnson care? Because he was a slave owner too.

In 1842, Johnson bought his first slave, a fourteen-year-old girl named Dolly. According to family lore, Dolly saw Andrew Johnson at a slave auction, and walking up to the white man, asked him to buy her "because she liked his looks." Purchased for five hundred dollars as household help, Johnson went back later to buy her twelve-year-old half-brother Sam, who would become his favorite slave. Over the course of his life, Johnson would own somewhere between six and ten slaves.

Johnson apparently wasn't a harsh slave master, likely because he was a businessman and not a plantation owner.

In fact, according to Mrs. Patterson, it was a mistake to call Sam a slave at all. She often laughed and said that Sam did not belong to her father but her father belonged to Sam. Tall and dignified, black as coal, Sam was one of the best known characters in Greeneville, and a thorough gentleman. He at least was an aristocrat.

Sam Johnson, slave of President Andrew Johnson, who followed him to Washington, D.C., and eventually ends up working for the Freedman's Bureau. PHOTO COURTESY OF THE NATIONAL PARK SERVICE

But Johnson's other children thought he was too lenient. In a letter to his father, Charles Johnson suggests selling Sam because of his attitude.

"A few days since Mother sent him word to cut wood at Pattersons,—he came up in the house and said, he would 'be damed' if he wanted to cut wood there; and if you wanted to sell him you could just do so, just as soon as you pleased, he did not care a dam," wrote Johnson. "You will see he is quite an independent gentleman and just to show his notions of himself and his rights, at another time he was asking Mother for his part of some money paid him for work."

Sam was never sold. But as he rose up the political ladder in the North, Johnson's wife Eliza knew that he wouldn't advance very far as a slave owner. Therefore, she gathered her family's slaves together at their East Tennessee farm on August 8, 1863, to deliver the news. Dolly's son, William, remembered it happening this way: "She said we were free now. She said we were free to go, or we could stay if we wanted. We all stayed."

This came just in time for Johnson to get the vice presidential nomination on Abraham Lincoln's reelection ticket. Once freed, some of the slaves chose to stay in Tennessee. For example, his body servant Bill ended up taking over Johnson's tailor shop in Greeneville. A *New York Herald* reporter wrote in 1869 "an old negro raised by President Johnson and assuming his name is the sole occupant of the building and he is the successor in the business of 'A. Johnson, Tailor.' He says, 'Massa Johnson been in the trade, boss tailor in dese diggings.'"

Other slaves stayed with the Johnsons, including Dolly's children, Florence and another slave named Henry; they followed them all the way to the nation's capital but instead of working for them as slaves, they worked for them as freemen servants, including inside the White House. Little is known about the White House time of Johnson's slaves, but it is known that his time in Washington ended with Sam Johnson deciding to work for the Freedman's Bureau, which assisted freed slaves.

Several of Johnson's now ex-slaves would return to Tennessee with him after his term in office, and continue to work for his family, now in their employ instead of being enslaved. They would stay with him in familiar roles, even though they were free.

For example, Bill would continue as Johnson's body servant, sleeping in the same room as the ex-president.

When night came he would stir around and get a pair of blankets and make a pallet in the same room with old Mas'r. When he would get back home, tall tales Bill would tell about his trip. "Old Mas'r," he would say, "let dem po' white folks know de body servant's place was in de room wid him," wisely shaking his woolly head and ha-ha-ing with laughter.

Other slaves may have had other reasons to stay with Johnson. During her life, Dolly would have three children: Liz; Florence, who went to Washington with the Johnsons; and William Andrew Johnson, who ended up with the first name of the president's beloved brother William and the president's first name as his middle name. Johnson was very fond of these children, with William saying later in his life "Mr. Andrew used to hold me on one knee and my sister on the other, and he'd rub our heads and laugh." Dolly's children did not go unnoticed by the public, and neither did the kindness Johnson showed them.

Although described by census takers as "black," her light-skinned children were listed as "mulattos." Their father might have been anybody in Greeneville, yet Johnson's gentleness toward her children, together with the fact that William was given the same forename as Johnson's brother, led Tennessee whites to speculate that Andrew Johnson maintained a "colored concubine."

Others have said the fathers of Dolly's children were Andrew Johnson's sons, but nothing has been proven conclusively either way. (William's death certificate lists Robert Johnson as his father, but obviously William Johnson didn't have any say on what that document said.) Either way, William Andrew Johnson, who was somewhere between five and seven years old when the president's wife freed his mother and himself, ended up staying with Johnson as well, and was at his bedside as he deteriorated.

"I used to sit by the side of his bed day and night," William Johnson remembered later. "He was paralyzed on one side. He would reach over with his good arm and take hold of his wrist and say, 'Is that your hand, William?' And I'd say, 'No, Mr. Andrew, that's your own hand.'"

Johnson would die of a stroke while out visiting his daughter Mary in Carter County, Tennessee. Dolly and William Johnson would take over the Johnsons' tailor shop and begin to sell baked goods out of the store. William would end up getting good as a chef, and would go on to become a well-known cook in Knoxville, Tennessee.

When William Johnson was older, President Franklin Roosevelt visited Tennessee to dedicate the Norris Dam. Johnson, like some earlier slaves, thought it would be a good idea to shake the current president's hand, feeling a connection to the officer through his service to the now-deceased President Johnson. However, the ex-slave couldn't get close enough to Roosevelt to actually shake the man's hand, and left feeling disappointed.

Along came famed newspaperman Ernie Pyle, who was back in the United States taking a break from his war correspondent work. Instead of writing about battles and death, Pyle had decided to tell some stories about interesting people and places he found in America. And one day, he came across William Andrew Johnson, and decided to write about him in his column.

"William Andrew Johnson is a happy old man with a distinction," Pyle wrote. "He is, so far as he knows, the only living ex-slave of a president. He's mighty proud of it."

Pyle wrote in his column about Johnson's attempt to shake Roosevelt's hand and his status as the last living slave of a US president. Roosevelt apparently read Pyle's column, and told the Secret Service to go and collect William Johnson and bring him to the White House. "A gentleman just come to me and asked if I wanted to come to Washington," Johnson would tell The United Press in 1937.

Followed by cameras, Johnson was escorted by the Secret Service to a snowy Washington, DC, in February 1937 by train, and picked up at Union Station by a presidential limousine and whisked to the White House, where some of his relatives stayed with President Johnson. "A few minutes later he was not only shaking hands with the president, he was sitting down and talking to him—talking to him for half an hour about the old days back in Tennessee when he was just a little boy in the home of another president," The United Press story says.

"I told him about when President Johnson died," he continued in an Associated Press story. "I slept with him six days and six nights down in Tennessee after he had a stroke."

Johnson had nothing but good things to say about Roosevelt, who financed his day-long trip to the District of Columbia. "FDR reminds me a heap of Andrew Johnson. That's what I like about him so much. He's my kind of white folks," he said in an International News Service story.

Roosevelt, after meeting with Johnson in the Oval Office, sent him on his way with a Secret Service escort that took him to see the sights in the nation's capital, including the Lincoln Memorial and the US Capitol where Johnson had presided over the Senate as vice president. But before he left the White House, Roosevelt noticed that the cane being used by the seventy-nine-year-old man was a bit worn.

"Mr. Roosevelt gave me a silver-headed cane," Johnson continued. "My old cane was just about worn out, and Mr. Roosevelt noticed it. I guess this new one will last me the rest of my life."

Johnson went back to his chef job in Knoxville, where he died in 1943, with that cane never leaving his side. An exchange with Ernie Pyle earlier in his life summed up what most of the slaves of the president seemed to have concluded about their lives with the chief executive.

"White folks have been awful good to me," William said. Pyle then followed up by asking him if he wasn't better off when Andrew Johnson owned him than as a poor cook in a southern restaurant.

William Andrew Johnson, former slave of President Andrew Johnson, in his younger days. Johnson would be one of the only presidential slaves honored by a sitting president during his lifetime. LIBRARY OF CONGRESS

William Andrew Johnson replied, "Yes, we were mighty well off then. But any man would rather be free than be a slave."

CHAPTER 12

CONCLUSION

So far, William Andrew Johnson is the only slave of a US president who has been honored by a holder of that office.

Having lost their youth to slavery, these African American men and women were part of the origins of this country and deserve to be honored along with all of the others who worked with and for the president. And their day may soon be coming.

The government in the past ignored the use of slaves in the construction of the US Capitol. But now, after years of research and lobbying, Congress dedicated the largest room in the newest portion of the Capitol Complex, the US Capitol Visitor Center, to those slaves by naming it "Emancipation Hall" and placing a bronze plaque inside the Capitol recognizing those slaves' work that reads: "This original exterior wall was constructed between 1793 and 1800 of sandstone quarried by laborers, including enslaved African Americans who were an important part of the workforce that built the United States Capitol." These meager efforts took a decade, a congressional panel, several media reports, and at least one book to accomplish.

In Philadelphia, some effort has been made to remember the nine slaves who lived inside the President's House with Washington. Their names have been listed in concrete at the excavation site, and included in the President's House exhibit is an explanation of who these slaves were, what Washington and his wife did to keep them enslaved, and even a description of Oney Judge's escape from the president at the site.

No similar effort has been made to honor the slaves who worked on and lived inside the White House, until now. A New York congressman,

Gary Ackerman, sent a letter to President Obama in February 2012 asking him to recognize the role played by African American slaves by putting an "appropriate acknowledgement" in a public area of the White House.

> *Slaves helped dig the foundation for the White House. They quarried stone that would be used for the walls, dug up clay for thousands of bricks, cut timber, sawed lumber, and performed carpentry inside the White House. Even after White House construction was completed, slaves continued to support White House operations. Slaves served in White House domestic staff from 1800 through the Civil War.*
>
> *While slavery is no monument worthy of national pride, the American way has always been to acknowledge our wrongs and constantly strive for better. It is wrong not to acknowledge wrongs. An acknowledgment of the role of slave labor displayed in the White House would be an important symbol that the United States does not run from its history, but rather learns from it. That is something of which all Americans can be proud.*

It is hard to say it better than that. Perhaps it won't be long before these brave men and women get their due.

Since Obama's election, at least some of the descendants of presidential slaves have gotten inside the White House to view some of the areas where their ancestors lived. The most prominent group of White House slave descendants is the family of Paul Jennings, the slave of James Madison.

Jennings is likely the best-known White House slave following the excellent book by Elizabeth Dowling Taylor. Following the publicity from Taylor's book, the plantation and presidential center where Madison lived, Montpelier, organized a tour of the White House for the Jennings family. It just so happened that the tour of the White House fell on the 195th anniversary of the rescue of the Gilbert Stuart Landsdowne portrait of George Washington, which Dolley Madison took credit for but Jennings wrote that she didn't do alone.

White House curator William G. Allman took the family into the East Room, where that painting hangs today. The family then got together for a picture with the portrait before touring the rest of the White House, including the Green, Blue, and Red Rooms, and State Dining Room.

Hugh Alexander, who is a great-great-grandson of Jennings, told National Public Radio that day that being inside the White House and seeing that painting of George Washington was one of the greatest thrills of his life. "To actually see the painting of George Washington that my great-great-grandfather played a part in saving," he said. "That painting means so much as being one of the key artifacts that's left over from that period. And it's just pretty amazing to actually see it close up."

As we have discovered, some slaves' time inside the White House turned out to be beneficial for them in the long run: Paul Jennings used his experiences with James Madison to write the first tell-all book about life inside the executive mansion after gaining his freedom; Fanny Hern and Edy Fossett would use the skills they learned while working for a White House chef to become celebrated, though still enslaved, chefs at Monticello; Oney Judge escaped from slavery while working in the presidential mansion in Philadelphia, while Hercules's time with Washington in Philadelphia likely led to his decision to try for his freedom.

For others, their time in the executive mansion was not as positive. These slaves would leave the President's House with their situation no better than it was when they first showed up in the nation's capital. Not only would they be forced to return to Mount Vernon, Monticello, or Montpelier as enslaved human beings, many of them would have to wait until the death of their president and his wife, or even the Civil War to taste freedom—this despite being around some of the greatest revolutionary thinkers of all time, despite being present in the blossoming days of what can be considered the freest country in the world, despite being owned by men who claimed to believe in the right of men to be free.

The end of this book does not mark the conclusion of the stories that need to be told about African American slavery inside the White House. There is still much more to be done before we understand the lives of the men and women who were brought to the nation's capital as slaves of the president.

It is very encouraging to realize that historians around the nation are now focusing on the lives of the African American slaves at the presidential plantations. I am also continuing my investigation, scouring records and books to update what I have already written, and I hope to one day update this book with more stories of the White House slaves. I'm sure that one day Americans will be holding a book that contains all of the stories of these remarkable men and women.

I hope this book will honor the presidential slaves' suffering and sacrifice, and that it will accurately portray their spirit in a way that would make them proud. Most of all, I hope that it ensures that future generations do not forget that before America had a black president living inside the White House, it had black slaves living in bondage inside those same walls.

It's worth remembering.

BIBLIOGRAPHY

Abbot, W.W., ed. *The Papers of George Washington, Retirement Series, Vol. 4, April–December 1799.* Charlottesville: University Press of Virginia, 1999.

Alexandria Gazette, January 3, 1887.

Anderson, James Douglas, and Bailie Peyton. *Making the American Thoroughbred: Especially in Tennessee, 1800–1845.* Plimpton Press, 1916.

Arnebeck, Bob. *Through a Fiery Trial: Building Washington 1790–1800.* Lanham, MD: Madison Books, 1991.

Arnebeck, Bob. "The Use of Slaves to Build the Capitol and White House 1791–1801," www.geocities.com/Bobarnebeck/slaves.html, accessed April 6, 2012.

The *Atlanta Constitution,* Thursday, January 30, 1873.

Baptist, Edward E. "'Cuffy,' 'Fancy Maids,' and 'One-Eyed Men': Rape, Commodification, and the Domestic Slave Trade in the United States." *American Historical Review* 106, no. 5 (December 2001), 1619–50.

Barnes, Thurlow Weed and Thurlow Weed. *Life of Thurlow Weed Including His Autobiography and a Memoir: Volume 2.* Houghton Mifflin and Co., 1884.

Bayard, Samuel John. *A Sketch of the Life of Com. Robert F. Stockton; with an Appendix, Comprising His Correspondence with the Navy Department Respecting His Conquest of California; and Extracts from the Defence of Col. J. C. Fremont, in Relation to the Same Subject; Together with His Speeches in the Senate of the United States and His Political Letters.* http://quod.lib.umich.edu/cgi/t/text/text-idx?c=moa&cc=moa&sid=95e3f6e828e116b80d4cccd93c806bc1&view=text&rgn=main&idno=ABT5063.0001.001.

Bergen, Anthony. February 21, 2015, "Deadly 'Peacemaker,' Unlikely Matchmaker," http://deadpresidents.tumblr.com/post/6872957404/deadly-peacemaker-unlikely-matchmaker.

Berlin, Ira. "The Structure of the Free Negro Caste in the Antebellum United States." *Journal of Social History* 9, no. 3 (Spring 1976), 297–318.

Betts, Edwin Morris, ed. *Thomas Jefferson's Farm Book*. Princeton, NJ: Published for the American Philosophical Society by Princeton University Press, 1953.

Bever, Lucia, ed. *Memoirs and Letters of Dolly Madison: Wife of James Madison, President of the United States*. Boston: Houghton, Mifflin and Co., 1886. Google e-book, accessed April 6, 2012.

Bibb, Henry. *Narrative of the Life and Adventures of Henry Bibb, an American Slave, Written by Himself*. http://docsouth.unc.edu/neh/bibb/menu.html, accessed April 6, 2012.

Billings, Warren M. *The Old Dominion in the Seventeenth Century: A Documentary History of Virginia, 1606–1700*. Chapel Hill: Published for the Omohundro Institute of Early American History and Culture, Williamsburg, VA, by the University of North Carolina Press, 2009.

Blackman, Ann. Accessed on April 30, 2015. "The Fatal Cruise of the Princeton," www.military.com/NewContent/0,13190,NH_0905_Cruise-P1,00.html.

Blackman, Ann. *Wild Rose: Rose O'Neale Greenhow, Civil War Spy*. New York: Random House, 2005.

Brinkerhoff, Roeliff. *Recollections of a Lifetime*. Cincinnati: The Robert Clarke Co., 1904.

Brooks, Elbridge S. *A Son of the Revolution: Being the Story of Young Tom Edwards, Adventurer, and How He Labored for Liberty and Fought It Out with His Conscience in the Days of Burr's Conspiracy*. Boston: W.A. Wilde, 1898.

Brown, Dale. *American Cooking*. New York: Time-Life Books, 1968.

Browning, James R. "Anti-Miscegenation Laws in the United States." *Duke Bar Journal* 1, no. 1 (March 1951), 26–41.

Bryan, Helen. *Martha Washington: First Lady of Liberty*. New York: Wiley, 2002.

Bryan, Wilhelmus Bogart. *A History of the National Capital from Its Foundation Through the Period of the Adoption of the Organic Act.* New York: The Macmillan Co., 1916.

Buell, Augustus C. *History of Andrew Jackson, Pioneer, Patriot, Soldier, Politician, President.* New York: C. Scribner's Sons, 1904.

Bushong, William. "The Horse and the White House," *Equestrian,* November 1, 2008, 42–49.

Carpenter, Frank G. "Our Presidents As Horsemen," *Magazine of American History* 17 (January 1, 1887).

Chernow, Ron. *Washington: A Life.* New York: Penguin Press, 2010.

"Chronicles of the Black Jockeys Volume I: When 'Monkey Simon' Dealt Defeat to 'Old Hickory', General Andrew Jackson," Ealy Mays Artworks, www.ealymaysartworks.com/news/art-narratives-in-focus/281-legend-of-the-black-jockey-when-monkey-simon-dealt-defeat-to-old-hickory-himself-president-andrew-jackson, accessed April 30, 2015.

Cleaves, Freeman. *Old Tippecanoe: William Henry Harrison and His Time.* American Political Biography Press, 1990.

Colonial Williamsburg, www.history.org, accessed April 6, 2012.

Cruz, Bárbara C. and Michael J. Berson. "The American Melting Pot? Miscegenation Laws in the United States." *OAH Magazine of History* 15, no. 4, Family History (Summer 2001), 80–84.

Custalow, Dr. Linwood "Little Bear" and Angela L. Daniel "Silver Star." *The True Story of Pocahontas: The Other Side of History.* Golden, CO: Fulcrum Pub., 2007.

Custis, George Washington Parke. *Recollections and Private Memoirs of Washington.* New York: Derby & Jackson, 1860.

Davis, T. R. "Negro Servitude in the United States: Servitude Distinguished from Slavery." *Journal of Negro History* 8, no. 3 (July 1923), 247–83.

"Debasing Tendency of Slavery—The President's House Converted into a Stall for Fattening Slaves," *Liberator,* August 4, 1837, 4.

Decatur, Stephen and Tobias Lear. *Private Affairs of George Washington, from the Records and Accounts of Tobias Lear, Esquire, His Secretary.* Boston: Houghton Mifflin Co., 1933.

DeGregorio, William A. *The Complete Book of U.S. Presidents.* New York: Dembner Books, 1984.

De Tocqueville, Alexis. *Democracy in America.* Indianapolis: Liberty Fund, 2012.

DeWitt, Dave. *The Founding Foodies: How Washington, Jefferson, and Franklin Revolutionized American Cuisine.* Naperville, IL: Sourcebooks, 2010.

Dillon, Merton Lynn. *Slavery Attacked: Southern Slaves and Their Allies, 1619–1865.* Baton Rouge: Louisiana State University Press, 1991.

Dorris, Mary C. *Preservation of the Hermitage, 1889–1915: Annals, History, and Stories.* Nashville: Smith & Lamar, 1915.

Drake, Samuel Adams. *Historic Mansions and Highways Around Boston: Being a New and Rev. Ed. of "Old Landmarks and Historic Fields of Middlesex."* Boston: Little, Brown, and Co., 1899.

Dusinberre, William. *Slavemaster President: The Double Career of James Polk.* New York: Oxford University Press, 2003.

"Early Days of the Turn in Kentucky and Tennessee," *Courier-Journal,* May 6, 1894.

Egerton, Douglas R. *The Wars of Reconstruction: The Brief, Violent History of America's Most Progressive Era.* New York : Bloomsbury, 2013.

"Elias Polk's Death. The Remarkable Man Who Was President Polk's Servant—Gen. Jackson's Kindness," *St. Louis Post Dispatch,* January 17, 1887.

"An Englishman's Opinion of Mr. Polk," *Eastern Carolina Republican,* August 8, 1849, 1.

Equiano, Olaudiah. *The Interesting Narrative of the Life of Olaudah Equiano: or, Gustavus Vassa, the African.* Google e-book, accessed April 6, 2012.

Farrow, Anne, Joel Lang, and Jenifer Frank. *Complicity: How the North Promoted, Prolonged, and Profited from Slavery.* New York: Ballantine Books, 2005.

Federal Writers' Project. *Washington, City and Capital.* Washington, DC: US Government Printing Office, 1937.

Finley, Randy, and Thomas A. DeBlack. *The Southern Elite and Social Change: Essays in Honor of Willard B. Gatewood, Jr.* Fayetteville: University of Arkansas Press, 2002.

"The First Black Americans," *U.S. News and World Report*, www.usnews .com/usnews/news/articles/070121/29african.htm, accessed April 6, 2012.

Fogel, Robert William, and Stanley L. Engerman. *Time on the Cross: The Economics of American Negro Slavery.* Boston: Little, Brown, 1974.

Francis, Mary Cornelia. *A Son of Destiny: The Story of Andrew Jackson.* New York City: Federal Book Company, 1903.

Free African Americans of Maryland and Delaware, www.freeafrican americans.com/Intro_md.htm, accessed April 6, 2012.

Freedom in the Archives: Free African Americans in Colonial America, www.common-place.org/vol-05/no-01/heinegg-hoff/index.shtml, accessed April 6, 2012.

Galle, Jillian E., and Amy L. Young. *Engendering African American Archaeology: A Southern Perspective.* Knoxville: University of Tennessee Press, 2004.

Garrett, Romeo B. *The Presidents and the Negro.* Peoria, Ill: Association for the Study of Afro-American Life and History, 1982. Print.

Garrett, Wendell D. *Our Changing White House.* Boston: Northeastern University Press, 1995.

"General Jackson" *Estherville Daily News*, December 1, 1892.

Gordon-Reed, Annette. *The Hemingses of Monticello: An American Family.* New York: W. W. Norton & Company, 2008.

Greeley, Horace. *The American Conflict: A History of the Great Rebellion in the United States of America, 1860–'64: Its Causes, Incidents, and Results: Intended to Exhibit Especially Its Moral and Political Phases, with the Drift and Progress of American Opinion Respecting Human Slavery from 1776 to the Close of the War for the Union, Volume 1.* Chicago: O.D. Case, 1864.

Greene, Richard Henry, et al. *The New York Genealogical and Biographical Record.* New York: The New York Genealogical and Biographical Society, 1892.

Griswold, Rufus Wilmot. *The Republican Court: or, American Society in the Days of Washington.* New York: D. Appleton, 1854.

Guild, Josephus Conn. *Old Times in Tennessee: With Historical, Personal, and Political Scraps and Sketches.* Nashville, Tavel, Eastman & Howell, 1878.

Gutzman, Kevin R. C. *James Madison and the Making of America.* New York: St. Martin's Press, 2012.

Hapgood, Norman. *George Washington.* New York: Macmillan & Co., 1901.

Harris, Jessica B. *The Welcome Table: African-American Heritage Cooking.* New York: Simon & Schuster, 1995.

Heinegg, Paul. *Free African Americans of North Carolina, Virginia, and South Carolina from the Colonial Period to About 1820.* Baltimore, Md: Clearfield, 2005.

Heiskell, Samuel Gordon, and John Sevier. *Andrew Jackson and Early Tennessee History.* Nashville, TN: Ambrose Print. Co., 1920.

Herbert, Leila. *The First American: His Homes and His Households.* New York: Harper & Brothers, 1900.

Hirschfeld, Fritz. *George Washington and Slavery: A Documentary Portrayal.* Columbia: University of Missouri, 1997.

The Historic Blue Grass Line. Nashville: Nashville-Gallatin Interurban Railway, 1913.

"Historical Record" *The New England Magazine and Bay State Monthly.* P 285-286.

The Historical Record: *A Quarterly Publication Devoted Principally to the Early History of Wyoming Valley and Contiguous Territory: With Notes and Queries, Biographical, Antiquarian, Genealogical.* Wilkes-Barre, PA: Press of the Wilkes-Barre Record, 1887, http://catalog. hathitrust.org/api/volumes/oclc/48064695.html.

Hodes, Martha Elizabeth. *White Women, Black Men: Illicit Sex in the Nineteenth-Century South.* New Haven, CT: Yale University Press, 1997.

Holland, Jesse J. *Black Men Built the Capitol: Discovering African-American History In and Around Washington, D.C.* Guilford, CT: Globe Pequot Press, 2007.

Horton, James Oliver, and Lois E. Horton. *Slavery and the Making of America*. Oxford: Oxford University Press, 2005.

Hotaling, Edward. *The Great Black Jockeys: The Lives and Times of the Men Who Dominated America's First National Sport*. Rocklin, CA: Forum, 1999.

Hudson, Charles M., and Carmen Chaves Tesser, eds. *The Forgotten Centuries: Indians and Europeans in the American South, 1521–1704*. Athens: University of Georgia Press, 1993.

Hunt, Gallaird, ed. *The Writings of James Madison: 1819–1836*. New York City: Knickerbocker Press, 1910. Google e-book, accessed April 6, 2012.

"Identifying Some Primary Documents on the Capture of the Portuguese Slaver on July 15, 1619 and the Delivery of 60 of Her African Captives to Virginia, (and to Virginia via Bermuda) Including the '20 and odd' Africans Who Arrived at Jamestown at the 'Latter End' of August, 1619, www2.vcdh.virginia.edu/HIST403/resources/ManchesterPapers.VCRPB.pdf, accessed April 6, 2012.

Irving, Washington. *Life of George Washington*. Philadelphia: Lippincott, 1871.

Jackson, Andrew, John Spencer Bassett, and David Maydole Matteson. *Correspondence of Andrew Jackson*. Washington, DC: Carnegie Institution of Washington, 1926.

Jackson, Andrew, Sam B. Smith, Harriet Fason Chappell Owsley, and Harold D. Moser. *The Papers of Andrew Jackson*. Knoxville: University of Tennessee Press, 1980.

"Jackson's Old Servants," *New York Times*, September 24, 1882.

Jacobs, Harriet. *Incidents in the Life of a Slave Girl*. Google e-book, accessed April 6, 2012.

James Madison's Montpelier, www.montpelier.org, accessed April 6, 2012.

James, Marquis. *Andrew Jackson, the Border Captain*. Indianapolis: Bobbs-Merrill, 1933.

James, Marquis. *Andrew Jackson, Portrait of a President*. Indianapolis: Bobbs-Merrill Co., 1937.

James, Marquis. *The Life of Andrew Jackson, Complete in One Volume.* Indianapolis: Bobbs-Merrill Co., 1938.

Jefferson, Thomas, Julian P. Boyd, L. H. Butterfield, Charles T. Cullen, John Catanzariti, and Barbara Oberg. *The Papers of Thomas Jefferson.* Princeton, NJ: Princeton University Press, 1950.

Jennings, Paul. *A Colored Man's Reminiscences of James Madison.* Brooklyn: George C. Beadle, 1865. Google e-book, accessed April 6, 2012.

Johnson, Andrew, and LeRoy P. Graf. *The Papers of Andrew Johnson*, Vol. 6. Knoxville: University of Tennessee Press, 1983.

Jordan, Winthrop D. "American Chiaroscuro: The Status and Definition of Mulattoes in the British Colonies." *William and Mary Quarterly*, Third Series, 19, no. 2 (April 1962), 183–200.

Kapsch, Robert J. "The Labor History of the Construction and Reconstruction of the White House, 1793–1817." PhD diss., University of Maryland, 1993.

"The Kentucky Derby's Forgotten Jockeys," *Smithsonian*, April 23, 2009, www.smithsonianmag.com/history/the-kentucky-derbys-forgotten-jockeys-128781428/?no-ist, accessed April 30, 2015.

"King Edward's Turf Career" *Cincinnati Enquirer*, July 3, 1909.

Klein, Lauren. "How We Know What We Know: Thomas Jefferson, James Hemings, and the Task of the Scholar (and Teacher) in the Digital Age," http://macaulay.cuny.edu/eportfolios/lklein/2011/03/17/how-we-know-what-we-know, accessed April 6, 2012.

Klein, Philip Shriver. *President James Buchanan, A Biography.* University Park: Pennsylvania State University Press, 1962.

Krainik, Clifford, and Michele Krainik. "A Special Space Lost and Found: Images of Abraham Lincoln's White House Stables." *White House History* 29, www.whitehousehistory.org/history/documents/White-House-History-29-Krainik-Lincoln-Stables.pdf, accessed April 28, 2015.

Kupfer, Barbara Stern. "A Presidential Patron of the Sport of Kings: Andrew Jackson." *Tennessee Historical Quarterly* 29, no. 3 (Fall 1970), 243–55.

Lawrence, Rachel Jackson. "Andrew Jackson at Home," *McClure's Magazine*, Vol. 9, 1897.

Lepore, Jill. *New York Burning: Liberty, Slavery, and Conspiracy in Eighteenth-Century Manhattan*. New York: Alfred A. Knopf, 2005.

"Life Among The Lowly, No. 1" *Pike County Republican*, March 13, 1873.

Lindsay, Rae. *The Presidents' First Ladies*. New York: F. Watts, 1989.

Louis, Philippe. *Diary of My Travels in America*. New York: Delacorte Press, 1977. Print.

Lovett, Bobby L. *The African-American History of Nashville, Tennessee, 1780–1930: Elites and Dilemmas*. Fayetteville: University of Arkansas Press, 1999.

Lovett, Bobby L. *The Civil Rights Movement in Tennessee: A Narrative History*. Knoxville: University of Tennessee Press, 2005.

Lusane, Clarence. *The Black History of the White House*. San Francisco: City Lights Books, 2011.

"MALUNGU: The African Origin of the American Melungeons," www.eclectica.org/v5n3/hashaw.html, accessed April 6, 2012.

McCartney, Martha W. "A Study of the Africans and African Americans on Jamestown Island and at Green Spring, 1619–1803," www.nps.gov/jame/historyculture/upload/African%20Americans%20on%20Jamestown%20Island.pdf, accessed April 6, 2012.

McCormac, Eugene Irving. *James K. Polk: A Political Biography*. London: Forgotten Books, 2013 (original work published 1922).

McFeely, William S. *Grant: A Biography*. New York: Norton, 1981.

McLaughlin, Jack. *Jefferson and Monticello: The Biography of a Builder*. New York: Henry Holt, 1988.

Meacham, Jon. *American Lion: Andrew Jackson in the White House*. New York: Random House, 2008.

Meaney, Jean Rawlings, "STOKELY DONELSON HAYS 1788–1831," Genealogy Trails, http://genealogytrails.com/tenn/madison/biohays.html, accessed April 30, 2015.

Minardi, Margot. *Making Slavery History: Abolitionism and the Politics of Memory in Massachusetts*. Oxford: Oxford University Press, 2010.

Moeller Jr., G. Martin. *AIA Guide to the Architecture of Washington, D.C.* Baltimore: The Johns Hopkins University Press, 2006.

"Monkey Simon, the Noted Black Jockey and a Sketch of His Famous Career," *Courier-Journal*, April 8, 1883.

Monticello, www.monticello.org, accessed April 6, 2012.

Moore, Harvey L. "Last of the Jacksons—Faithful Old Uncle Alfred, Guardian of the Hermitage," *Florida Star*, October 25, 1901.

Moore, John Trotwood. *Hearts of Hickory: A Story of Andrew Jackson and the War of 1812.* Nashville: Kessinger, 2005.

Moore, John Trotwood. "The Measure of a Man," *Trotwood's Monthly, Devoted to Farm, Horse and Home*, November 1906.

Morgan, George. *The Life of James Monroe.* Boston: Small, Maynard and Company, 1921.

Morrel, Martha McBride. *Young Hickory, the Life and Times of President James K. Polk.* New York: E.P. Dutton, 1903.

Morris, Thomas D. *Southern Slavery and the Law, 1619–1860.* Chapel Hill: University of North Carolina Press, 1996, Kindle edition.

Mount Vernon, www.mountvernon.org/meet-george-washington/biography-and-influence/view-slavery, accessed April 6, 2012.

"Mrs. Madison and Her Slaves," *The Liberator*, March 31, 1848.

"Mrs. Madison's Slaves Again," *The Liberator*, March 31, 1848.

Mumford, Kevin. "After Hugh: Statutory Race Segregation in Colonial America, 1630–1725," *American Journal of Legal History* 43, no. 3 (July 1999), 280–305.

Mundy, Liza. "When Presidents and Slaves Mingled at the White House," *Washington Post*, February 15, 2010.

Murrell, Amy. Appendix of report in Ash Lawn–Highland research files, 1997.

National Park Service. *White House and President's Park.* US Department of the Interior, National Park Service, 2009.

Nelson, Anson, and Fanny Nelson. *Memorials of Sarah Childress Polk, Wife of the Eleventh President of the United States.* New York: A.D.F. Randolph & Co., 1892.

Nelson, Lee H. *White House Stone Carving: Builders and Restorers.* Washington D.C: U.S. Dept. of the Interior, National Park Service, National Capital Region, White House Liaison, 1992.

Oberg, Barbara B., and J. Jefferson Looney, eds. *The Papers of Thomas Jefferson Digital Edition.* Charlottesville: University of Virginia Press, Rotunda, 2008. http://rotunda.upress.virginia.edu/founders/default .xqy?keys=TSJN-print-01–32–02–0094, accessed July 3, 2012.

"Once The Slave of Thomas Jefferson," *New York World,* January 30, 1898.

Pacheco, Josephine F. *The* Pearl: *A Failed Slave Escape on the Potomac.* Chapel Hill: University of North Carolina Press, 2005.

Parton, James. *Life of Andrew Jackson, Volume 3.* New York: Mason Bros., 1861.

Paynter, John H. *Fugitives of the* Pearl. New York: AMS Press, 1971.

Pogue, Dennis J. "Interpreting the Dimensions of Daily Life for the Slaves Living at the President's House and at Mount Vernon." *Pennsylvania Magazine of History and Biography* 129, no. 4 (October 2005), 433–43.

Poore, Benjamin Perley. *Perley's Reminiscences, Vol. 1-2 of Sixty Years in the National Metropolis,* www.gutenberg.org/files/20290/20290.txt.

"President Polk's Servant," *New York Times,* December 30, 1886.

The President's House in Philadelphia, www.ushistory.org/presidents house/slaves/oneyinterview.htm, accessed April 6, 2012.

"Project 1619: Arrival of the First Africans in Colonial America at Point Comfort, Fort Monroe, Virginia," http://project1619.org, accessed April 6, 2012.

Publications of the Southern History Association. Washington, D.C: The Association, 1898.

Randall, Willard Sterne. *Thomas Jefferson: A Life.* New York: Henry Holt, 1993.

Raphael, Ray. *Founders: The People Who Brought You a Nation.* New York: The New Press, 2009.

"Recalling The Old Days," *Greensboro Patriot,* February 25, 1880.

Remini, Robert V. *Andrew Jackson and the Course of American Democracy, 1833–1845.* New York: Harper & Row, 1984.

Reuter, Edward Byron. "The Mulatto in the United States; Including a Study of the Role of Mixed-Blood Races throughout the World." PhD diss., University of Illinois, 1919.

Ricks, Mary Kay. *Escape on the* Pearl*: The Heroic Bid for Freedom on the Underground Railroad.* New York: William Morrow, 2007.

Rodman, Leslie J. "The Evolution of Slavery in Colonial Virginia," www.amtour.net/downloadable/SlaveryInColonialVirginia.pdf, accessed April 6, 2012.

Russell, Hilary. "The Operation of the Underground Railroad in Washington, D.C., c. 1800–1860," www.nps.gov/subjects/ugrr/discover_history/upload/dc-UGGR-Report-H-Russell.pdf, 2001.

Scharff, Virginia. *The Women Jefferson Loved.* New York: Harper, 2011.

Schrock, Patrick. *The White House: An Illustrated Architectural History.* Jefferson, NC: McFarland, 2013.

Schwarz, Philip J. *Slavery at the Home of George Washington.* Mount Vernon, VA: Mount Vernon Ladies' Association, 2001.

Seale, William. *The President's House: A History.* Washington, DC: White House Historical Association with the cooperation of the National Geographic Society, 1986.

"The Servants' Plot of 1663," *Virginia Historical Magazine*, 1906, www.archive.org/stream/virginiamagazin03socigoog/virginiamagazin03socigoog_djvu.txt, accessed April 6, 2012.

"Served Gen. Jackson: Death of Alfred Jackson. The Oldest Servant Who Saw the President Die," *Iola Register*, October 9, 1901.

Sharfstein, Daniel J. "The Secret History of Race in the United States." *Yale Law Journal* 112, no. 6 (April 2003), 1473–1509.

Sioussat, George L., "The Accident on Board the U.S.S. *Princeton*, February 28, 1844: A Contemporary News-Letter." *Pennsylvania History: A Journal of Mid-Atlantic Studies* 4, no. 3 (July 1937), 161–89.

The Slave Rebellion Website, http://slaverebellion.org, accessed April 6, 2012.

"Slavery | Andrew Jackson's Hermitage Plantation," The Hermitage, http://thehermitage.com/learn/mansion-grounds/slavery/, accessed April 30, 2015.

Smith, Harry. *Fifty Years of Slavery in the United States of America.* Grand Rapids, Mich.: West Michigan Printing Company, 1891, Google e-book.

Smith, Jessie Carney. *Encyclopedia of African American Popular Culture.* Santa Barbara, CA: Greenwood, 2011.

Smith, Margaret, and Gaillard Hunt. *The First Forty Years of Washington Society, Portrayed by the Family Letters of Mrs. Samuel Harrison Smith (Margaret Bayard) from the Collection of Her Grandson, J. Henley Smith.* New York: Scribner, 1905.

Stanton, Lucia C. *Free Some Day: The African-American Families of Monticello.* Charlottesville, VA: Thomas Jefferson Foundation, 2000.

Stanton, Lucia C. *Slavery at Monticello.* Charlottesville, VA: Thomas Jefferson Memorial Foundation, 1993.

Stanton, Lucia C. *"Those Who Labor for My Happiness": Slavery at Thomas Jefferson's Monticello.* Charlottesville: University of Virginia Press, 2012.

Stanton, Lucia C. "A Well-Ordered Household: Domestic Servants in Jefferson's White House." *White House History* 17 (2006). http://www.whitehousehistory.org/whha_publications/publications_documents/whitehousehistory_17.pdf.

Stephenson, Nathaniel Wright, and Waldo Hilary Dunn. *George Washington: 1778–1799.* New York: Oxford University Press, 1940.

Still, William. *The Underground Railroad: a Record of Facts, Authentic Narratives, Letters, &c., Narrating the Hardships, Hair-Breadth Escapes, and Death Struggles of the Slaves in Their Efforts for Freedom, as Related by Themselves and Others or Witnessed by the Author: Together with Sketches of Some of the Largest Stockholders and Most Liberal Aiders and Advisers of the Road. Volume 1.* Cirencester: The Echo Library, 2007.

Sutherland, Jonathan. *African Americans at War: An Encyclopedia, Volume 1.* Santa Barbara, CA: ABC-CLIO, 2003.

Taylor, Elizabeth Dowling. *A Slave in the White House: Paul Jennings and the Madisons.* New York: Palgrave Macmillan, 2012, Kindle edition.

Tennessee Department of Conservation. *Tennessee Conservationist,* Volume 19–20.

Thompson, Mary V. "Different People, Different Stories: The Life Stories of Individual Slaves from Mount Vernon and Their Relationships with George and Martha Washington." A talk given at a symposium entitled "George Washington & Slavery," Mount Vernon, VA, November 3, 2001.

Thompson, Mary V. "They Appear To Live Comfortable Together: Private Life of the Mount Vernon Slaves." Speech given at a conference entitled "Slavery in the Age of Washington," Mount Vernon, VA, November 3, 1994.

Thornton, John. "The African Experience of the '20. and Odd Negroes' Arriving in Virginia in 1619." *William and Mary Quarterly*, Third Series, 55, no. 3 (July 1998), 421–34.

Toplin, Robert Brent. "Between Black and White: Attitudes Toward Southern Mulattoes, 1830–1861." *Journal of Southern History* 45, no. 2 (May 1979), 185–200.

The University of Virginia, http://gwpapers.virginia.edu/education/life/quest11.html, accessed April 6, 2012.

"Virginia's First Africans" in *Encyclopedia Virginia*, www.encyclopedia virginia.org/Virginia_s_First_Africans, accessed April 6, 2012.

Virtual Jamestown, www.virtualjamestown.org, accessed April 6, 2012.

Wallace, John Hankins. "Early Tennessee Turf History," *Wallace's Monthly: An Illustrated Magazine Devoted to Domesticated Animal Nature*, February 1, 1878, 33–43.

Walton, Eugene. *The Slaves Who Built the White House and the Capitol.* Washington, DC: EWEmedia.com, 2012, Kindle edition.

Warshauer, Matthew S. "Andrew Jackson: Chivalric Slave Master." *Tennessee Historical Quarterly* 65 (Fall 2006), 202–29.

Washington, George. *Letters and Recollections of George Washington.* New York: Doubleday, Doran & Co., 1906, http://archive.org/stream/lettersrecollect00wash/lettersrecollect00wash_djvu.txt, accessed April 6, 2012.

Washington, George, and John H. Rhodehamel. *George Washington: Writings.* New York: Library of America, 1997.

Washington, George, Tobias Lear, William Keeney Bixby, and William Holland Samson. *Letters from George Washington to Tobias Lear: With an Appendix Containing Miscellaneous Washington Letters and Documents.* Rochester, NY: Genesee Press, 1903.

Watson, Robert P. *Life in the White House: A Social History of the First Family and the President's House.* Albany: State University of New York Press, 2004.

Webb, William Benning, John Wooldridge and Harvey W. Crew. *Centennial History of the City of Washington, D.C.* Dayton, OH: United Brethren Pub. House, 1892.

West, Elizabeth Howard. *Calendar of the Papers of Martin Van Buren: Prepared from the Original Manuscripts in the Library of Congress.* Washington: Government Printing Office, 1910.

West, Thomas G. *Vindicating the Founders: Race, Sex, Class, and Justice in the Origins of America.* Lanham, MD: Rowman & Littlefield Publishers, 2000.

Whitcomb, John, and Claire Whitcomb. *Real Life at the White House: 200 Years of Daily Life at America's Most Famous Residence.* New York: Routledge, 2003.

The White House Historical Association, www.whha.org, accessed April 6, 2012.

Wiencek, Henry. *An Imperfect God: George Washington, His Slaves, and the Creation of America.* New York: Farrar, Straus and Giroux, 2003.

Wills, Garry. *Negro President: Jefferson and the Slave Power.* Boston: Houghton Mifflin, 2003.

Wise, Henry A. *Seven Decades of the Union the Humanities and Materialism, Illustrated by a Memoir of John Tyler, with Reminiscences of Some of His Great Contemporaries; The Transition State of This Nation—Its Dangers and Their Remedy.* Philadelphia: J.B. Lippincott, 1876.

Woodson, Carter G. "The Beginnings of the Miscegenation of the Whites and Blacks." *Journal of Negro History* 3, no. 4 (October 1918), 335–53.

Woodson, Carter G., ed. *The Journal of Negro History.* Washington, DC: The Association for the Study of Negro Life and History, 1916. Google e-book, accessed April 6, 2012.

"The Writings of George Washington from the Original Manuscript Sources 1745–1799," http://etext.lib.virginia.edu/washington/fitzpatrick/index.html, accessed April 6, 2012.

"The Writings of George Washington from the Original Manuscript Sources, 1745–1799; Prepared under the Direction of the United States George Washington Bicentennial Commission and Published by Authority of Congress," http://archive.org/stream/writingsofgeorge37wash/writingsofgeorge37wash_djvu.txt, accessed April 6, 2012.

Wunder, William L. "Andrew Jackson and Horse Racing in Early America," https://suite.io/william-l-wunder/5xwd2d0, accessed April 30, 2015.

Yarbrough, Fay A. "Power, Perception, and Interracial Sex: Former Slaves Recall an Interracial South." *Journal of Southern History* 71, no. 3 (August 2005), 559–88.

INDEX

ABOUT THE AUTHOR

Jesse J. Holland is the author of *Black Men Built the Capitol: Discovering African-American History In and Around Washington, D.C.* A longtime writer for The Associated Press, Holland graduated from the University of Mississippi and received a Master of Fine Arts in creative nonfiction from Goucher College in Maryland. He lives in Bowie, Maryland, with his wife and children. Follow him on his website, www.jessejholland.com.